Digital Libraries for Cultural Heritage

Development, Outcomes, and Challenges from European Perspectives

Synthesis Lectures on Information Concepts, Retrieval, and Services

Editor
Gary Marchionini, *University of North Carolina, Chapel Hill*

Synthesis Lectures on Information Concepts, Retrieval, and Services publishes short books on topics pertaining to information science and applications of technology to information discovery, production, distribution, and management. Potential topics include: data models, indexing theory and algorithms, classification, information architecture, information economics, privacy and identity, scholarly communication, bibliometrics and webometrics, personal information management, human information behavior, digital libraries, archives and preservation, cultural informatics, information retrieval evaluation, data fusion, relevance feedback, recommendation systems, question answering, natural language processing for retrieval, text summarization, multimedia retrieval, multilingual retrieval, and exploratory search.

Digital Libraries for Cultural Heritage: Development, Outcomes, and Challenges from European Perspectives
Tatjana Aparac-Jelušić

ISBN: 978-3-031-01182-5 print
ISBN: 978-3-031-02310-1 ebook

DOI 10.1007/978-3-031-02310-1

A Publication in the Springer series
SYNTHESIS LECTURES ON INFORMATION CONCEPTS, RETRIEVAL, AND SERVICES, #58
Series Editor: Gary Marchionini, University of North Carolina, Chapel Hill

Series ISSN: 1947-945X Print   1947-9468 Electronic

Digital Libraries for Cultural Heritage

Development, Outcomes, and Challenges from
European Perspectives

Tatjana Aparac-Jelušić
University of Zadar

SYNTHESIS LECTURES ON INFORMATION CONCEPTS, RETRIEVAL,
AND SERVICES #58

Dedication

To my former assistants and great colleagues Martina Dragija Ivanović and Sanjica Faletar Tanacković.

ABSTRACT

European digital libraries have existed in diverse forms and with quite different functions, priorities, and aims. However, there are some common features of European-based initiatives that are relevant to non-European communities. There are now many more challenges and changes than ever before, and the development rate of new digital libraries is ever accelerating. Delivering educational, cultural, and research resources—especially from major scientific and cultural organizations—has become a core mission of these organizations. Using these resources they will be able to investigate, educate, and elucidate, in order to promote and disseminate and to preserve civilization. Extremely important in conceptualizing the digital environment priorities in Europe was its cultural heritage and the feeling that these rich resources should be open to Europe and the global community.

In this book we focus on European digitized heritage and digital culture, and its potential in the digital age. We specifically look at the EU and its approaches to digitization and digital culture, problems detected, and achievements reached, all with an emphasis on digital cultural heritage. We seek to report on important documents that were prepared on digitization; copyright and related documents; research and education in the digital libraries field under the auspices of the EU; some other European and national initiatives; and funded projects.

The aim of this book is to discuss the development of digital libraries in the European context by presenting, primarily to non-European communities interested in digital libraries, the phenomena, initiatives, and developments that dominated in Europe. We describe the main projects and their outcomes, and shine a light on the number of challenges that have been inspiring new approaches, cooperative efforts, and the use of research methodology at different stages of the digital libraries development. The specific goals are reflected in the structure of the book, which can be conceived as a guide to several main topics and sub-topics. However, the author's scope is far from being comprehensive, since the field of digital libraries is very complex and digital libraries for cultural heritage is even moreso.

KEYWORDS

digital libraries, cultural heritage, European cultural heritage, European digital libraries, research in digital libraries, European Union, European Commission, education in digital libraries

Contents

Figures

Preface

Previous analysis of the multitude of definitions, as well as mission statements and project proposals, indicates that digital libraries are seen from different perspectives and sometimes with different concepts as well. Many elements that characterized the early digital library positioned it as a separated set of resources and activities within but not necessarily associated with a traditional library. However, a growing interest in computational aspects has brought to the "stage" professionals from archives and museums, scientists and programmers from computer science, and researchers from the social sciences and humanities. The concept of the "hybrid library," which originated in Europe, reflected the realities already being faced by many actors on the "digital scene" at the beginning of 1990s. Today, "digital library" is still looked at not only as a new term and concept that covers a great many diverse activities, but also as a new paradigm related to processing and managing information in the digital environment.

Although digital libraries in Europe have existed in diverse forms with quite different functions, priorities, and aims, as in other parts of the globe, there are some common features of European-based initiatives that are worthy of presentation to non-European communities. Being politically, economically, and culturally so diverse, many European countries have started digital libraries with an impetus derived either from innovative thinking about the future role of libraries, archives, and museums in preservation and usage of their rich cultural heritage, or about the future role of these institutions inside the fast growing networked environment. Other motivations, too, have led various digital libraries' own personalities, and reflected the circumstances of their birth, their cultural environment, and their leaders. The approaches of the European Union, regionally, nationally, and even transnationally based sets of regulations, recommendations, and funding possibilities, made developmental efforts more feasible, and the results gave the research and professional arena more vitality and visible results.

Challenges and changes that are happening today, even more intensively than before, show an intention of digital libraries to appear as a process of constant acceleration. The need to deliver educational, cultural, and research resources, especially from major scientific and cultural organizations, has become an imperative closely associated with the core mission of these organizations to investigate, educate, and elucidate, to promote and disseminate and to preserve civilization.

Extremely important in conceptualizing the digital environment priorities in Europe was its cultural heritage and the feeling that this wealth of resources should be opened up to Europe's and the world's community. Is is also important to shine a light upon cultural heritage infrastructural elements in European society, which are so diverse and yet so bound by many historical, cultural, and political ties.

Undoubtelly, the interest in cultural diversity, domination by certain cultures, and cultural imperialism has grown with globalization trends. The issues that relate to the cultural diversity are not only the actual questions posed by scientists and politicians, but indeed among the most important ones in regard to perspectives of the human civilization. Europe made a significant effort to answer to the problem of cultural and national tensions by actualizing those values that could guarantee stability, homogenity, and identity among its citizens and strengthening its position in today's world. Its rich heritage plays an important role in these attempts.

In this book we intend to concentrate on European digitized heritage and digital culture and its potentials in the digital age. A new digital culture has been transforming the whole cultural field, encouraging new forms of creative expression, offering new resources to be used for various purposes, intensifying educational, scientific, business, and leisure fields, and offering new perspectives to intercultural communication inside Europe and worldwide. We will specifically look at the EU and its approaches to digitalization and digital culture, problems detected, and achievements reached, with an emphasis on digital cultural heritage. We seek to report on important documents that were prepared on digitization, copyright and related topics, research and education in the digital libraries field under the auspices of EU, and some other European and national initiatives and funded projects.

The aim of this book is to discuss the development of digital libraries in the European context by presenting, primarily to non-European communities interested in digital libraries, the phenomena, initiatives, and developments that dominate in Europe. Following this aim, we intend to describe the main projects and their outcomes and to shine a light on the number of challenges that have been inspiring new approaches, cooperative efforts, and the use of research methodology at different stages of digital libraries' development. The specific goals are reflected in the structure of the book that can be seen as a guide to several main topics and sub-topics. However, the author's intention is far from being comprehensive. The reasons for this are threefold: first, digital libraries cover a wide range of fields, activities, scientific disciplines, educational paradigms, and business models to be covered in one single book; second, the number of initiatives and ongoing or finished projects is too high and results are often not so visible, not as influential as expected, or as interesting for wider user communities; and third, there are several literature reviews that cover either certain periods or special topics of the digital library developments in Europe, that could supplement our study.

The content of the book is divided into several chapters. After an introduction to the main characteristics of Europe and its visions and developmental plans, Chapter 1 looks at European and national policies and initiatives that intend to coordinate activities related to culture and cultural heritage, primarily in European Union countries. In Chapter 2 we discuss related terminological issues, definitions, and basic notions of the digital library from the perspectives of the digitization of cultural heritage and its meaning to the new digital environment.

In Chapter 3 we look at the development of information infrastracture, in particular that which aims to support digitization and digital libraries for cultural heritage. Following, there is a description of the main characteristics and features of some digital libraries' projects from the early stage of their development to recent attempts and results. This chapter will cover principles and criteria of digitization, especially in relation to the cultural heritage in Europe, and Europeana in particular.

Chapter 4 is devoted to the research projects that investigated the challenges and possibilities of digital libraries from various perspectives (e.g., considering principles and models, users and use, preservation, and evaluation).

Chapter 5 discusses education on digital libraries and the changes in the information profession on the European scene, as well as future trends in digital library education, research, and development.

In the Conclusion, Chapter 6, we intend to summarize main findings and present our view about the challenges and possible future paths.

Acknowledgments

This book would not have been possible without support from Gary Marchionini, a long-term colleague and a great supporter of LIDA conferences, who persistently and kindly kept reminding me of my promise. It was his idea to present European Digital Libraries to American students, academicians, and professionals in the Information Science and related fields, and it is only my fault if I have failed to meet his expectations.

I would like to express my gratitude to my colleagues Primož Južnič, Mirta Matošić, and Dora Rubinić who were helpful in providing literature that was out of my reach; and to Emil Levine who patiently read and commented some chapters.

I thank Ivana Katavić and Katja Ivaković, students from the Department of Information and Communication Sciences, Faculty of Philosophy in Zagreb, who kindly helped me with the scanning of some important documents.

I am particularly indebted to my reviewers for their helpful comments to improve and refine the content of my manuscript and to Diane Cerra at Morgan & Claypool who offered friendly encouragement and support over the course of the whole process.

I appreciate the support that I received from the Morgan & Claypool team, especially from Deborah Gabriel and Sara Kreisman who spent—I am sure!—a lot of time editing and polishing this book.

I would also like to thank many friends and colleagues who have helped me prepare this book through discussions and their valuable research, especially Tefko Saracevic for his lead and support over the last 25 years.

Abbreviations

ALM – Archives, Libraries, and Museums (see also: LAM)

APIs – Application Programming Interfaces

CASPAR – Cultural, Artistic, and Scientific knowledge for Preservation

CDCPP – Steering Committee for Culture, Heritge, and Landscape

CEE – Central and East Europe

CENL – Conference of European National Librarians

CERL – Consortium of European Research Libraries

CH – Cultural Heritage

CILIP – Chartered Institute for Library and Information Professionals

DAE – Digital Agenda for Europe

DARIAH – Digital Research Infrastructure for the Arts and Humanities

DCH – Digital Cultural Heritage

DCC – Digital Curation Center

DILL – Digital Libraries Learning

DL – Digital Library

DPE – DigitalPreservationEurope

DRM – Digital Rights Management

ERA-NET – Network for the European Research Area

ERPANET – Electronic Resource Preservation and Access Network

EC – European Commission

ECL – Extended Collective Licenses

ECo – European Council

ECTS – European Credit Transfer System

EDL – European Digital Library

EHEA – European Higher Education Area

EP – European Parliament

EPOCH – Excellence in Processing Open Cultural Heritage

ERA – European Research Area

ERASMUS – European Regional Action Scheme for the Mobility of University Students

ERIC – European Research Infrastructure Consortium

ERPANET – Electronic Resource Preservation and Access Network

ECTS – European Credit Transfer System

ERA – European Research Area

ERASMUS – European Regional Action Scheme for the Mobility of University Students

EU – European Union

FP – Framework Program (EU)

FRBR – Functional Requirements for Bibliographic Records

GDP – Gross Domestic Product

GII – Global Information Infrastructure

HAITII – Humanities Advanced Technology and Information Institute

HEI – Higher Education Institution

HEREIN – European Heritage Heads Forum

HOPE – Heritage of the People's Europe

ICT – Information and Communication Technologies

IFLA – International Federation of Library Associations and Institutions

II – Information Infrastructure

InterPARES – International Research on Permanent Authentic Records in Electronic Systems

IPR – Intellectual Property Rights

IS – Information Science

IST – Information Society Technologies

LAM – Libraries, Archives, and Museums (see also: ALM)

LIBER – Ligue des Bibliothèques Europénnes de recherche (Association of European Research Libraries)

LIS – Library and Information Science

LOD – Linked Open Data

MALVINE – Manuscripts and Letters via Integrated Networks in Europe

METS – Metadata Encoding and Transmission Standard

MICHAEL – Multilingual Inventory of Cultural Heritage in Europe

MINERVA – Ministerial Network for Valorising Activities in Digitization

MLA – Museums, Libraries, and Archives Council

MOSAICA – Semantically Enhanced, Multifaceted, Collaborative Access to Cultural Heritage

MultiMATCH – Multilingual/Multimedia Access to Cultural Heritage

NEDLIB – Networked European Deposit Library

NGA – Next Generation Access

NPLD – European Network to Promote Linguistic Diversity

NSF – National Science Foundation (U.S.)

OpenAIRE – Open Access Infrastructure for Research in Europe

OAIS – Open Archival Information Systems

PATHTS – Personalized Access To Cultural Heritage Spaces

PLANETS – Preservation and Long-term Access through NETworked Services

PPS – Purchasing Power Standard

TEL – The European Library

R&D – Research and Development

RCUK – Research Councils UK

RDA – Research Data Alliance

RDM – Research Data Management

RDLP – Memory of Russia and Russian Digital Libraries

RIN – Research Information Network

ROADS – Resource Organization and Discovery in Subject-based services

ROW – (European) Registry of Orphan Works

RTD – Research and Technological Development

SCRAN – Scottish Cultural Resource Access Network

SHAMAN – Sustaining Heritage Access through Multivalent ArchiviNg

SPAM – Supporting Digital Preservation and Asset Management in Institutions

STREP – Specific Targeted Research Projects

TEL-ME-MOR – The European Library: Modular Extensions for Mediating Online Resources

TEMPUS – Trans-European Mobility Scheme for University Studies

TNT – The Neanderthal Tools

UKWAC – United Kingdom

UNESCO – United Nations Educational, Scientific, and Cultural Organization

VSA – Voluntary Stakeholders Agreements

CHAPTER 1

Introduction

In an attempt to present various approaches to digitization of the rich European cultural heritage (CH), and to build up and develop digital libraries (DLs) that would offer content and services to European citizens and worldwide, it seems necessary to offer even a surface look at the European CH scene.

European culture is considered one of the cornerstones of civilization. Yet, it is almost impossible to make even a brief sketch of the main elements of European culture. One might start with the evidence found in archeological sites and ancient art objects—from the cave paintings of Altamira and the Cave of Lascaux, Stonehenge, Homer and the Iliad, the Venus de Milo, the Acropolis of Athens, and Ancient Epidaurus, to the Roman Theatre of Merida, Les Ferreres Aqueduct, Diocletian's Palace—all of which reveal the high structures of state organization, life, and art; or the roots of democracy in Athens that led to great philosophical thought, literary works, and sculptures. Through many centuries, each period of growth resulted in a myriad of cultural objects that are now treated as European CH par excellence. Later phenomena, such as the Renaissance, Enlightenment, science, Romanticism, or postmodernism, came hand-in-hand with socio-political constructs such as nationalism, liberalism, imperialism, or totalitarianism, which influenced European culture in many ways.

Europe is rich in cultural institutions—museums like the Louvre, Prado, Hermitage, and British Museum; galleries like the Uffizi, Pinakothek München, Luisiana in Denmark, or Narodni Galerie in Praha; libraries and archives like astonishing medieval or Baroque libraries, national libraries, or Vatican Archives; film and creative industry, music, and literature, etc.—that form a base of modern civilization.

There are a number of perspectives from which one can look at modern Europe, and in particular, rich European CH, which is the focus of this book. Indeed, it is impossible to form a single, all-embracing concept of European culture, although a number of core elements could be generally agreed upon as a base for interpretations of the cultural foundation of modern Europe. In his well-known work, K. Bochmann (1990) pointed out a common cultural and spiritual heritage derived from Greco-Roman antiquity, Christianity, the Renaissance and its Humanism, the political thinking of the Enlightenment period, the French Revolution, and the developments of modernity. Moreover, European culture had influenced culture on other continents in many ways, especially during the period of the "Great Divergence." European philosophers, sociologists, theoreticians of culture and their conceptions of the "individual," "collective," "human rights," and the "liberty of the individual," to name just few of the topics, inspired leading thinkers throughout the world (cf. Berting, 2007).

Figure 1.1: Stonehenge and the Last Judgment from the Sistine Chapel.

European culture also reflects a specific way of living in states that have different religious backgrounds and political orders, a tradition that was often enriched by close relationships between states during centuries of international alliances, fights, wars, and foreign regimes. The concept of European culture is often linked to the classical definition of the Western world, e.g., the Western canon represented as a set of literary, scientific, political, artistic, and philosophical principles that differentiate it from other civilizations' canons.

With such a rich and diverse cultural background forming an important ground for overall development, Europe entered the 21st century full of positive energy and plans in many sectors to become more powerful and competitive. It has been building new infrastructure. Some European countries were already members of the European Union (EU), some approaching it, and some remaining neutral or with other focuses of their socio-political pursuits.

Education and culture have been regarded as two main pillars of Europe's future. Europe has been developing various educational systems since the 11th century. According to J. Rupnik (1989) the rebirth of Europe as a single educational entity toward the end of the 1990s has been emerging over the 1,500 years since the collapse and division of the Roman Empire, accompanied by ethnic and religious divisions and economic and political rivalries, particularly those that culminated in several major wars in the 19th and 20th centuries. These situations have continually shaped and altered the boundaries of the nation states that exist today. Today this system is submitted to coordination and harmonization by EU policy-making documents as it pertains to the member states, as well as stimulated by UNESCO's policies and documents as they pertain to the world. Visions and approaches to the future development presented in documents of non-EU countries should not be neglected, as they make an important contribution to the efforts related to the coordination of numerous activities, especially in relation to cultural, educational, and scientific ones. The cultural sector has been in a transitional period due to the growing influence of information and communication technology (ICT) in every part of life, but also due to the need to overcome economic constraints by strengthening its resources with digital technology and empowering its social role by coordination and networking supported by the EU and national-like funding mechanisms.

According to the United Nations' statistical data from 2015,[1] Europe has 48 countries with 743,122,816 inhabitants, Russia being the largest and most populous (comprising 15% of its population), while the Vatican City is the smallest both in terms of area and population. As of 2013 the EU has 28 member states,[2] covering over 4 million km,[2] and has 508 million inhabitants—the world's third largest population after China and India.[3] By surface area, France is the biggest EU country and Malta the smallest. Europe's population is increasing through a combination of natural growth (more people are born each year than die) and net migration, especially during the last several years when more people settled in the EU than left it, mostly due to the high migration from coutries that are hit by wars and uncertain political or deprived economic situations. At the same time, the population of Europe is aging, as life expectancy increases and fewer children are born. Living standards are usually compared by measuring the price of a range of goods and services in each country relative to income, using a common national currency called the purchasing power standard (PPS). Comparing gross domestic product (GDP) per inhabitant in PPS provides an overview of living standards across the EU. Bulgaria is still the country with the lowest GDP per capita in PPS (47) and Luxemburg with the highest (266).

The major goal of the EU[4] is to promote peace, European values, and the well-being of its peoples. In doing so, the EU strives to improve living standards by protecting the environment, encouraging job creation, reducing regional disparities, connecting formerly isolated areas by devel-

---

[1] Data was extracted from the website: http://statisticstimes.com/population/european-countries-by-population. php (2016-05-06).

[2] On May 1, 2004, ten new countries joined the EU—Poland, Lithuania, Czech Republic, Slovakia, Hungary, Malta, Slovenia, Cyprus, Estonia, and Latvia. Bulgaria and Romania joined the "family" in 2007 and Croatia did so in 2013.

[3] Data was selectively extracted from the website: https://europa.eu/european-union/about-eu/figures/living_ en#quality-of-life (2016-05-06).

[4] The EU is comprised of the following institutions: the European Parliament (EP), European Council (ECo) the European Commission (EC), often referred as "the Commission," Court of Justice of the European Union, European Central Bank, and the Court of Auditors. The nomenclature of some of these institutions is at times confusing, especially in regard to the European Council and European Commission. The EC is an executive agency, ultimately subordinated to the European Parliament. The regular meetings of the ECo, whose members are heads of government of the member states, have a strategic role, being charged with defining "the general political directions and priorities." None of these bodies should be confused with the Council of Europe, a separate forum for all the parliamentary democracies in Europe (cf. Johnson, 2013: 64).

oping cross-border infrastructure, and encouraging the acquisition of language skills from an early age to support language and cultural diversity (EC, 2012).

> As for languages spoken, there are 24 official languages with which the EU institutions work.[5] In addition, some 80–90 regional, minority, or endangered languages are also spoken across Europe and enjoy different degrees of official recognition. These range from communities with full co-official status such as Basque, Catalan, Galician, or Welsh, to linguistic communities with little or no official recognition but with a strong will to keep their languages alive (NPLD, s.a.:16).

> In accordance with the EU population, the most widely spoken mother tongue is German (16%), followed by Italian and English (13% each), French (12%), then Spanish and Polish (8% each). For the majority of Europeans their mother tongue is one of the official languages of the country in which they reside; 54% of European citizens are able to hold a conversation in at least one additional language; 25% are able to speak at least two additional languages; and 10% are conversant in at least three languages. The five most widely spoken foreign languages are English (38%), French (12%), German (11%), Spanish (7%), and Russian (5%) (EC, 2012: 5).

Because linguistic communities, like other human groups, are dynamic phenomena and do not have fixed frontiers, their contacts with other linguistic communities usually result in numerous multilingual and polyglossic situations on collective and individual levels, so that it is really impossible to draw a territorial borderline that would separate two or more communities (cf. Škiljan, 2001: 91). Europe's linguistic diversity is what best defines the continent and, at the same time, expresses and reinforces the cultural identity of Europe. Thus, it is not suprising that the motto "United in Diversity" was adopted by the EU (in 2000) and that the EC's first ever Communication on Multilingualism was adopted in 2005 (EC, 2005c).[6] A set of appropriate measures was intended to extend the benefits of language learning to all citizens as a lifelong activity. The 2008 Council's document (ECo, 2008) also stressed that languages and multilingualism played a major role in the European economy and that all mechanisms should be employed to encourage all citizens to learn and speak more languages, in order to improve mutual understanding and communication. These documents

---

[5] Bulgarian, Croatian, Czech, Danish, Dutch, English, Estonian, Finnish, French, German, Greek, Hungarian, Irish, Italian, Latvian, Lithuanian, Maltese, Polish, Portuguese, Romanian, Slovak, Slovene, Spanish, and Swedish.

[6] This document was superseded by the ECo's Resolution on Strategy on a European strategy on multiculturalism (ECo, 2008), which complemented EC's Action Plan Promoting Language Learning and Linguistic Diversity from 2003 (EC, 2003), which set out measures aimed at supporting initiatives carried out at local, regional, and national levels.

highlighted the idea of linguistic and cultural diversity as a part and parcel of the European identity and an asset for Europe.[7]

By strongly supporting and funding language and information and communication skills, the EU has been attempting to ensure that all EU citizens, whether they speak a major European language or a lesser-known one, have equal access to the policies and legislation of the EU as well as to the various online resources within the European Digital Library (EDL)[8] or other access points to rich scientific, cultural, or educational resources.

On the other hand, language skills are becoming increasingly important, as globalization leads to more and more contact with people from other countries and an interweaving of different cultures. The most conservative estimate of the number of cultures would take the number of nation states or countries as its baseline, that is, 28 cultures are represented in the EU. But it is obvious that inside every country, from Spain or Germany to the UK or Croatia, people from different inner regions have a different culture. In major cities like Paris, London, Stockholm, Warsaw, Bucharest, or Madrid there exist different cultures in their different areas.

The complex European composition, with many languages and culture, dates from centuries ago, namely from the 16th century when Guttenberg's discovery and geographic and colonial expansion provided impetus in searching for new kinds of identity, when traditional national bonds such as territory, history, culture, and political traditions had the same role as the identification with the nation. It should be mentioned here that, in the 1970s, the idea of European identity became one of the important issues in discussions among politicians and bureaucrats within the EU. The declaration of European identity, accepted in 1973, stressed the importance of the legal frameworks, respect for human rights, and common marketplace as basic characteristics of Europe (cf. Božić-Vrbančić, 2008:10).

There is a great wealth of literature on European identity covering topics on European culture (issues on language, multiculturalism, heritage, belonging, boundaries, and identification). During the 1970s the domination of the traditional, neo-functional approach toward integration was ubiquitous. Such an approach departed from presumptions that European integrative processes could legalize a number of instruments as a vehicle for getting in tune with various national policies (cf., for example, Shore, 2004). However, not a single one of these proccesses was successful in shaping the unified European feeling about European identity. Thus, during the 1980s it became clear that the uncertainty about European identity could disrupt the development of a common EU market, and the issues related to the idea of European citizenship became topical at the beginning

---

[7] Much of the funding has supported foreign language learning initiatives, under the Lifelong Learning programs. However, investment in non EU-official language projects has been and continues to be much lower and it has been showing a downward trend in recent years (NPLD, s.a.: 20).

[8] The creation of the EDL began in 2001; from 2004 it has been supported, used, and developed by a growing number of members of the CENL and LIBER, and with generous funding from the EC.

of the 1990s, when it was realized that economic integration was not enough for the stability of the EU. As Castells pointed out, European integration is, at the same time, a reaction to the process of globalization and its most advanced expression (cf. Castells, 2000: 348).[9]

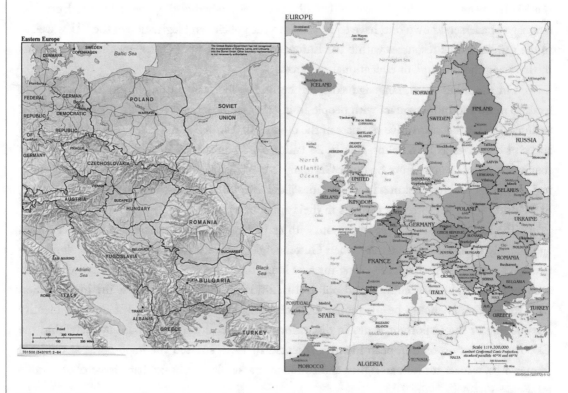

Figure 1.2: The map of East Europe before the fall of the Berlin Wall (left) and of Europe from 2012 (right).

These socio-political barriers also mark the European continent. Western Europe is a known term, but Central, South, Mid-Europe, Balkan, and West Balkan or Eastern Europe are used often for covering different countries. Among these concepts Central and East Europe (CEE) is probably the most problematic one.[10] In her book, Borgman (2000: 245) uses the term CEE, which refers to the region of Europe that was under Soviet control until 1989, plus Yugoslavia, which was a nonaligned nation.

[9] Indeed, recent events around Brexit proved that a common EU market could be disrupted within a short period of time and that the idea of a unified Europe is vulnerable.

[10] In both literature and politics, CEE sometimes includes the entire former Soviet Bloc and the former Yugoslavia and sometimes refers to a subset, distinguishing former Soviet satellite states in the western part of the bloc from "the former Soviet Union," the Commonwealth of Independent States, the present and former Yugoslav republics, or other subsets such as the Baltic States or the Caucasus.

Indeed, Europe is a mosaic of nations and minorities. For instance, before 1989 many of the CEE countries had various national minorities living within their borders.[11] The change of the geo-political map of this part of Europe also meant a change in the relationships between the countries belonging to this region.[12] This also meant a new cultural neighborhood for each country. As the fall of the Berlin Wall and the breakup of the socialist/communist systems in Eastern Europe and Yugoslavia led toward the disappearance of multinational states, the reunion of Germany, and the birth of new countries, Europe was witnessing many new challenges, one of these being the growing interest in cultural issues related to identity, ethnicity, and nationalism. Although, of course, cultural relations with Western Europe existed before the 1990s, the exchanges and contacts were largely manifestational in character and lacking in content. Albeit an interest in different European cultures and civilizations was present (for instance since the 19th century for folk culture from the Balkan region, Russian music and literature, or ancient Greek culture), there were few opportunities for real exchanges of ideas, experience, and knowledge, the most visible ones being those stemming from the defection of a number of cultural figures and artists (film makers, writers, musicians) from eastern parts of Europe, who simultaneously promoted the cultural traditions from their native countries. In such a way, the changes that had taken place in Central/Eastern Europe also influenced the changes in other parts of Europe and brought in novelties in international cultural relations. In Huntington's words (1993: 31), "(T)he Velvet Curtain of culture has replaced the Iron Curtain of ideology as the most significant dividing line in Europe." These, and other circumstances relating to the notion of multiculturalism, weigh on the nation-states' attitudes toward the international environment and, by all means, on cultural circumstances (cf. Krzysztofek, 1997: 65), e.g., on creative achievements, mobility, and much closer interrelations.

In the context of Europe, this process of change of socio-political paradigms opened up space for a more flexible interpretation of national and ethnic values. In fact, the influence of a global cultural space seems to be supportive of the definition and redefinition of local cultural spaces (individual and regional) and of the readiness to promote local creativity and local cultural values through global cultural communication. The new paradigms led and are still leading toward finding one's own cultural space within the European cultural space. At the same time, such an approach calls for the acceptance of European basic standards as regulatory elements in designing cultural development (cf. Švob-Đokić, 2004).

---

[11] For instance, Slovakia, Lithuania, and Croatia had between 10 and 20% of national minorities, Estonia and Latvia had between 30–40%, and even in the countries that are considered homogeneous, like Poland, the Czech Republic, and Hungary, up to 10% of the population were members of national minorities. At the same time, for instance, large numbers of Hungarians used to live as national minorities in a number of countries in the region, in Romania, Czech Republic, Slovakia, Ukraine, Croatia, Serbia, and Austria (cf. Švob-Đokić, 1997, p. 26.).

[12] As noted by Krzysztofek (1997), at the beginning of the 1990s Poland had three neighbors: the German Democratic Republic, the Soviet Union, and Czechoslovakia; none of them exist anymore.

Moreover, these changes strongly influenced the discussions about the role of culture in the future of Europe, especially when connected with the challenges of the digital era. Thus, during the late 1990s the ideas of "European culture" and "perception of Europe" started to be implemented in the economic and political goals of EU policy. Many discussions about "Europeanization" as a proccess were marked by the attempt to assure a unique European identity that involved issues related to the diverse nature of the notion of identity, including language and culture (cf., for example, Howarth, 2005; Stavrakakis, 2005). More and more politicians and theoreticians claim that Europe means "education and culture" (cf. Sassoon, 2012; Gielen, 2016) and that its highest value is Europe's cultural diversity. In Konrád's words, Europe's special quality is sensitive attraction to diversity, kept coherent by European humanism (cf. Konrád, 2016). Cultural diversity is one of the key objectives of the Council of Europe and is frequently being addressed in programs and measures of national or regional cultural policies.

It is worth mentioning that modern European-based discourses, such as "envisaged unity of Europeans," take over cultural differences as something that could co-exist peacefully, without contradictions. Diverse cultural (and national) styles characterize the diversity of Europe, while at the same time there exists another peculiarity—the assumption that all these differences could be assimilated in a body of the "supra-nation." Along these lines, new symbols of Europeanism have been designed and created: European passport, European driving license, European anthem, European health-insurance card, and European statistics, as well as school and university courses on "European themes" (e.g., culture, history, legal issues, and collaboration), European Higher Education Area (EHEA), collaborative projects and initiatives such as Active European Remembrance, European City of Culture Project, European Film Awards, Europe's Culture Award, Enlargement of Minds, Born in Europe, Mosaic, Captain Euro, European heritage label, and European Union prize for cultural heritage (Europa Nostra Awards), not to mention projects funded by the EU, such as the frameworks projects, Tempus,[13] Erasmus,[14] etc. (cf. Božić-Vrbančić, 2008: 13).

As can be seen, Europe is a patchwork quilt, a diversity of national and regional cultures. But Europe has a common CH. The creation of the EU would not have been possible without this common heritage and the endeavor to have a common future. Paradoxically, as Berting (2007) points out, Europe's specificity, its common heritage, is threatened by one of its major exports, the ideology of modernity and modernization. Thus, a very important task that Europe confronts is to be at the same time modernizing and preserving its specificity and diversity.

---

[13] Tempus was a trans-European mobility scheme for university studies, adopted by the Council of Europe in 1990, with the goal to respond to the modernization needs of the higher education sector in CEE countries, following the fall of the Berlin Wall in 1989.

[14] Erasmus was launched in 1987 with the aim to increase student mobility within the European Community. The program was extended later to include many other activities (e.g. teacher mobility, joint curriculum development, international intensive programs, thematic networks, language courses, and ECTS). Recently it adopted the term Erasmus + for the 2014–2020 period.

As Europe struggles with the tension between its past and its future, authors from different scientific and professional communities discuss broader social, cultural, and political issues (e.g., Stivenson, 2003; Berting, 2007; Cameron and Kenderdine, 2007; Segers and Albrecht, 2016). Certainly, the influence of the ICT and new communication paradigms significantly marked socio-political, cultural, educational, scientific, and business developments. Due to the growing importance of ICT in knowledge generation and distribution in the 1990s, the discussion shifted increasingly to the envisioned role of ICT, which stimulated new approaches, connections, and collaboration inside the framework of a "networked society" and an "information society." New approaches and interpretations stressed "the power changes that are related to the control of the continuously (in speed and wideness) increasing flows of information, the knowledge management, the networking and communication infrastructures and the automation" (van Rij, 2015: 11).

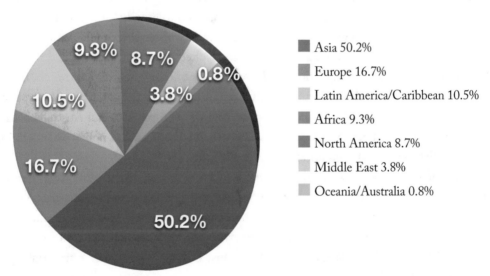

Source: Internet World Stats - www.internetworldstats.com/stats.htm
Basis: 3,675,824,813 Internet users on June 30, 2016
Copyright © 2016, Miniwatts Marketing Group

Figure 1.3: Internet users in the world by regions, June 3, 2016. From www.internetworldstats.com/stats.htm.

The Bangemann Report (1994) was considered an important pillar for EU policies. In the report it was pointed out that the information society had the potential to improve the quality of life of Europe's citizens and the efficiency of European social and economic organization, and to reinforce cohesion. However, the idea of developing an information society in which "everyone can share," including marginalized and vulnerable groups, is linked more closely to social and economic policies than cultural ones. Another impetus for the policy-making area was the approach of UNE-SCO (2005), which promoted the concept of a knowledge society inside which the cultural aspects of knowledge were embedded and (re)shaped in local communities. The rising issues of web archiving and harvesting strategies, discussions and decisions taken in relation to intellectual property rights (IPR) legislation, digital rights management (DRM), and the open-access movement—the new ways of making resources available online, free or via suitable business models—strongly influence the goal to promote Europe's achivments to its citizens and to the rest of the world.

Research projects investigating issues that relate to the information/knowledge society and the rising concept and context of DLs became more and more dependent upon the participation of researchers and practitioners from a variety of disciplines and professional fields, including but not limited to library and information science (LIS) and information science (IS), cultural communication and learning theory, cognitive science, artificial intelligence, visual art history and theory, information management, history, anthropology, film, and music studies. In order to support digitization activities, researchers also began developing a variety of novel technologies and tools for the digitization of specific types of CH objects, which resulted in various national libraries, museums, archives, and government organizations and new services offering their digital content through organizational websites, specialized online exibitions or portals and aggregators. At the same time, the influence of the growing research and development in DLs in the U.S. and Australia became one of the important incentives for European researchers, practitioners, and policy makers to intensify their capacities in order to keep up with new challenges.

All these novelties have been by all means enriching and, at the same time, transforming cultural organizations and "old" paradigms, as well as users and the ways they approach information and culture. When we have users in mind, it should not be forgotten that anyone can be a user of a DL. Users can access the DL from anywhere, they can be of any age, have various educational backgrounds, and speak any language. However, most DLs are constructed with certain groups of users and their needs in mind.

But, as S. Chowdhury (2015) wisely questioned, is there such a thing as a "European user" (or "world user") for whom the digital products and services are built? It has already been stated that Europeans live in different countries and regions, speak different languages, have different ages, different educational backgrounds, different levels of digital and information skills, and, most of all, many different cultures. Designing a digital environment that can meet the information needs of this diverse population is a big challenge in itself.

While some authors state that many reflections about development seem to have "a fascination with technology as 'the' solution to development problems" (e.g., Mansell and Tremblay, 2013), others are stressing that ICT has been developing with lightning speed, deeply influencing society as a whole (e.g., Castells, 2000; Gleick, 1999; Bawden and Robinson, 2013). In Europe, given that the unpredictable ways in which technological innovations are interconnected with other changes in all areas of society, the situation is even more complex, due to the different levels of economic growth, investments in information infrastructure or improvement of information and media skills, and different cultures and traditions, to name some of the most notable ones.

The need for collaboration and the advanced supporting infrastucture and mechanisms for digitization and preservation of digital heritage has been highlighted by many authors, policy makers, and (even) governments. Sula (2013: 16) observes that "the 21st century has seen a dramatic rise in social networks and crowdsourcing, access to digitized CH materials, and interfaces for archives and collections that exploit the capabilities of linked data and visualization." The implications of digital technology for knowledge creation, the possibilities for "virtual CH," and the preservation and interpretation of cultural and natural heritage through real time, require immense and interactive techniques that have been continuously investigated and tested.

CHAPTER 2

The Digital Aura in Europe

2.1 INTRODUCTION TO CULTURAL HERITAGE ISSUES

In recent decades, the concept of heritage has evolved and expanded. Digitization and digital environments in general have been playing a notable role in how heritage is perceived today. The first decade of the 21st century recorded significant changes that had been occurring across the whole CH sector, including the noticable tendency toward an inflationary use of the notion of "heritage."

The higher aspiration to understand the entire heritage sector, reaching beyond museums or libraries, often considered as the most valuable and most used heritage institutions, became obvious in theory and practice. The definition of the term "cultural heritage" has been evolving throughout the 20th century from an approach referring exclusively to archeological sites and monuments to a definition that includes both tangible and intangible heritage and the close interrelations between the two. CH covers a wide area of many human activities, involves many different types of individual and group actors and monument sites, as well as organizations such as memory institutions (archives, libraries museums—LAM, etc.), local, national, and transnational authorities, voluntary sector organizations (e.g., preservation trusts, local history societies, arts organizations), researchers and organizations providing services that involve CH venues (cultural industry, research institutions, tourism, education, etc.).

According to the definition by UNESCO (1972), objects and land/seascapes belonging to CH distinguish themselves for their "outstanding universal value from the point of view of history, art, or science." The close interrelation between the CH and (national, regional, local) identity introduced in the last decades of the 20th century led to the consideration of intangible heritage as the mainspring of cultural diversity and a guarantee of sustainable development. UNESCO's (2003b) Convention on the Safeguarding of the Intangible Cultural Heritage states that "intangible CH" means the practices, representations, expressions, knowledge, skills—as well as the instruments, objects, artifacts, and cultural spaces associated therewith—that communities, groups, and, in some cases, individuals recognize as part of their CH. This intangible CH, together with tangible cultural objects, transmitted from generation to generation, is constantly recreated by communities and groups in response to their environment, their interaction with nature, and their history, and provides them with a sense of identity and continuity. Both the tangible and intangible heritage as well as digital heritage are covered by another UNESCO document—the Charter on the Preservation of Digital Heritage (UNESCO, 2003c). UNESCO holds that the disappearance of heritage in whatever form constitutes an impoverishment of the heritage of all nations, and recalls that the main goals of UNESCO are instrumental for maintaining, increasing, diffusing, and preserving knowledge. UNESCO's programs, Information for All and Memory of the World, provide a base for the comprehension of the nature of heritage and all activities on information policies and the safeguarding of oral and recorded knowledge, and serve as an impetus "to ensure the preservation and universal accessibility" of the world's heritage (UNESCO 2003a: 1).

Theoretical reflections on heritage, usually framed by the theory of cultural approach, have also been changing under influences from different disciplines and theories: R. Barthes's semiotic; P. Bourdieu's concept of the symbolic fields; and discourse analysis of the style elaborated by M. Foulcault; as well as the theory of narrative by P. Ricouer. Also influential was C. Geertz with his approach to the ethnology discourse and R. Girard with his contributions to the new discipline of cultural studies. (cf. Hecken, 2007; Müller-Funk, 2006). T. Eagleton (2000), one of the strongest representatives of the British postmarxsism theoreticians, empowered the theory of culture with his thoughts on the recent state-of-the-art of science and culture, considering all levels of culture's practical presence, its existence, reflections, and experience in life.

European history of culture, alongside the traditional approach to material culture that provided a framework for identification and interpretations of different art styles, artifacts, and architecture, has contributed to the general theory of culture with new ethnology- and anthropology-based approaches, that brought in new cross-cultural typologies of the behavior represented in the material remains. New interpretations of the Vučedol culture, the Thracian tumulus near Kazanlak, or the Old City of Herakleion, for instance, are among the examples of the better understanding of European culture. As Silberman (cf. 2007: 98–99) explains, there was a myriad of approaches and intellectual streams (processualists, structuralists, and post-processual scholars, for example) that represent "a distinctive methodology of study, with particular preferences for certain kinds of data and distinctive and differing criteria for documenting and analyzing the evidence." He also points out that the present fragmentation and inconsistency of information sources is to a considerable degree the result of distinct and long-established disciplinary epistemologies, which determine how the scholars in the specialized sub-fields and methodological traditions conceive objects of study and make them see different types of data as significant. Yet Silberman admits that the effort to establish interoperable tools for data collection, management, and analysis "can be the first step in creating innovative, new multidisciplinary forms of historiography." In accordance with this statement we might consider that he understood well how the widening of the access to new classes of networked data could encourage a deeper consideration of their commonalities and contrasts. Indeed, todays research activities and practices in any discipline, as well as interdisciplinary or multidisciplinary projects, could not be possible without a networked, approachable, well-managed, shared, and preserved data (often call "big data" or "scientific data").

The concept of "heritage" is constantly evolving as new meaning and values are continuously being attributed for a range of different, overlapping, and possibly conflicting purposes, be they economic, cultural, political, or social (cf. Lowenthal, 1998: 2). It is widely recognized that "heritage" means different things to different people, even within the same culture. Inside Europe it is characterized by its diversity and the presence of its manifestations: heritage is everywhere and, as Lowenthal stresses, one can barely move without bumping into a heritage site. Heritage has been an inspirer of the growth and advancement on one side, and a dangerous weapon in the hands of warmongers on the other.

According to Graham et al. (2000: 17), "Nineteenth-century conceptualizations of heritage emerged in the ethos of a singular and totalized modernity, in which it was assumed that to be modern was to be European, and that to be European or to espouse European values (even in the U.S.) was to be at the pinnacle of cultural achievement and social evolution." However, since heritage is inherently a spatial phenomenon, characterized by location, distribution, and scale, it is a fundamental part of cultural geography's concern with signification, representation, and identity, which is in Europe reflected in national, regional, and local identity on one side, and the strong feeling of the power of multicultural approaches on the other.

The socio-political changes also resulted in a new approach to the concept of heritage, especially in Eastern Europe, where heritage used to be more ideologized. Expectations from institutions and culture that were part of the social and political project in this part of Europe (cf. Šola, 2015: 12) started to change after the 1990s and communication inside different parts of Europe became intensified and contributed to the flow of ideas and multicultural and multilingual projects, and an exchange between cultural institutions and creative actors in the whole of Europe.

As Y. Albrecht (2016: 9) observes, Europe presents a unique experience in developing "cities and landscapes, works of art, music, and painting, the welfare state, the constitutional state, and democracy." On the other hand, Europe and its culture have been exposed throughout history, and especially during the 20th century, to genocide, war, exploitation, and persecution, which provoked constant tension. And, indeed, it is evident from Europe's rich and turbulent history that "European culture has steered a course between extremes of rationalism, expansionism, and bureaucracy on the one hand, and romanticism, adventure, and nationalism on the other" (Albrecht, 2016: 11).

Why has heritage become so important for society? Maybe because, as Le Goff (1995: IX) stated: "Europe is in the making," and without its history it "would be orphaned and unhappy." European CH's worth certainly lies in a combination of historical, symbolic, spiritual, aesthetic, and social values (cf. Sable and Kling, 2001; Throsby, 2003; Hansen, 2003). The historical character of heritage and its content provides a connection with the past and a sense of continuity, which is appreciated as an important proof of human history and the development of civilization. The symbolic meaning and power of certain places and objects add to people's and nation's cultural identity. The aesthetic quality of the cultural object obviously contributes to its enjoyment, inspiration, and creativity. While the difference between the intrinsic value of heritage (ethical and philosophic property, value that an object has "in itself") and its instrumental value (manifested in its social and economic implications) has been underlined in studies, the intrinsic value of heritage as the collective memory of the society is often neglected.

In recent years, the instrumental value of heritage has been claimed by various advocates of heritage and recognized by many policy makers. Culture (and heritage, as its indispensible part) is considered as one of the four pillars[15] of sustainable development on an equal footing with the others. As confirmed by multiple studies, heritage, if properly managed, can be instrumental in enhancing social inclusion, stimulating and supporting intercultural dialog, shaping the identity of a territory, improving the quality of the environment, providing social cohesion, and—on the economic side—stimulating tourism development, creating jobs, and enhancing investments in culture.

At the social level, heritage facilitates connection with others and it helps to promote local values and social cohesion and experience. As Arnold and Gezer (2008: 186) pointed out, CH places and objects can enhance the cultural and social capital and community welfare in a number of ways, based upon this multitude of values. The concept of heritage value, though, was not seen earlier as an important player in the economic sense. From the 20th century onward, and especially supported by digitization policies and practicies, the value of CH assets started to show the multitude of benefits that can be wheedled from its direct and indirect use and, even, non-use. In the past, especially from the 19th century, heritage was an important stimulus for artists and rich leisure people to plan their voyages. Heritage was, even earlier, a goal for pilgrims who studied old books and manuscripts hidden in monasteries around Europe. Nowadays, it is the most important single resource for international tourism, which is seen in its dual role: a resource of economic and cultural capital. Because of its ubiquity, heritage cannot be examined without addressing the implied questions—who decides what is heritage, and whose heritage is it? Moreover, with the digitization strategies and processes, it opened up questions related to the role of people who decide what of these valuable cultural assets is going to be digitized in order to be made visible and available to everyone. Although heritage is an economic instrument in policies of regional and urban development and regeneration, the economic uses of heritage are often ignored in literature, being regarded as somehow inferior to the cultural domain (cf. Graham et al., 2000: 256).[16]

By discussing digitization phenomena in a European context one should not neglect the fact that cultures are formed through complex dialogs and interactions with other cultures. Usu-

---

[15] It is commonly accepted that these four pillars are: environmental responsibility, social equity, economic health, and cultural vitality.

[16] The economic potential of CH and DCH has been a topic of several funds and projects (for instance, Creative Europe, the fund which helps the cultural and creative sectors to seize the opportunities of the "digital age" and globalization; the RICHES project, which investigates fiscal and economic aspects of cultural consumption in the European Union); strategic documents, plans, studies, and reports (for instance, Unesco and EU documents, Europeana goals, S. Tanner's reports, 2005, 2006).

ally associated with a variety of "players" (including museums, libraries, schools, cinemas, and the media), today the term "culture" includes digital resources and new services offered through numerous internet portals and social networks. As Benhabib (2002: 326) states, "the boundaries of cultures are fluid, porous, and contested." There is no doubt that the internet has added a new dimension to these relationships by constantly changing our attitude toward knowledge and culture in general, deregulating the circulation of cultural goods and services, and influencing deeply our understanding of creativity (cf. Le Glatin, 2007). In such a situation all cultural institutions have been acting in two basic directions: one relates to the effective and efficient content presentation of their collections, and the other allows them to generate new knowledge that can be transferred and complemented in intercultural communication and cooperation.

On the other hand, the development of the concept known as "memory communication" became an important issue that has been stimulating communities to develop themselves in the digital environment and at the same time to build bridges between different communities and cultures. Memory communication is based upon the concept of representations of past experience in line with the needs of present communities. This concept used to be well managed up until recently by the LAM and other institutions containing cultural objects and offering related services. However, the change in communication patterns has been challenging these institutions to answer to the needs of today's communities/users and find new ways of communicating CH assets. It is noted that, since the 1990s, LAM and other memory institutions have become visible in EU programs as important instruments for the implementation of EU's strategic objectives (cf. Manžuch and Knoll, 2007). Despite significant efforts in coordination activities and financial resources allocated to finding effective heritage communication solutions, it seems that the issues of how memory is communicated are not discussed in a satisfactory way, and "the terms are mainly used metaphorically" (Manžuch, 2009: 1). The concept of communication of cultural memory as a complex phenomenon that foresees the synergies between LAM studies and ICT is widely spread among researchers and practitioners. As it is known, cultural memory used to be mediated by designated institutions, primarily LAM institutions, which selected, collected, processed, and presented what was percieved and interpreted by these institutions as valuable assets worth preserving. In the digital environment many new players have been entering the field, offering their own interpretations and services. However, as Manžuch (2009: 3) noticed, EU programs from the first half of the 2000s, failed to start from "an understanding of the cultural and social roles of heritage" and focused on "pre-conditioned technological determinism" and economic aspects of CH.[17]

It was soon shown that digital culture reduces barriers and difficulties emerging in communication based upon analog documents, linked to time and place. Digital culture allows people to

---

[17] CH and memory institutions research was performed under the FP5 entitled, "Creating a User-friendly Information Society" (1998–2002) as well as in the "Information Society Technologies" (IST) priority in the FP6 (2002–2006).

adopt new forms of interaction and participation, especially through Web 2.0 and social networks, that widen the experience of community and allow audiences to become more creative. Undoubtely, digital culture changes the relationships between actors. "Collaboration in the digital era" became a slogan for cultural institutions, above all for museums and libraries, in communicating with their audiences (visitors and users).

From the theoretical point of view the digitization of CH "refers to the dynamic and evolving interdisciplinary domain that encompasses philosophical, social, cultural, economic, and managerial aspects and consequences of management of CH in the technological environment" (Manžuch et al., 2005).

When discussing the concept of public conversation at the core of digital heritage (DH) practices involving artifacts and their digital representations, Dalbello (2009b) recognizes two waves of practice that memory institutions pursued to extend their role as repositories to becoming participants in a broader discourse about heritage with the consuming public: the first wave of DL development characterized by isolated and fragmented efforts, and the other that is characterized by engagement of online audiences through social networking platforms.

Different models for collecting and presenting, as well as for preserving and using digital assets, have been designed and tested. Experts in the general theory of culture, heritage, and digital society have been contributing with conceptual elaboration and reflections on the social value of digital cultural heritage (DCH). Computer scientists have been engaged in such projects by providing and pondering technology-based conceptual framework(s), such as the DELOS Reference Model, or the 5S Model, for example (more about these models in Chapter 4).

Moreover, over the years, digital heritage's standing as heritage has been a source of considerable debate about an entity in its own right. The UNESCO's Charter on the Preservation of Digital Heritage (UNESCO, 2003c: 1) articulates this turn by creating a new legacy—the DH—which "consists of unique resources of human knowledge and expression. It embraces cultural, educational, scientific, and administrative resources, as well as technical, legal, medical, and other kinds of information created digitally, or converted into digital form from existing analog resources. Where resources are 'born-digital,' there is no other format but the digital object." Various resources of information and creative expression are increasingly produced, distributed, accessed, and maintained in digital form (Cameron and Kenderdine, 2007: 3).

At the beginning of 21st century, a small but significant part of the digital world was digital cultural content, which helped to capture cultural memory and preserve the human record for future generations. However, it was widely recognized by professionals from various disciplines that a large portion of such a small amount of digitized and digitally born heritage was not well captured and preserved. Obviously, the notion of the digital cultural content became a broad and not well-defined concept including digital multimedia surrogates for cultural artifacts that were usually held in the collections of the world's museums, libraries, and archives, as well as "born-digital" resources of that kind. Much of the digital cultural content originates from trusted and respected information pro-viders, such as LAM institutions, and is of high quality. For many centuries these objects have had an intrinsically high value for education and research and have been relatively stable over time. The same providers started to digitize their own material, adding to the richness of digital surrogates collections and contributing to the promotion of a sense of cultural identity at local, regional, and national levels. However, it was soon noticed that, in the process of the creation of a digital future, cultural policies were focusing their attention more on the digitization of heritage items than on the emergence of a new culture for which interactivity and convergence were becoming the main aspects. Although it was understood that digital culture reduces barriers and difficulties emerging in the communication of culture, as well as transforms the whole cultural field and encourages new forms of creative expression, until recently, cultural policies in Europe did not give digital culture a particular space in most cases.[18]

Finally, in all attempts to capture and manage digital assets, digital preservation plays a special role. Cultural resources have faced various threats during the rise of civilization, and in the digital era a number of new threats have appeared. For instance, the need to preserve not only dig-ital cultural objects but also the data stream's integrity and the means to interpret the data stream, as well as the means by which the resource is experienced. According to Deegan and Tanner (2008: 236) "digital data is in danger, not because it is inherently fragile or flawed, but because there is a continually accelerating rate of replication, adaptation, and redundancy of hardware, software, and data formats and standards, which may mean that the bit stream may not be readable, interpretable, or usable long into the future." All CH institutions, digital services providers, and policy makers face new challenges in regard to digital curation.

As we are primarily looking at heritage organizations that "have institutionalized authority to act as custodians of the past in Western societies" and hold a significant part of the "intellectual capital" (cf. Cameron and Kenderdine, 2007: 1) of today's society, their use of emerging digital technologies is crucial when it comes to the idea that this "intellectual capital" has to be activated, engaged, transformed, and preserved.

Of course, technology alone is not sufficient to meet these expectations and growing user demands. Equally important is the role of European CH institutions that "hold the key to a treasure chest of unique resources" and have "the potential to turn the key to unlock the true value of our rich cultural heritage" (EC, 2002: 12).

If we uphold the definition of CH consisting of manifestations of human life that repre-sent a particular view of life and witness the history and validity of that view, there is no better testimony than European CH. Moreover, digitization of CH objects became a key tool by which

---

[18] For instance, Flemish cultural policy listed e-culture among its priorities for the 2004–2009 period, with stra-tegic objectives to digitize CH and encourage digital creativity; or, the Netherlands whose new cultural policy encourages digital creativity.

citizens could engage with their own history, culture, and language while also being of enormous value in restoring cultural artifacts to public view where the original is lost or too fragile for normal display (Deegan and Tanner, 2008: 220). There are unfortunately many examples of such loss, even in recent days.[19]

2.2   CULTURAL HERITAGE AND INSIDE EUROPEAN POLICIES AND STRATEGIES

Heritage has been an important topic covered not only in digitization strategies but in cultural policies at national or transnational levels, as cultural policies today focus on two main issues: cultural diversity and intercultural communication. Indeed, it is impossible to deal with the European and global dynamic of cultural diversity without referring to intercultural communication and dialog. This communication became a dynamic process containing various forms of interrelations, transmissions, and exchanges of cultural values. Moreover, the interaction between different cultures under the impact of ICT opened many questions in regard to the concepts of cultural diversity and their position in the global society. In such a changing environment the concept of cultural policy became an important starting point for cultural development at local, national, and international levels.

Cultural policy refers to institutional support that provides a base for both aesthetic creativity and collective ways of life, and is reflected in systematic and regulatory guides to actions that organizations adopt in order to achieve their own goals. In the last 30 or so years, Europe has gone through a period characterized by the mixture of different approaches to cultural policy issues as well as to digitization strategies, as one of the newest approaches that relates to modern culture. But some authors (e.g., Miller and Yudice, 2002: 1) claim that cultural policy is "bureaucratic rather than creative or organic," although it can stimulate organizations and individuals to promote culture by providing appropriate working frameworks.

In the European context, the use of the term "cultural policy" reflects these activities and products that directly or indirectly come within the competency of the European bodies and agencies as well as national ministries of cultural and arts councils. Out of all public policies and systems, cultural policies can be distinguished as key resource structures that support and assist cultural organizations in their attempts to adopt to the changes in society and more specifically in order to reach wider audiences. Cultural policy provides structural guidelines and legislative frameworks that include legal acts on founding cultural/heritage organizations and their governance and financing. Since the focus of this book is on European approaches, goals, and outcomes to the DL field covering CH, and due to the complex nature of the DL, we intend to shine light primarily

---

[19] For instance, the City Library of Vinkovci, that burned to the ground during the bombing in 1991, in Croatia, was only able to renew its lost special collection with photocopies that were later digitized.

on policies related to the digitalized and born-digital cultural assets as one of the underpinnings of modern Europe.

In the mid 1990s, the EC launched a remarkable program to boost the use of ICT in the emerging information society, anticipating economic growth, a growing employment market, and an overall increase of quality in all aspects of our lives. Prompted by Al Gore's "White Paper for Building a National Information Infrastructure" (1993) and the "Bangemann Report" (1994), Europe and the Global Information Society, new technologies were considered as one of the key drivers of future prosperity in both continents.

The legal basis for the creation and development of information infrastructure on a national level constitutes a number of the laws that affect the field of information, informatization and protection of information, science development, education, libraries, and other heritage institutions, copyright and associated rights, legal protection of software and databases, preservation, etc. These documents governed the relationship between the participants of information processes and defined the principles of work of the whole information infrastructure sector, as well as provided a framework for building up national digital collections on the basis of legal deposits and relevant curation regulations. In some countries, the legal basis laid the foundation for the active involvement in the international information exchange, enabling joint projects and presentations of outcomes. This was especially important for countries that were behind the Iron Curtain, as the new legal regulations secured citizens' rights to free access to information and reinforced international cooperation and participation in a Global Information Infrastructure (GII) movement.

Between 1996 and 2001, the EC and national governments managed to create regulatory frameworks removing some of the obstacles to the accessibility of future e-business markets. One important step was breaking up the national telecommunication monopolies to lower access costs, which allowed a faster buildup of an information infrastructure (EC, 2002).

The Council of the EU and the EC gave impetus to the e-Europe Initiative (EC, 2000), expecting that new funded programs should develop advanced systems and services that would help improve access to Europe's scientific and educational resources and improve their visibility.

From the beginning of the 2000s, the EC and member states have invested millions of Euros in supporting CH institutions to digitize their collections and make them available on the internet. Between 2005–2009 the EC invested €149m in the eContentPlus Program alone.[20]

When it comes to the visions of ICT development, and its applications for purposes that are specific to the CH sector, from a European perspective, the first point of reference was the Lisbon

---

[20] From the statistical data published by the EU it is clear that, for instance, the Erasmus plus program was given 1.834,2 EUR millions, compared with 9,626,8 EUR millions for Horizon 2020 from which the amount of 24,7 EUR millions was allocated for ICT. Find more details at: http://ec.europa.eu/budget/figures/interactive/index_en.cfm.

Strategy. Launched in 2000, the Lisbon Strategy[21] stated that by 2010 the EU should become the most competitive and dynamic knowledge-based economy in the world. This was certainly a fearless vision, although some succeeding events, especially those provoked by economic reasons, made expected progress much slower. The development of the "information society" has been placed at the heart of the Lisbon Strategy, with the eEurope 2002 Action Plan (issued in 2000) and eEurope 2005 Action Plan (issued in 2002).

One of the objectives of the Action Plan 2002 was to stimulate European content in global networks in order to fully exploit the opportunities created by the growing use of digital technologies. Since digitization at that time was highly fragmented, and involved duplication of efforts and risks that could have jeopartized best use of the investment, it was felt that a specific action for member states and the EC should have been taken jointly to create a coordination mechanism for digitization programs across member states. The actions ranged from bottom-up involvement of cultural institutions (by spreading best practice) to top-down policy initiatives for European Frameworks[22] projects that were funded in order to find solutions for growing problems with interdependency and multimedia and multilinguality of digitized items and services offered to specialists and the general public.

In 2001, in Lund, Sweden, representatives and experts from member states accepted the document known as Lund principles, which served as a basis to make recommendations for actions meant to "support coordination and add value to digitization activities in ways that would be sustainable over time" (ECo, 2001: 1). The document identified that the diversity and richness of Europe's cultural resources are extremely important for the future information society. The coordination across Europe was needed, and, as a logical consequence, the Lund Action Plan (EC, 2001) proposed a set of actions to be undertaken by the EC and the member states. Its overall objectives related to the increase of the visibility of ongoing activities and share of experiences, as well as to the identification, promotion, and exchange of best practices and the adoption of common standards and compatible procedures that were expected to enable the creation of a common cultural area by offering e-services to citizens and researchers, that are interoperable, extendable, and offered from a unified European platform. The plan also envisaged opportunities for the whole e-content industry in Europe.

---

[21] The Lisbon Strategy was born as a European commitment to overcome the differences in growth and productivity between the EU and its leading global competitors at the time, the U.S. and Japan. Europe's deficit in terms of technological capacity and innovation became the symbol of need to assure EU competitiveness; this was at the heart of the emphasis laid on advancing toward a "knowledge society," which became the strategy's best-known slogan (Rodriguez et al., 2010: 11).

[22] From its launching in 1984, the idea of the Framework Programs has expanded in scope and scale, shifting from industrial sectors, as it used to be in practice since the 1950s, or energy, environment, and molecular biology to other research fields, including ICT and DL research. European Frameworks projects include: FP1 (1984–1987), FP2 (1987–1991), FP3 (1990–1994), FP4 (1994–1998), FP5 (1998–2002), FP6 (2002–2006), FP7 (2007–2013), and FP8 – Horizon 2020 (2014–2020).

As a basis for further development, the MINERVA network was established as a valuable forum for open discussion on the harmonization of digitization policies and for an exchange of best practices in which national representatives from partner institutions and government bodies took part.[23] One of the first issues addressed was to build a shared platform of recommendations and guidelines and develop common data models and services, which was done through two major projects—MINERVA and MICHAEL. These programs were funded in order to create a proper basis from which two branches of development started: toward citizens (the national cultural portals and, later, Europeana—more details in Chapter 3) and toward researchers (building up and developing dedicated e-infrastructures in the CH sector, which started to rapidly transform into a data-based science).

The CALIMERA network of professionals from the CH sector produced some valuable documents on digitization processes, copyright, licensing models, orphan works, etc.[24]

A number of projects under FP6 and FP7 were supported with the goal of helping the EC propose new lines of funding that would bring in new analysis and recommendations for the better organization and management of digital resources and their sustainability. These plans were major drivers and coordination frameworks for digitization projects and future funding and were soon implemented in new strategic documents on digitization, not only by member states but also by some of the non-EU countries as well.

Following the Council Resolution on Preserving Tomorrow's Memory from 2002 (cf. Justrell, 2003; EC, 2004) an experts workgroup was proposed to identify the state-of-art and plan the developments needed to implement the resolution's principles. The workgroup was led by the ERPANET and MINERVA projects, chaired by the EC and the Italian presidency. One of the outputs was the Firenze Agenda, which was intended to stimulate and coordinate ongoing initiatives in Europe.

The DigiCULT Report (EC, 2002)—prepared for the Directorate-General for the information society—recognized that Europe's cultural and memory institutions were facing very rapid and dramatic transformations that were not only provoked by the use of increasingly sophisticated technologies, but also by the need to re-examine the role of modern public institutions and the related fast-changing user demands. The report suggested that heritage institutions can utilize ICT "as

---

[23] A series of working groups had been set up to address specific thematic issues using the methodology of benchmarking, identification of good practices and competency centers, and fostering interoperability and IPR, and contributing to the creation of inventories of digital content. Issues relating to quality and user needs were also considered.

[24] It should be stressed that copyright law is not consistent across Europe and for content involving multiple rights holders and territories, such as films or television broadcasts, the situations can be complex. In most of Europe, copyright lasts for 70 years after the death of its longest living creator. If copyright is held by a corporation, then it lasts for 70 years after publication. Once this temporary protection has come to its end, all legal restrictions cease to exist.

effective instruments to direct public interest back to the original objects in their trust, by providing contextual information, enlightened with narratives and visualizations with computer-aided renderings and displays" (EC, 2002). The experts who participated in the DigiCULT study identified several challenges they considered indispensable. They suggested that European and each national CH policy should include issues related to the future development of the digitization of CH and its public use and re-use. The diverse and multilingual approach to CH and the need for a systematic, comprehensive, and transparent methodology for digitization were seen as starting points that would support attempts to integrate content from small CH institutions across the sectors and in the regions, to lower barriers for access to the digital culture, and to improve its effectiveness and cost-efficiency. It was evident that there were more new users' target groups whose needs and demands vary from those of users known so far in heritage institutions.

Such a recognition was emphasized even more in the EC's i2010 Program (EC, 2005a), which was seen as a thoughful attempt to foster the boost of Europe's digital economy. ICT services, skills, media, and content were recognized as a fast and growing part of the economy and society. In 2006, the i2010 Program—the EC's strategic policy framework in this field—centered on three priorities:

- "to create a Single European Information Space, which promotes an open and competitive internal market for information society and media services;

- to strengthen innovation and investment in ICT research; and

- to support inclusion, better public services, and quality of life through the use of ICT" (EC, 2008c).

In 2007, the Council of the European Union adopted the first-ever European Working Plan for Culture (2008–2010) based upon its Agenda for Culture (EC, 2007b). This document lists digitization as one of the five priority points in the context of intercultural communication and dialog promotion. Basically, the promotion of access to culture, in particular the promotion of CH, multilingualism, digitization, cultural tourism, synergies with education, especially art education, and greater mobility of collections, became priorities for the period 2008–2010 (EC, 2007a; EU, 2008). In the following plan for 2011–2014 (adopted in 2010) CH was listed as priority area D,[25] including mobility of collections.[26]

---

[25] The other priorities were: cultural diversity, intercultural dialog, and accessible and inclusive culture; cultural and creative industries; skills and mobility; culture in external relations; and culture statistics.

[26] The other three are: accessible and inclusive culture, cultural and creative sectors, creative economy and innovation, and promotion of cultural diversity, culture in EU external relations, and mobility. Later on, the Work Plan for Culture 2015–18, adopted by EU Culture Ministers in 2014, listed CH among four main priorities for European cooperation in cultural policy-making.

Another document, i2010 Digital Libraries (EC, 2008c), focused on the future of the DL in Europe, and the EDL was seen as a flagship project. This focus had become a major reference point of funding programs such as the eContent Plus program. The EDL was considered actually both as a vision and an emerging reality. The purpose, generally accepted by the EDL, is still to further democracy, equality, and social justice, increase access to information, disseminate culture and knowledge, and contribute to a meaningful and informative leisure time.[27]

Being considered as the most visible element of the EDL, the Europeana—European portal to digitized and born-digital heritage—was highlighted by the European Parliament and the Council both as a showcase for the CH of the member states on the internet and a unique access point to that heritage for everyone. At the same time, they had underlined the economic potential of making European cultural treasures available online as a source for creativity and new products and services in areas such as tourism and learning. In the document Europeana–Next Steps, the next phase of development of Europeana and its orientation for the future were presented. The main challenges for the coming years were detected in relation to enriching Europeana's content with both the public domain and copyright material of the highest quality and relevance to users, as well as to a sustainable financing and governance model (cf. EC, 2009a: 2). In accordance with the communication i2010 Digital Libraries from 2005 and the Recommendation on the Digitization from 2006 (EC, 2006a) that provided a basis for the development of strategic and operational frameworks, many EU institutions produced a series of strategic documents related to the Europeana in order to help to bring the vision of the EDL to life.

Thereafter, with the strategic document "Europe 2020" (cf. EC, 2010a), which aimed to achieve smart, sustainable, and inclusive growth in the European digital environment,[28] the vision and development of the new economy in Europe was foreseen as a strength if based on knowledge, innovation, and sufficient use of ICT, and it follows the targets based upon the accepted seven pillars.[29] Digital technology played a crucial role in each of these seven pillars when it came to interoperability and standards, security, and fast and ultra-fast internet access, for example. "The Digital

[27] As several authors suggest (Aabø, 2005; Audunson, 2005), the role that was previously played by public libraries and museums has to be continuously re-evaluated and its outcomes monitored according to the new waves of changes in today's and tomorrow's digital society, bringing the digital assets and services to the center of their existance and future development.

[28] Job creation at the end of 2009 witnessed a decade-long wipeout, since European GDP fell by 4% in 2009, industrial production dropped back to the levels of the 1990s, and 23 million people—or 10% of Europe's active population—were unemployed. The crisis was a huge shock for millions of citizens and exposed some fundamental weaknesses of the European economy. Moreover, Europe was falling behind on high-speed internet, which affected its ability to innovate, as well as on the online dissemination of knowledge and distribution of goods and services (cf. EC, 2010a: 5, 10).

[29] These pillars are: the digital single market; interoperability and standards; trust and security; fast and ultra-fast internet access (Broadband Europe, open Internet, for example); research and innovation; enhancing digital literacy, skills, and inclusion; ICT-enabled benefits for EU society. Some of the pillars already have lists of specific actions (over 120 at the time of writing).

Agenda for Europe" (DAE) was considered a compelling strategic document, as it stressed that for the development of a digital single market the potential of ICTs for development, innovation, and economic growth should be better exploited (cf. EC, 2014b). CH also plays a vital role in several of the Europe 2020 flagship initiatives (such as the DAE, the Innovation Union, or the Agenda for New Skills and Jobs). More specifically, the DEA is considering CH to be one of the crucial elements in achieving smart, inclusive, and sustainable growth. The DAE also strives to connect the activities planned in the frame of three interlinked pillars, one of which relates to the design of the best framework conditions for the creation and diffusion of cultural assets. This attempt covers copyright issues and open access policies and strategies that are supposed to be indispensable in forming a legal framework for digitizing CH, making it accessible to all, and unlocking the potential for its re-use. The ICT-enabled benefits for EU society were seen as a base for the support of various efforts in the digitization of European cultural content, e.g., by providing a platform for aggregating digitized cultural resources with an easy and single access point—Europeana.

Moreover, to be able to digitally connect as many of the European citizens as possible, proposals for projects that aimed to enhance digital literacy, improve skills, and foster social inclusion have been stimulated and funded from EU funds.[30] The value of the digital heritage was also recognized in the agenda in regard to the online accessibility of Europe's CH, which required close collaboration between EU member states and cultural institutions, and also between these cultural institutions and other stakeholders. The agenda stressed the following topics: participatory governance of CH; skills, training, and knowledge transfer; traditional and emerging heritage professions; risk assessment and prevention for safeguarding CH (cf. EC, 2014b).

The EC's Recommendations from 2011 also provided guidelines for the selection of CH objects in the context of selection for digitization, in particular in regard to Europeana. These guidelines were supposed to help cultural institutions in selection of the material to be digitized by taking into account criteria such as the beauty of the content, and historical or highly important items. The recommendations also considered that content should be user-oriented, e.g., that selected items for digitization had to follow the preferences of users. Special attention was paid to the inclusion of the content that could make hidden treasures generally available, known only to experts, and make them attractive to users once digitized. Also, many items that are too fragile for users to consult, or to be displayed, require the attention of those responsible for digitization selection processes. The recommendations also suggested that appropriate mechanisms should be developed so that the same objects from different collections should not be digitized twice and that related collections are digitized in a shared context.

Not only was digitization generally seen as an important means for ensuring greater access to, and use of, cultural material, but it was also expected that it would add new dimensions to the

---

[30] Around 100 M€ per year was assured for the technological developments for digital content and CH (cf. Rouhana, 2011: 3).

benefits of the use of CH. For example, by improving online accessibility to cultural material, citizens throughout Europe and worldwide would be able to use it for leisure, studies, or work; it would give Europe's diverse and multilingual heritage a clear profile on the internet; and it would help Europe's cultural institutions to continue carrying out their mission of giving access to and preserving Europe's culture and heritage in the digital environment. New approaches had been taken and new networks built, one of them being the Comité des Sages, which was challenged to make recommendations to the EC and to cultural actors, governments, and agencies throughout the EU, concerning how best to capture, foster, share, and celebrate the diversity and excitement of European culture and creativity online. In particular, the Comité addressed three areas: funding sources for digitization; interaction between public and private organizations in the digital age; and solutions for digitization of public domain and in-copyright material (cf. Poole, 2010: 9).

Moreover, the European Council, in its Conclusions (ECo, 2012) on the EC's Recommendation on the Digitization, confirmed its statement that digitized cultural material is an important resource for European cultural and creative industries, which account for about 4% of the EU's GDP and jobs. The council, though, invited the European member states to several actions, in particular to consolidate their strategies and targets for the digitization of cultural material; to consolidate the organization and provision of funding for digitization; to promote public-private partnerships; to improve the framework conditions for the online accessibility and use of cultural material; to contribute to the further development of Europeana and the EDL; and to ensure long-term digital preservation (cf. ECo, 2012: 5).

The new, fast-growing digital culture became a "hot" topic of cultural policy development and debate. According to the Compendium of Cultural Policies and Trends in Europe,[31] only a few countries adopted a strategy in the mid 2000s, which, in the context of new technologies, includes digital cultural content (Finland, Great Britain, Greece, Ireland, the Netherlands, Norway, Poland, Portugal, Moldova, and Slovakia).[32]

Also, it should be mentioned that a new strategy on European CH for the 21st century, which is under discussion, focuses on several priorities: the contribution of heritage to the improvement of European citizens' quality of life and living environment; the contribution of heritage to Europe's attractiveness and prosperity; education and lifelong training; and participatory

---

[31] The Compendium of cultural policies and trends in Europe is a major project set up in 1998 jointly by the Council of Europe and the ERICarts Institute (ERIC – European Research Infrastructure Consortium).

[32] Interesting examples of cultural strategies were those of Great Britain ("White Paper on Competitiveness," issued in 1998 and Culture Online issues in 2002). The key aim of the British Culture Online was to mobilize the resources of the cultural sector to enrich school education, particularly in subjects such as history, literature, music, art, and design, strengthening new links between digital technology and cultural resources). In Finland Content Creation Strategy, issued in 2007, defined digital content creation as the production of cultural, documentary, educational, research, entertainment, and marketing content for the electronic media.

governance in the heritage field. This strategy was drafted by the Steering Committee for Culture, Heritage, and Landscape (CDCPP). [33]

In 2016[34] the EC presented a set of measures to support and link up national initiatives for the digitization of industry and related services across all sectors and to boost investment through strategic partnerships and networks. The EC also proposed concrete measures to speed up the development of common standards in priority areas, such as 5G communication networks or cybersecurity, cloud computing, the internet of things, data technologies, and cybersecurity, which are crucial in modernizing public services. As part of these plans, the EC started activities to set up a European cloud that, as a first objective, could give Europe's 1.7 million researchers and 70 million science and technology professionals a virtual environment in which to store, manage, analyze, and re-use a large amount of research data.[35] The European cloud initiative is focusing on five priority areas: 5G, cloud computing, the internet of things, data technologies, and cybersecurity.[36]

When it comes to digital public services it was recognized that people and businesses are still not reaping the full benefit from digital public services that should be available seamlessly across the EU. In this respect, the EC put forward 20 measures to be launched by the end of 2017 that include the setting up of a digital single gateway enabling users to obtain all information, assistance, and problem-solving services needed to operate efficiently across borders.[37]

It is evident that the vision of the ECo and EC included digitization, accessibility, and digital preservation of CH and scientific knowledge, highlighting the role and benefits of DLs. By building and developing the digital culture framework on Europe's rich heritage, the policy documents also drew upon the multicultural and multilingual environment with technological advances and new business models for the heritage assets and services.[38]

---

[33] The HEREIN (European Heritage Heads Forum) System was launched in April 2015 as a consultation on the methodology for drawing up the European Cultural Heritage Strategy for the 21st century (http://www. ehhf.eu/news/european-cultural-heritage-strategy-21st-century-%E2%80%93-herein-consultation). More at: https://www.coe.int/en/web/culture-and-heritage/cultural-heritage (accessed: 2017-02-07).

[34] http://europa.eu/rapid/press-release_IP-16-1407_en.htm.

[35] For example, the EU is investing €500 EUR million in a pan-EU network of digital innovation hubs (centers of excellence in technology) where businesses can obtain advice and test digital innovations. (EC press release, April 19, 2016. http://europa.eu/rapid/press-release_IP-16-1407_en.htm).

[36] The public and private investment needed to implement the European Cloud Initiative is estimated at €6.7 billion. The commission estimates that, overall, €2 billion in Horizon 2020 funding should be allocated to the European Cloud initiative. The estimation of the required additional public and private investment is €4.7 billion in the period of 5 years (EC, 2016b).

[37] More at: http://europa.eu/rapid/press-release_IP-16-1407_en.htm.

[38] More data can be found in each of three reports published by the DigiCULT program. The first two reports cover the period between the 2006–2010 after the publishing of the "Recommendations on the Digitisation" (EC, 2006a), and the third report, covering the period between 2011–2013, draws on "Recommendation on the Digitisation from 2011" (EC, 2011b), as well as on the related "Council Conclusions" of May 10, 2012.

Nevertheless, it is worth noting the high level of awareness from heritage institutions of their duty to provide low-cost access to materials to the public prior to the need to make a profit from those materials. Obviously, CH represents a significant power for the current century in Europe, and contributes to the strengthening of the position of LAM and other players in the CH sector in the turbulent digital arena. As considered in EC's document Getting Cultural Heritage to Work for Europe (EC, 2015a), CH is at the heart of what it means to be European. Furthermore, it is considered by both governmental institutions and citizens as a powerful solution for improving economic performance and people's lives.

2.3   DIGITAL LIBRARIES FOR CULTURAL HERITAGE: A LITERATURE PERSPECTIVE

The representations, interpretations, and usage of CH as digital objects have been housed in so-called "digital libraries." The term DL has been in use since the 1990s, but the perspectives of DLs and professionals from different fields used to be quite different, although several initiatives have been undertaken to establish a framework for the exchange of ideas and comprehension between them. In our approach, we see a DL is an organization that provides various resources to its users through competent staff, who should be responsible for selection of content, design, and management of appropriate structure, as well as for offering access through thoughtfully organized information services. The goal of the DL that offers CH content is closely connected to the ability to interpret the content and its context, including the need to preserve the integrity of each item, and to ensure the persistence over time of each item and collection it belongs to. Such an interpretation of the notion of a DL also includes necessary functionalities and the need for its interoperabilitiy based upon capable information infrastructure and linguistic principles that allow mediation of content through multilingual approaches. Since the mediation of CH through DLs strongly depends upon a developed and innovative technological infrastructure, many such new technologies, tools, and standards for digitization and management of different kinds of digital objects and artifacts have been explored, tested, and offered for use to various users' groups.

These effort are presented in the literature on DLs, mostly in journals and proceedings arising from conferences or on respective project-based websites, and continue to make valuable contributions to the ongoing development of the sector, albeit they have yet to foster a body of sustained critical thinking about the meanings and implications of the apparent transformations, challenges, and possibilities posed by communications technologies. However, much of the discourse about the relationship between culture/CH and digital technology has been descriptive and introspective, focusing on projects and their technical considerations or overall outcomes.

There are a number of publications and reports that cover the early stage of the development of DLs in Europe (for detailed overviews or further reading see: Raitt, 2000; Dalbello, 2004 and 2009a; Liu, 2005).

A number of publications covering different aspects of digital culture with an emphasis on the role and outcomes of DLs, cooperation within the digital environment, and empowerment of the European CH as one of the key elements of European society, have appeared in Europe over the past 15 years (e.g., Schreibman et al., 2004, 2016; Manžuch et al., 2005; Kajberg and Lörring, 2005; Cohen and Rosenzweig, 2006; Feather, 2006; Cameron and Kenderdine, 2007; Siemens and Schreibman, 2008; Boot, 2009; Ruthven and Chowdhury, 2015; Salarelli and Tammaro, 2006; Béquet, 2014). Authors discuss broader social, cultural, and political issues, e.g., DCH as a political concept and practice and the need to reshape social, cultural, and political power in relation to cultural organizations and education through communication technologies. The issues concerning the representation and interpretation of CH as digital objects provoked new approaches in theory and practice (e.g., Dahlström, 2015; Warwick et al., 2012; Myburgh and Tammaro, 2013; Dalbello, 2015; Ruthven and Chowdhury, 2015), bringing into focus the relationship between digital objects and consumers of digital heritage, in particular relationships between wider communities and heritage institutions, by using new technologies and social tools.

It is necessary to remind readers that in the 1990s major journals that initiated discussions about DLs and sharing of the research results were established and that a number of new journals have grown since then (e.g., *Ariadne, D-lib* magazine, *International Journal on Digital Libraries, International Journal of Digital Curation, Journal of Digital Information, Digital Humanities Quarterly, Digital Humanities Now, Digital Medievalist, International Journal of Humanities and Arts Computing, Literary and Linguistic Computing*). From 1997 onward, professionals in LIS and CS have been organizing European or internationally based conferences and workshops in Europe covering broad and specialized topics of DLs (such as, European Digital Library Conference, Libraries in the Digital Age, the International Digital Curation Conference, the International Symposium on Information Science, CO:Opyright: Challenges and Practices of Copyright and Licensing of Digital Cultural Heritage). Professional societies, such as the International Federation of Library Associations and Institutions (IFLA), Liber, European Bureau of Library, Information, and Documentation Associations (Eblida),[39] or the European Association for Library and Information Education and Research (Euclid),[40] have been organizing their annual conferences and workshops covering a wide range of DL-related topics.

---

[39] EBLIDA is an independent umbrella association of library, information, documentation, and archive associations and institutions in Europe www.eblida.org.

[40] EUCLID is the only active association that connects LIS teachers and researchers from HEIs in Europe. www.euclid-lis.eu.

Dozens of national and federal grants have increasingly been awarded to projects in the area of DLs, digitization projects in particular, with a goal to create more digital content and make it available to audiences in Europe and worldwide.

Digitization guidelines of various kinds and purposes soon became an important reference point for digitization activities. A variety of handbooks and best-practice guidelines have been produced over 15 years by experts (see, for example, Beagrie and Jones, 2001; Deegan and Tanner, 2001, 2006b; Lee, 2001; EC, 2002; Drake et al., 2003; Hughes, 2004; Bestandsaufnahme, 2007; Greengrass and Hughes, 2008; Kolb, 2008; Pinninger, 2008) as well as by institutions and specialized centers. Good examples are various guidelines that appeared under the "Jisc Digitization Workflow Guidelines" (cf. Abu-Zayed, 2009), the British Library digitization strategy from 2008 and British Library digital preservation strategy from 2013, DigiCULT, MINERVA, or CILIP publications, as well as those that come out as a result of conducted DL projects. Examples of how to plan a digitization project can be found in journal articles as well, S. Tanner's (2001) being one of the most used at the time of publishing, because it was taken as a kind of guide that offered a list of useful recommendations. There are also books that discuss LIS/IS trends and research and development of DLs in Europe (cf. Bawden and Robinson, 2013; Spink and Heinstrom, 2012). All of these events and products were developed almost parallel or with a certain delay compared with similar attempts in the U.S. or Australia.

Two overviews covering the most important themes in regard to the DLs (Fox and Urs, 2002; Bearman, 2006) that presented the state-of-the-art of relevant literature in the studied periods include some European policies, institutions, and projects. It is interesting to note that some of the themes and topics that were presented in the former study do not appear in the later one, but in general both review papers cover the most important trends, methods, and tools that had been in use, and shed light upon the most active actors in the early and more advanced phase of the development of DLs, a number of them from Europe.

Also, an increasing number of books on DLs have been published since 2000. They dealt with general themes—such as an introduction to DLs, principles and practice of DLs, DL and digital humanities; and specialized issues—such as the use of digital resources from cultural institutions in teaching and learning, preservation of digital material, technical and economic aspects of DL, education for DLs, etc. (for instance, Lehmann, 2004; Harvey, 2005; Tedd and Large, 2005; Jacobs, 2006; Rydberg-Cox and Jeffrey, 2006; Carr, 2007; Jones, 2007; Nicholas and Rowlands, 2008; Baker and Evans, 2009; Blandford and Bainbridge, 2009; Verheul et al., 2010; Gillman, 2010; Hughes, 2011a; Jochum and Schlechter, 2011; Chowdhury and Chowdhury, 2011; Díez Carrera, 2013).

Many novel tools and techniques have been developed over the past years to facilitate digitization, protection, promotion, and access to CH information. Undoubtedly, digital technologies enabled cultural organizations to overcome the traditional constraints imposed by physical sites. The ICT, and especially digitization technologies, have been crucial in expanding their audience reach, empowering the social value of culture, opening new possibilities for new areas of activity and services, and adding a new dimension to the cultural value of heritage. Nevertheless, it has been understood that the processes of building up and managing DCH information involves a number of challenges. The sources of CH information include a variety of objects, ranging from stone carvings to manuscripts, paintings, sound from various objects, film, video games, etc., whose digital copies might be included in DLs, following a range of carefully chosen selection criteria. It is obvious that each of these objects may require different metadata, indexing, retrieval, and filtering techniques, whose aim is to support much richer functionality (Ruthven and Chowdhury, 2015).

In her study of the five libraries—Library of Congress and European national libraries—Dalbello (2009a) concluded that national libraries were playing a key role in the construction of ideas around DH, and that digitization was conceived as a formative national event. The American Memory, Memory of Portugal, or Gallica digital libraries had as their primary purpose the recreation of national heritage along familiar national collecting strategies.

From the late 1990s onward, the use of cultural content in DLs has increased exponentially and continues to do so. This is mostly due to changing circumstances that the CH sector itself cannot influence, such as changes arising through research, development, and innovation in the ICT industry and wider content markets (cf. Poole, 2010:11–12). There is no doubt that DLs have significantly improved the accessibility of material for research, learning, and enjoyment and the visibility of the European CH. Yet, at the same time, they have created new concerns about quality, sustainability, return on investment, and long-term cost. Ideally speaking, a socially sustainable digital information service should be ubiquitous, i.e., it should be embedded in the work and culture of people in such a way that they get access to the information that is relevant to their work or activities without even actively asking or searching for it (cf. Chowdhury, 2015b).

Because the volume of DCH data is growing quickly, it is a priority to manage such a huge amount of data in an efficient and selective way, making it available to the researchers and the citizens in a European as well as a global dimension. As the idea of making more citizens aware of the value of digitized and born-digital material was not in focus from the beginning of digitization projects and programs, efforts were made from the mid-2000s to assure that treasures of heritage institutions originally "hidden" to the public become available and accessible to all who are interested in these valuable special collections.

Needless to say, a great percentage of these collections are unique all over the world. It is also the same case in regard to the collections in languages other than English. A lot of DLs, especially DL projects of national libraries, focus on collections in their own languages. The focal point of all these activities should be the users. One of the major goals of any DL is to provide easy access to information and knowledge to the general public, or to specific communities of users, and to be accessible over time. The users of CH information may vary from experts and professional users in a specific domain, like history, archaeology, or music, to schoolchildren and novice users. Each of these user categories may have different information needs and information-seeking behavior that need to be considered while designing user-centered information access systems (Ruthven and Chowdhury, 2015: 4). Beaudoin (2012) highlights the need for DL frameworks that would enable CH to be used in different situations, by different users. In her view, contextual information is fundamental to the understanding of many aspects of digital content. Through the development of eight dimensions of context (technical, utilization, physical, intangible, curatorial, authentication, authorization, and intellectual) she proposed a fuller record of digital content with the intention of ensuring that digital preservation efforts include recording contextual information about each object to enable future retrieval, assessment, management, access, and use.

Moreover, Liew (2012) warned that there is also a problem regarding the indigenous cultural knowledge "hidden" in a number of CH institutions. In Europe, such collections of indigenous cultural knowledge are held in many local LAM institutions from northern parts of Europe to the Mediteranian islands, from isolated rural areas with rich traditional practices in Poland to small village museums in Normandy. These are part of oral heritage collections and could be digitized only if the institutions that collected them consult with indigenous communities, putting in place internationally acceptable guidelines, policies, and practices.

According to Beagrie (s.a), digitization activities related to CH are very resource intensive, as well as crucially dependent upon the relationship between different stakeholders, including users. Therefore, using a holistic lifecycle approach for digitization initiatives is needed to develop a sustainable and successful DL.

By discussing the changing environment of 21st-century life, Tanner (2005) expressed the view that highlights the need to deliver cultural resources, especially from major cultural organizations, such as museums or national libraries, which are seen as a crucial part of their mission in society, e.g., to educate and elucidate, to promote and disseminate, and to preserve culture. These attempts that are basically connected with a goal of every DL—to reach out to new audiences and to offer to current audiences new resources and services—were and still are major driving factors behind many DLs and digitization programs. Tanner also stated that "the justifications for delivering cultural resources digitally are rarely made on economic or mercantile grounds, as the returns on investment are relatively small, but the cultural, educational, and prestige returns are quite high" (Tanner, 2005: 6).

It is not suprising though that DLs were seen as opportunities to capitalize upon this important and priceless heritage for the benefit of education, research, creative re-use, tourism, and other human activities. For the communication of digitized heritage conditions sine qua non is the infrastructure that could bring closer those who are responsible for CH in various cultural institutions and goverments, as well as users who need to be well prepared to be able to use digital materials and services as well as to understand and appreciate the criteria for selection of materials for digitization.

Another indispensible aspect of DLs for CH in general is the constant fear that data might be destroyed or lost, which raises a concern for its protection and preservation. The documentary heritage has always been at risk of damage or destruction through natural or human forces: fire, flood, warfare, or neglect (cf. Deegan and Tanner, 2006b). The main reasons for the threat to digital heritage or, more precisely, digital obsolescence, are two factors that put in jeopardy current efforts in archiving and preserving what has been digitized or digitally born: first, since the technology develops ever more rapidly, the time before a particular technology becomes obsolete is getting shorter; and second, "unlike their analog counterparts, digital resources are much more 'unstable,' with the effect that the integrity and authenticity of digital cultural resources is corrupted" (Geser and Mulrenin, 2002: 210).

Another important element of DL growth and usage is e-learning as an important pillar of the knowledge society, based upon hybrid collections as a mix of physical and digital libraries. In EU strategies, e-learning was given much of the attention and its implementation and sharing of resources have been supported by a number of innovative educational projects (some of them will be discussed in Chapter 5).

As Hargreeves' report (2011) indicated a number of challenges in today's digital environment and called for the adaptation of the existing approach and rules, there has been substantial interest in, and investigations of, copyright issues which couldn't be considered "fit for the digital age when millions of citizens are in daily breach of copyright, simply for shifting a piece of music or video from one device to another" (Hargreeves, 2011: 5). Many approaches have been documented and opinions presented in the literature on copyright issues: from the ideas of Open Access and Creative Commons to the proposal that calls for the abolishment of the copyright.

There are a number of emerging issues connected with DLs in general that provoked lively discussions, such as those related to the decentralization of responsibilities and resources, as in Europe where different approaches have been taken, ranging from the centralized national systems for DLs and especially for the representation of the DCH, to scattered agencies that are responsible for only certain aspects of DL development, as well as to growing attempts to build rich digital resources that sometimes are not easily approachable. This was a noticable characteristic of the "European approach" to digitization at the early stage of DL development when DCH was localized in cultural communities of small reach and specialization, without much concern or awareness of a broader audience or scalable meanings.

The review literature covers in detail these and other trends focusing either on some projects (for a more detailed overview see, for instance, Chowdhury and Chowdhury, 1999; Raitt, 2000; EC, 2002; Liu, 2005; Tanner, 2005; Tariffi et al., 2004; Altenhöner et al., 2011; Ross, 2012), or digitization plans and reports presented in the EU and national information and digitization policy documents, which reveal their visions, intentions, and plans (cf. for instance, EC, 2002, 2004, 2008b, 2009b, 2010c, 2012, 2014c, 2015a, 2016a; Invest to Save, 2003; DPimpact, 2009; Hargreeves, 2011).

2.4   CONCLUDING REMARKS

CH covers a wide range of human activities. It involves many different types of individual and group actors, as well as monuments' sites and organizations, such as memory institutions. CH is considered to be an important topic, in particular today with new approaches to culture supported by ICT. Culture and CH, if properly managed in the digital environment, can be instrumental in proving the value and benefits of culture for human civilization in general, for they shape the identity of a territory, improve the quality of life by providing social cohesion and strengthening intercultural dialog, stimulate and support education and science, and strengthen business by adding value to tourism development, creating jobs, and enhancing investments in cultural development.

The policy documents and strategies—at EU and national levels of almost every European country—place emphasis on encouragement and preservation of cultural and linguistic diversity, multiculturalism, and cultural dialog. New IC technologies helped in expanding cultural content and access to European cultural wealth. Following these lines, important documents have been prepared on many new issues related to digitization, use, management, and preservation of CH.

It is evident that CH and digital cultures, which include DCH as well, have been exceptional themes in the last two decades. The EU and different professional and scientific communities have put a tremendous effort into making cultural, educational, and scientific resources publicly available, in spite of the global economic decline that began in 2007 and the tendency of the fragmentation of efforts along national and sectoral lines. Although fragmentation, as is evident in many reports, has been caused by the involvement of multiple ministries in European countries, by different funding models and the lack of skilled personnel, or by different rates of economic growth—to name the most obvious causes—it is evident that the EU, national policy making bodies, and professionals from various disciplines have been making tremendous efforts to overcome barriers by jointly looking for new cooperative working models.

Today, enabling and developing a Europe-wide virtual research community dedicated to CH is still seen as a top priority. Alongside UNESCO's Memory of the World Program, CH in the EU initiatives and program calls for building an unprecedented and inclusive cultural landscape in Europe, seeking to assure access to cultural content through the networks of heritage institutions that participate in digitization projects, to offer new tools and new services, and to seek for interoperability and new business models for cross-domain content navigation.

As was seen in previous sub-chapters, in Europe—as in any other parts of the world where information infrastructure is developed and available to citizens—digital culture became an important political concept and practice that reshapes social, cultural, and political power in relation to cultural organizations and all aspects of life.

CHAPTER 3

Digitization and Coordination of Digitization in the European CH Sector

3.1 INTRODUCTION

Most of the services offering cultural information in digital form are based on national or thematic aggregators and initiatives like Europeana, and provide a myriad of digital cultural resources for people, not only in Europe but worldwide. To facilitate the use of heterogeneous CH in mainstream services and applications, a number of projects have been conducted, e.g., dealing with principles and criteria for CH resources to be digitized, systems for content creation and usage, and systems that enable integration of cultural digital resources in the tools and services familiar to the user, including interoperability issues, different metadata models, and automatic application of their mappings. In parallel, the development of the Semantic Web and the availability of many linked open-data resources have opened new dimensions in searching and using scientific and cultural resources (cf. Orgel et al., 2015).

As presented in Chapter 2, the EC has been stimulating and funding development and research projects in the LAM sector, and promoting innovations and cooperation since 1990.[41] Cooperation and investigation of new methods for presentation of valuable heritage was not a novelty for the LAM community. As Terras (2015)[42] documented, since the 1970s there has been growing cooperation between LAM institutions in promoting and encouraging the use of ICT and, thereafter, digitalization as potential tools in attempts to increase access to CH material through various forms of digital media. As to libraries, it all began early in 1988 with the Libraries Program, when the role of libraries in the information society was recognized and appreciated. It continued with Framework Programs (FP3, FP4, FP5, FP6, and FP7) that included not only libraries but also, gradually, museums, archives, and other institutions containing valuable CH items and collections.

European heritage institutions (LAMs, archaeological sites, audiovisual repositories, etc.) started to digitize their content with two intentions: to preserve it in a digital format and to enable access to digital content and services for the variety of users from different geographical origins or educational backgrounds. Today, it is estimated that only a very small part of the European CH have been digitized, although many projects have been carried out, and a growing number of new

---

[41] The Appendix lists the most important facts about European DL projects mentioned in this book.

[42] See Terras (2012) for a fuller account of the history of digitization in the LAM sector.

projects for digitization are ongoing. Moreover, having in mind that a huge amount of born-digital material has also been generated, the heritage sector has been facing huge organizational challenges.

It could be said that almost all of the first batch of DL projects were finished at the end of the last century. A great number of achievements came from the exploration and experimentation phases taken by the "big" players, such as Bibliothèque de France (BNB), the British Library (BL), the Czech National Library, or the Royal libraries in the Netherlands and Denmark. In most member states various committees, expert groups, and newly established authorities started to work devotedly to provide a more accurate basis for cooperative efforts in digitization processes, including accepted guidelines and recommendations, as well as in evaluation of the outcomes.

Links with commercial information providers, such as Google and Microsoft, and mass digitization of printed content, continued or started in the 2000s. Commercial providers had the resources to digitize everything they possibly could, often in conjunction with world-leading institutions that could not have afforded to digitize their holdings alone. However, such new digitization initiatives brought with them very complex issues, not only regarding copyright and access, but also political debates and oppositions.[43] In some way, mass digitization was used to show to others a range of capacities, knowledge, and skills in one institution or nation as a kind of point of pride, which was a trigger to action. The mass digitization initiatives also raised questions about the potential exploitation of the dominance of ownership of digitized versions of cultural and heritage content. The growing use of social media brought in non-easily estimated issues related to new ways of communication between institutions and the individual user, such as the relationship of social media to more thoughtful digitization practices (cf. Terras, 2012).

Indeed, among many technological developments that brought up new formats, platforms, and new media, there was one of the most disruptive technologies—Web 2.0—which had an important impact on web publishing, introducing new types of publishers (for instance, online samizdat, heritage institutions as publishers). Additionally, the questions related to interdependency and interoperability in DLs in general, and in particular in the DCH systems, as well as challenges of multimedia and multilingual approaches to the digital content, could be taken as the growing tendencies of the DL activities in Europe from the mid-2000s onward.

---

[43] It is well-documented and cited that Jean-Noel Jeanneney of the French National Library had raised concerns about Google's potential influence on global culture with its creation of an immense database of content from the U.S. The fear was felt in the way that Jeanneney foresaw the possible interpretation of history and culture based upon only one culture's digital heritage. In an article in *Le Monde* entitled, "When Google Challenges Europe," he warned of "the risk of a crushing domination by America in the definition of how future generations conceive of the world." While welcoming the BL's joint digitization program with Microsoft—since in his view it diminished the risk of a Google monopoly—he also saw the BL/Microsoft deal as an act of "anglo-saxon solidarity" with a big American enterprise and, as such, counter to the close cooperation with the European national libraries that were working toward the development of the EDL (cf. Brindley, 2008, p 69). It is interesting to read the interview with Jeanneney by A. Riding (2005) published in the *New York Times* to get a complete picture of the topic.

In the last few years, issues related to the trustworthiness of digital copies have been raised. Alongside information professionals, digital humanists also find it necessary to stress that the digital object needs to be enhanced with large amounts of metadata, indexing, descriptive encoding, paratexts, and bibliographical information. Such an approach and persuasion contributed to the development of critical digitization as a qualitative process in which experts and digital humanists are concentrating on what is unique and contingent in the documents. Undoubtedly, up until now, digitization processes have been creating core content for digital resources, increasingly augmented by born-digital material. Additional infrastructure is felt to be required in order to deliver digitized material in a useful manner. As is commonly known, project management, records creation, and adding metadata for each digital item are often more time consuming than the creation of digital surrogates themselves. Even more, as M. Dahlström (cf. 2015: 479–480) highlighted, the constant consideration of the need to apply standards and new tools (such as Metadata Encoding and Transmission Standard—METS for metadata, the Functional Requirements for Bibliographic Records—FRBR for descriptive cataloging, and Linked Open Data—LOD for sharing and reusing data through, for example, Application Programming Interfaces—APIs) is needed in order to gain the best outcomes of digitization initiatives.

Gradually, metadata became a popular topic of conversation between experts around the globe. According to Arnold and Gezer (2008), as a digital representation of an artifact is a representation of certain relevant characteristics of the artifact, it does not represent the original and complete artifact itself. Thus, the role of metadata describing the context of the original and its digital replica and possibilities of "linked data" are crucial.

The richness of digital resources has been extended and strengthened through a multitude of innovative collaborations between different parts of the LAM, education and cultural sectors, and public and private spheres. Professionals also started to be involved in digitization projects and developments of international standards together with colleagues from outside Europe (for instance, in regard to Dublin Core or Warwick Framework).

In Follett's (2008: 55–56) words, the electronic trends[44] at the beginning of the first decade of the 21st century had many virtues, but the trends anticipated certain distortions. In this chapter we are presenting the main goals and trends with outcomes that shaped and influenced the development of DLs in Europe, in particular DLs that cover the CH sector. For a better understanding of the circumstances in which the single or joint projects in digitization of CH in Europe have been developing, insights on the approaches and current state of the information infrastructure are presented, followed by an overview of the rise and development of DLs in Europe, as well as an overview of Europeana as a most visible and used digital portal in Europe.

---

[44] In the UK, the term "electronic library" was widely used in the 1990s; in France "bibliothèque numérique" stands for digital library.

3.2   DEVELOPING INFRASTRUCTURE FOR DIGITIZATION

"What can possibly be said about the state of digital technologies that will not be woefully and embarrassingly incorrect by 2030?" (Tanner, 2010: 37)

All infrastructures embed social norms, networks of various kinds of relationships, and ways of thinking and acting (cf. Borgmann,2000; Monteiro et al., 2014; Mongili and Pellegrino, 2014). As aftereffects, they provoke another chain of changes that leads to the redistribution of authority, influence, and power. Knowledge infrastructures are no different; they create tensions and raise many concerns, and infrastructure for CH is no exeption.

E-infrastructure came under the focus of the European research and development agenda at the beginning of the 1990s when it was recognized that researchers need to be empowered with the possibility of easy and controlled online access to various resources and services. Basically, ICT-based infrastructures and services were seen as a useful aid in strengthening collaboration between scientists and scientific institutions from different research disciplines. Following these trends in science, the EU took new steps toward the building up of an overall e-infrastucture, aiming to enable citizens of Europe to access various kinds of information material and services for their education, cultural, business, and leisure needs.

There is a common understanding that infrastructures (and in particular information infrastructures—IIs) allow, facilitate, mediate, saturate, and influence in many ways human material and immaterial surroundings. As stated by Mongili and Pellegrino (cf. 2014: XXI), IIs are not static and immobile in time and space; they are rather vulnerable and demand constant care, renewal, and catching up with technological innovations. Furthermore, all kinds of infrastructures, including IIs, are often shaped and intertwined with networks of various types of relationships and distributed institutions, agencies, professionals, and policy makers. IIs are characterized by openness to a variety of users, interconnections of numerous modules/systems designed to satisfy a multiplicity of purposes and goals, and by creating new systems and practices that often tend to restrict the scope of design, as traditionally conceived. Today, a growing opinion is that the key to infrastructures is their multilayered, modular, and rough-cut character.

IIs, like all infrastructures, are "subject to public policy," which was also evident in EU policy documents since 1994, when the EU proposed the European Information Infrastructure. The idea and later developments evolved from Bangemann's report that outlined the EU vision of the information society and pointed to areas in which action was needed. IIs were among these sectors that needed urgent actions toward better connectivity and a common regulatory mechanism. European II was seen as evolving into an ever-tighter web of networks, generic services, applications, and equipment, the development, distribution, and maintenance of which occupy a multitude of sources worldwide (cf. Bangemann Report, 1994). On the other hand, IIs depend upon policy making, regulatory frameworks, and the involvement of human resources capable of dealing with constant changes and challenges. Being a constituent element of the global II (Borgman, 2000), people—information and computer specialists and many others involved in digital activities—have to follow trends, learn how to cope with challenges, gain new skills in using technology, and show their competency in performing old and new tasks as well as foresee future challenges.

Many actions related to the building up of IIs were started in the 1990s and continued either at national or European levels, or both. Here, an overview of the main approaches, activities, and development trends is given based upon the review literature that covered two decades—the last of the 20th century and the first 15 years of the 21st century. The latest plans and actions are presented by the method of extracting from the most important ideas, plans, and projects from primary literary sources, including websites of relevant institutions and projects.

The Follett report in the UK (1993), which can be taken as one of the earliest examples of foreseeing the changes in society, influenced the common understanding of libraries as containers of information and suggested their new social roles in providing information. Following Follett's recommendations, national networks, such as JANET (Joint Academic Network), were supported in their attempt to initiate and coordinate projects that dealt with new models for navigation through documents of different kinds, building up databases and datasets, designing and presenting national information strategies, supporting training initiatives, etc. (cf. Earnshaw, 2008: XVIII). In the UK, the JISC,[45] which was the parent organization of eLib,[46] funded a number of development programs aimed at supporting universities by piloting the use of appropriate new technologies. Parallel to these and some other national initiatives, such as national IIs in the Netherlands, Germany, or France, were the programs eEurope 2003+, eEurope 2005, and i2010, which began to form a base for the further development of IIs in Europe in the first decade of the 2000s.

Many information institutions across Europe at that time expressed their intention to change their existing II. However, when changing an organization's II, changes in its philosophy and strategy are also needed. According to van Veen (2005), "big" information institutions like national or university libraries gradually started to be seen as a part of global knowledge, which influenced vigorously their traditional image as closed systems.

In line with these attempts, national ICT strategies for the cultural sector became vital to support both the retro-conversion of existing heritage resources into the digital form, as well as the creation of new digital collections for which activities a proper II was needed (cf. Ross, Economou, 1998). In Brindley's (cf. 2008: 66) opinion, II at that time had to be improved and constantly upgraded, as the concept of information strategy was emerging, whereby information

---

[45] The Joint Information Systems Committee (JISC) supported UK universities and their libraries on innovative paths and new services and funded the Electronic Libraries program (eLib), which started in 1995 (Pinfield, 2004; Baker and Evans, 2009: 2).

[46] In contrast to the U.S. Digital Libraries Initiative (DLI), the eLib program characterized itself right from the start as "development" rather than research (cf. Rusbridge, 1998: 2).

and libraries were seen as important knowledge resources underpinning academic education and research activities.

Approaches to the building up of sophisticated infrastructures taken by national governments were based upon the socio-political structure and traditions. For example, the French internet industry and other communications sectors used to be more heavily regulated than those of Germany, but, as members of the EU, these and other member countries have been making a continuous effort to take an active part in decision-making processess that result in legal frameworks, including those related to the development and use of advanced technology. They also became active in research projects and collaborative programs that later aimed to build EDL.

In regard to DCH, the European e-infrastructure was not seen at the level of European common policy-making as something that had to be built from scratch—a new infrastructure—but somehow was conceived as a new approach based on the interoperation and federation of national and regional systems, with the scope of valorizing existing resources. In other words, "the keyword was interoperability among national, regional, and thematic systems" (Fresa, 2013: 31), which varied in size, capacity, and developmental stage, as well as in organizational structure and financial resources. In many aspects IIs stemmed from existing cultural, educational, or scientific infrastructural elements such as ICT networks, CH organizations, or educational programs.

As part of the national IIs, there were new established expert centers for digitization of CH, such as the center at Göttingen State and University Library and the center at the Bavarian State Library in Munich (cf. Brahms, 2001). In Germany—imbedded in the Information Infrastructure Program of the German Federal Government for the years 1996–2000—Global-Info[47] aimed to provide an infrastructural basis that would enable all researchers in Germany to have direct access to literature, research results, and other relevant information. In contrast to the American Digital Libraries Project, the German program was based on furthering cooperation with universities, publishing houses, book dealers, special subject information centers, and learned societies, as well as academic and research libraries, rather than with the public (cf. Raitt, 2000; Ball, 2009).

Moreover, in several countries IIs for research were initiated with a goal to stimulate the use of ICT by a wider audience than just libraries. The focus was on the improvement of the research-related IIs and support for innovations, primarily in digital academic publishing. The

---

[47] Global-info was initiated by the Information and Communication Commission of the German Research Council (Deutshe Forschungsgemeinschaft). The German Digital Libraries Program, which was funded by the Federal Ministry, since 1998 managed to involve many German libraries and information centers to offer new ideas and deliverables of the various research projects that were in the form of tested, workable prototypes to be implemented in the German national II (cf. Raitt, 2000).

approach of the Dutch Government in the Netherlands[48] and governmental decisions in Scandinavian countries[49] are good examples of the early awareness of the need to build IIs in the early 1990s.

On the other hand, in East European countries that used to belong to the so-called "Soviet block," a complete absence of publicly accessible digital information was present before the 1990s. The penetration rate of telephones was well below the EU average in some countries, for both fixed and mobile telephony as well as for the availability of computers. In an article on the social impact of the "digital divide" in Central and East Europe (CEE), N. G. Dragulanescu (2002a) compared and contrasted access to new technologies and electronic information in various countries, focusing on Romania, which was placed at one of the lowest positions in Europe in terms of penetration and availability of ICTs.[50]

It was obvious at that time that CEE countries had to take strong-willed steps in order to become part of the international information society, dealing in the first place with some noticable obstacles, such as the insufficient interest in e-business in these countries, the lack of legislation in the information technology field, and the low remuneration of IT professionals. Several countries had presented their road maps, for instance Poland (cf. Grabowska and Ogonowska, 1993) and Estonia (cf. Kalvet, 2007). In Bulgaria a national strategy was adopted in 1999 (cf. Chobanova, 2003) and in Romania in 2002 (Bakó, 2007). The national plans indicated how governments planned to address obstacles that prevent free access to information and knowledge, development of new competencies, consolidation of democracy and government institutions, and improvement of the quality of life in general. These plans also highlighted new opportunities for LAM institutions to join the digital world by connecting to broadband internet, developing a web presence for each institution, creating national networks, digitizing documents, creating virtual libraries, and introducing e-government and e-business (cf. Dragulanescu, 2002b).

At the beginning of the 1990s, considerable support from the EU, the U.S., Japan, the World Bank, the Mellon and Soros Foundations, and other countries and agencies assisted the

---

[48] The SURF Foundation, established in 1987 to coordinate the implementation of a multi-year plan for the improvement of the application of ICT, had become a nationwide supplier of services (cf. Pieters, 1996).

[49] In Denmark, the Ministry of Research, the Ministry of Education, and the Ministry of Culture initiated, in 1996, Denmark's Electronic Research Library (DEF) as a national virtual library service involving national policies for infrastructure, national licenses to full-text databases, digitizing of printed material, and retro-conversion of catalogs, etc. (cf. Thorhauge and Petersen, 2001).

[50] As stated by Anghelescu (2005: 448), statistics indicated that in 2003 11.11% of Romania's population used a computer, out of which 31% were personal and 69% were institutional. In 2001, 3.3% of Romania's population had internet access; some more, 7.4%, had it in 2003 and 18.6% in 2004. Aabø (2005), who presented some statistical data from Norway for 2002, noted that 70% of the Norwegian population between the ages of nine and 79 used a personal computer in an average week. According to NUA, (2003) as of July 2002 Denmark had 62.73% of the population online; the Netherlands had 60.83%; Norway had 59.2%; Belgium had 36.62%; and Italy had 33.37%; while France had 28.39%. The smallest percent of the population online in the EU was in Greece, 13.5% (NUA, 2003). At the same period, for example, only 10% of the Russian population had internet access (EC, 2004).

CEE countries in developing their IIs through monetary grants and loans and contributions of technical expertise (cf. Borgmann, 2000). By analyzing the notion of II, Borgman claimed that they became one of the key issues in national development policies, pointing at the rising problems and the specific issues in different regions, especially in Eastern Europe. Almost immediately after the political changes of 1989–90, these countries began large-scale investments in telecommunications and computer networks, by creation of the physical IT network infrastructure backbone systems, which made it possible for major research and higher education institutions, libraries, public museums, and archives to use a rapidly developing IT infrastructure. The issue was elaborated also in a follow-up study by Caidi (2001), as well as in published articles, conference papers, and reports written by authors from that part of Europe (cf. Anguelova, 2005; Šimić, 2007; Németh, 2014; Digitisation, 2004). In Russia, the Interagency Program for the creation of the national network of computer telecommunications for science and education was launched,[51] as was, at the same time, the LibWeb project aimed at network integration of information resources of major libraries and information centers of Russia.[52]

In 1998 the Working Group on Telecommunications of the Russian-American Commission on Economic and Technological Cooperation (the "Gore–Chernomyrdin" Commission) approved the concept of the interagency DL program, its purpose, and main elements.[53]

At the turn of the century in every European country some kind of II was set up, and digitization activities were directed toward nationally coordinated programs and key institutions. In 2003, for example, Austria took a first major step toward a systematic approach by initiating the building up of an infrastructure for digitization activities and the Austrian coordination mechanism for digitization works.[54] An important contribution came from the Vienna Computer Center, which provided external connections to the internet to countries with low-level infrastructure or to those that for various reasons could not manage it on their own (i.e., to Croatia, which was ex-

---

[51] The initiative was jointly taken by the Russian Ministry of Science, the Russian Foundation for Basic Research (RFBR), the Russian Ministry of Education, and the Russian Academy of Science. The program aimed at the creation and use of IIs, including regional infrastructure, which provided priority directions to scientific research and higher education, taking into account the economic conditions (cf. Syuntyurenko and Hohlov, 2000).

[52] By the beginning of 2000, these projects helped in opening access to more than 4.7 million bibliographic records, 540,000 titles of magazines, and about 4.3 Tb of full-text information from major libraries and information centers of Russia. The result of the first phase of the project in 1995–1998 was the creation of the LibWeb infrastructure and the organization of access to bibliographic, technological, and other types of information of the project participants (cf. Ershova and Hohlov, 1999; Syuntyurenko and Hohlov, 2000; Akimov et al., 2005).

[53] This idea was supported further at parliamentary hearings organized by the Committee on Information Policy and Communication of the State Duma of the Russian Federation (cf. Syuntyurenko and Hohlov, 2000).

[54] The Austrian coordination mechanism consisted of the Austrian Federal Ministry for Education, Science, and Culture (strategic and funding level), a domain expert from the Austrian National Library (professional expertise), and Salzburg Research, an independent research unit that is well situated within the European research community (operational level) (cf. EC, 2002; Mulrenin and Greser, 2002).

periencing war circumstances). The network access in these countries expanded quickly thereafter. However, network growth in the region continues to be constrained by the lack of high-capacity telecommunications lines (cf. Borgman, 2000: 246–247).

In other EU countries, the end of the 1990s was characterized by discussions and acceptance of national information policies and IT strategies. According to the results of the IFLA survey in 1999 (cf. Niegaard, 1999), Austria and Liechtenstein had national information policies; national IT strategies were accepted in Denmark, Ireland, Italy, and Portugal; and both documents were in Finland, France, Germany, Island, Lithuania, the Netherlands, Slovakia, and Sweden. Furthermore, in some countries stronger regulatory reforms provided a solid foundation for further progress (for instance in Spain, when the Spanish government made significant progress in adopting the regulatory principles prescribed by the EU and WTO, in particular, the General Telecommunications Law in 1998). It can be said that in the first decade of the 2000s telecommunication networks had been strengthened throughout Europe, and the number of users had grown. Moreover, the development of a homogeneous infrastructure for electronic access to academic information, standardization, and unification at the national level started at the beginning of the 2000s, when several countries joined GEANT, the pan-European data communications networks.

The situation in Eastern and Central Europe in the 1990s mirrors the statement that technology does not develop independently of its social context, including a number of historical, cultural, and economic as well as technical factors. Starting from the assumptions that DLs are a mixture of content, technology, and people, Caidi (2001) reported on the development of IIs and DLs in four CEE countries studied (the Czech Republic, Slovakia, Hungary, and Poland). In her conclusions, Caidi states that the transitional period for these countries was characterized by the attempt to establish a climate of cooperation as a basic prerequisite for any further developments, which was obviously an attempt that had to deal with the tradition of the goverment-related and institution-oriented working culture from socialist times. In fact, the earlier initiatives, mostly helped by western library-oriented philanthropic foundations, were instrumental in the management of change, enabling the building of II and encouraging the transfer of technology. The financial incentives and the new approach to the resource-sharing concept led to a series of consortia that resulted in projects such as the Krakow Library Project and NUKAT in Poland (cf. Burchard, 2001), CASLIN in the Czech Republic and Slovakia (cf. Stoklasová and Krbec, 2002), and HUSLONET in Hungary (Németh, 2014). These and other projects developed later, especially after joining the EU, were tightly connected with the adoption of internationally recognized standards in the field of networking, technology, library and information services, and building the DLs.

In ex-Yougoslav countries the level of the IIs also reflected the differeneces between so-called "developed" and "underdeveloped" republics. Although initial experiments with computer networks in academic and research environments in Croatia began in the mid-1980s, with SRCE (University of Zagreb Computer Center), the "Rugjer Boskovic" Institute, and some other academic institutions in the country, in 1991 the initial idea of the national communication network was born, and the new CARNet network[55] started to offer its services first to higher education and research institutions and later to all schools and some public institutions (such as public libraries and museums). Both institutions, SRCE and CARNet, have been working on building a strong information infrastructure with elements related to physical status (integrated and interconnected network), information organization in its various forms (applications and programs for the access, processing, and management of information), network standards and protocols (for connecting networks, protecting privacy of an individual, security of information, security of networks), and people (content, application, and service developers, education of users, in particular university and school teachers).

In Slovenia, the development of the Cobiss network enabled not only the informatization of Slovenian libraries, but also has been constantly improving its network by adding participants from other ex-Yugoslavian countries and improving its services as a vivacious contributor to the development of cooperative services and DL content in the Balkan region.[56]

The Agreement on the Establishment of the COBISS.Net Network and the Free Exchange of Bibliographic Records, created in autonomous library information systems of Bosnia and Herzegovina, Montenegro, Macedonia, Slovenia, and Serbia, was signed in 2003, later (in 2006) the Bulgarian National Library and some libraries from Albania (2013) joined the network (cf. Seljak and Seljak, 2002).

At the EU level the extension of the existing IIs and building of new ones in order to foster the development of a network-based knowledge economy and stimulate growth was strongly supported after 2010. The DAE included a set of specific broadband coverage targets forming the base of further developments, e.g. universal broadband coverage by 2013 and universal broadband coverage of speeds of at least 30 Mbps by 2020. In order to monitor the progress of the broadband coverage DAE's objectives, DC Connect (the European Commission Directorate General for Communications Networks, Content, and Technology) has commissioned the Broadband Coverage in Europe project to measure the household coverage of all the main fixed and wireless broadband technologies with a specific focus on Next Generation Access (NGA) technologies. Up to 2016 there were two reports published covering 31 countries across Europe—the EU28, plus

---

[55] CARNet (Croatian Academic and Research Network), which was approved by the Croatian Ministry of Science and Technology, established its connection through the pan-European research network GEANT. In 1995 the official status of CARNet changed when it became a Croatian government institution (cf. Aparac and Vrana, 2001).

[56] In 1987, when a shared cataloging system was adopted by the then Association of the Yugoslav National Libraries as a common ground for the library information system and the system of scientific and technological information of Yugoslavia, the role of the organizational solutions and software development was taken over by Institut informacijskih znanosti (Institute of Information Sciences—IZUM) from Maribor. In 1991 IZUM promoted the COBISS (Co-operative Online Bibliographic System and Services) as an upgrade of the shared cataloging system. At that time, the same acronym started to be used for the related software and services (cf. Seljak and Seljak, 2002; http://www.cobiss.net).

Norway, Iceland, and Switzerland. The second report (EC, 2015b) analyzes the availability of nine broadband technologies across each market, at national and rural levels, and compared the data with those from 2013. The results showed that over 216 million EU households (99.4%) had access to at least one of the main fixed or mobile broadband access technologies (excluding satellite) at the end of 2014. While the overall broadband coverage remains unchanged, an increase in the absolute coverage by over three million households has been recorded compared to 2013. One of the major problems detected was the access to fast broadband services in rural areas, which remains the major priority at the European level and a target for further investments in rural NGA deployments.

EU law covers fixed and wireless telecoms, internet, broadcasting, and transmission services. The Electronic Communications Regulatory Framework, adopted in 2002 and revised in 2009 (EC, 2009c), is composed of a series of rules (directives, regulations, recommendations, etc.) that apply throughout the EU member states. It encourages competition, improves the functioning of the market, guarantees basic user rights, and pursuit of lower prices, higher quality, and innovative services for customers.

The rapid development of ICT brought along several major problems concerning the issues of complexity and the predictions related to socio-economic changes and technological development trends, as well as to sustainability issues. The EU supported the development of digital infrastructure in the first decade of the 21st century with a main goal to answer these problems, e.g., by investing in the design and building of top-quality ICT systems "that are reliable, easy to use, adaptive, capable of development and efficient" in both performance and cost (Jeffery, 2006: 1).

On the other hand, it became clear that a new type of governing the cultural sector was needed. Among the first countries that came up with new solutions was Norway, which set up the unified body the Norwegian Archive, Library, and Museum Authority, known as ABM-utvikling at the beginning of 2003. This was, and still is, the main strategic and consultative body at the national level that promotes partnership and cooperation among these institutions and works as an intermediary between cultural institutions and the Norwegian government (usp. Østby, 2003).

The infrastructure for the particular set of activities (preservation, for example, for which UKWAC has laid the foundations of a national web archiving strategy and a shared technical infrastructure for the UK) or sectors (Higher Education—HE or CH) was developed separately. The experience of UKWAC[57] showed that it was important to focus on two key areas of strategic development: the future coordination of web archiving at the national level, taking into consideration the requirements of legal deposit legislation; and the evaluation and appraisal of software, platform, and tools to ensure a future shared technical infrastructure for web archiving. The problem faced

---

[57] The technical development work is being carried out largely under the auspices of ITPC. Current ITPC membership comprises: BNB, National Library of Italy—Florence, Helsinki University Library—the National Library of Finland, Royal Library—National Library of Sweden, National and University Library—Iceland, Library and Archives Canada, National Library of Norway, National Library of Australia, the BL and the Library of Congress.

not only by UKWAC was and still is a low level of successful permissions to archive from website owners, which jeopardize the viability and sustainability of web archiving on a voluntary rights-cleared basis.

As the development of e-infrastructures with powerful computing systems was supported for science in general, the needs of the DCH sector were also included. In the FP6 program, for example, access to CH was considered one of its strategic objectives. The IST program included the specific objective of stimulating the participation of the new EU member states in IST activities, such as TEL-ME-MOR, which helped in extending the The European Library (TEL) service to the national libraries of the new member states, or a strategic objective, such as Access to and Preservation of Cultural and Scientific Resources. The IIs for these activities were continuously improved, in particular when related to the goals of the FP7 program, which defined the ICT and DL research priorities for 2007–2008. Under the challenge entitled Digital Libraries and Content, a number of projects were funded in order to generate the conditions for the creation of large-scale European-wide DLs of cultural and scientific multi-format and multi-source digital objects, assisting communities of practice in the creative use of content in multilingual and multidisciplinary contexts with a support of robust and scalable environments, cost-effective digitization processes, semantic-based search facilities, and tools for the preservation of digital content (cf. EC, 2010b).

Later on (2013), to address the growing global need for data infrastructure, the Research Data Alliance (RDA) was launched as an international, community-powered organization.[58] In practice, RDA members focus on both the technical infrastructure needed for data sharing and exchange, including its underlying structures and components, such as persistent digital identifiers, shared metadata frameworks, etc., as well as the social infrastructure needed for community collaboration, such as common policy and organizational practice, harmonization of standards, common approaches to data access, and preservation, etc. (cf. Berman et al., 2014). RDA aims to provide infrastructure for all scientific disciplines and investigations in CH, which produce a huge amount of data—for instance, with excavated archeological findings, or forensic studies of art objects—and indeed need a trustworthy technology for sharing and preserving such data.

A big step forward for the whole CH sector was the establishment of DARIAH-EU (Digital Research Infrastructure for the Arts and Humanities), a Pan-European infrastructure for arts and humanities scholars and a network that connects hundreds of scholars from 22 countries. Virtual Competency Center's (VCC) e-Infrastructure is responsible for DARIAH's technological

---

[58] In 2011 and 2012, the need for more effective infrastructure to accelerate research data sharing and exchange worldwide drove discussions between the U.S. National Science Foundation and National Institute of Standards and Technology, the European Commission, the Australian Government, and others. RDA's vision is that of researchers and innovators openly sharing data across technologies, disciplines, and countries through the creation, adoption, and use of the social, organizational, and technical infrastructure needed to reduce barriers to data sharing and exchange (cf. https://www.rd-alliance.org).

foundations that allows one to share community-developed data and tools to ensure the quality, permanence, and growth of e-infrastructures and technical services in the arts and humanities.[59]

As research infrastructures play an increasingly important role in the advancement of knowledge and technology in all scientific and applied disciplines, digital humanists also depend upon the availability of these resources and funding programs. In this regard, ERIC[60] played an important role in facilitating the joint establishment and operation of research infrastructures of European interest, including the needs of the CH sector.

In the framework of initiatives to support the development of the DCH e-infrastructure, two initiatives are worth mentioning: DC-NET (Network for the European Research Area) and INDICATE (Concrete Approach within an International Dimension). According to Fresa (2013), both networks, funded under the EC FP7 e-infrastructures program, were meant to start pondering the European program Horizon 2020 for research, development, and innovation, by establishing a common awareness of perspectives, priorities, constraints, and capabilities across the DCH and e-infrastructures communities in Europe as well as access and use of DCH.

The OpenAIRE infrastructure was conceived as a "horizontal" EC initiative, i.e., cross-discipline and cross-country, aimed to connect research outcomes from scientific "vertical" infrastructures, i.e., discipline specific. The infrastructure was seen as an important vehicle for promoting the Open Access culture[61] for both publications and datasets; speeding up the research life-cycle by identifying and providing all actors in the scholarly communication chain with new meaningful links between information objects of different types; and leveraging multi-disciplinary research (cf. Manghi et al., 2012).

Over the years, as the large and heterogeneous collections of digital resources were created, the challenge to build a comprehensive and interoperable European infrastructure has been obtaining new dimensions, in particular related to technical and organizational interoperability and multilinguality. The EDL has been participating in Europeana Cloud, a project that aimed to establish a cloud-based infrastructure that could enable easy sharing, enhancement, and storage of content and data across the Europeana family of services, interested LAM insitutions, and other content

---

[59] This includes: local data stores for the trustworthy management of research data (large national data archives as well as smaller specialized collections); digital scholarly tools (infrastructure components as well as digital research environments); and standards to ensure interoperability across different locations, different disciplines, different scholarly and cultural traditions, as well as different languages. VCC e-Infrastructure is coordinated by the Austrian Academy of Sciences, and the Society for Scientific Data Processing (Gesellschaft für wissenschaftliche Datenverarbeitung mbH) in Göttingen, Germany (cf. www.dariah.eu).

[60] The community legal framework for ERIC entered into force on August 28, 2009 (cf. https://ec.europa.eu/research/infrastructures/index_en.cfm?pg=what).

[61] In Germany, for example, the OA Network that started in 2007 was characterized by highly controlled data sources, elaborated browsing features (according to subject classifications, institutions, authors, document types, etc.), a clear focus on German repositories, and an open architecture (cf. Müller et al., 2009).

providers and aggregators.[62] The decision was based upon the data on external internet connectivity in, for example, national libraries.[63]

However, there are still many actions to be taken in order to make the DH sector more advanced and open to users. In regard to the infrastructure, international cooperation is an important issue since e-infrastructures are operating globally—thanks to the EU investment in international links of the GEANT European network. As cultural and memory institutions are sharing methods and standards for digitization and managing a huge amount of digital data, the need to capitalize on these results and progress on the level of international cooperation was and remains very important. It is expected that a faster approach, based upon robust and reliable II, would speed up the development and take-up of technologies, such as smart grids, mobile services, etc. Such a direction should enable CH institutions to participate in research and development projects that tend to propose and implement innovative approaches to the digitization and management of DCH.

3.3   A SHORT OVERVIEW OF DIGITAL LIBRARY DEVELOPMENTS IN EUROPEAN COUNTRIES

It is evident from the published literature, especially from articles by Raitt (2000) and Liu (2005), that small-scale initiatives in creating digital images of CH objects in information institutions can be traced back to the early 1980s (in the UK or the Netherlands, for example). A series of exploratory activities in libraries, in particular, were initiated at the beginning of the 1990s in order to determine the size and impact of the library sector to the development of information society.

During the initial phase of the development of DLs in Europe, several approaches were evident. Most of the institutions that started their own or nation-based digitization project preferred rare books and other valuable materials created in the ancient (i.e., *Codex Sinaiticus*, International

---

[62] For example, the HOPE (Heritage of the People's Europe) aggregator has three main functional objectives: collecting the data from content providers (harvesting, transformation, and storage); curating the records (editing, cleaning, enrichment); and disseminating the records to third-party systems (pull or push) (cf. Bardi et al., 2011: 27; Artini et al., 2014).

[63] The research showed that out of the 39 national libraries only 9 had external internet connectivity of at least 1 Gbps. Only 5 of these were the old EU member states and 2 are non-EU members (Serbia and Russia-Moscow). Among the 10 national libraries with the weakest connectivity, i.e. less than 9 mbps, 3 were some of the old EU member states (cf. Knoll, 2006).,

Dunhuang Project,[64] *Gutenberg Bible* (1450),[65] *Magna Carta, Book of Kells, Fragmenta Membranea,*[66] *Beato de Liébana: códice de Fernando I y Dña. Sancha,*[67] *Cosmographie universelle,*[68] *Memoria Mundi* [69]). Still, to date, this has been one of the favorable approaches coming out from the awareness of the universal value of these heritage examples. One of the most important outcomes of these efforts is that researchers, especially in the humanities, started using new technology in examining the valuable and easily approachable digital copies of these and similar heritage items. On the other hand, copyright issues with such materials do not cause any discomfort, since they are nonexistant when related to the original analog form.

> *Codex Sinaiticus,* the oldest surviving Bible, dated in the middle of the fourth century. Codex is an extremely important landmark in the history of the book. It was preserved for many centuries at the Monastery of Saint Catherine, but later dispersed between the Monastery, the BL, Leipzig University Library, and the National Library of Russia in St. Petersburg. Due to the extreme age and fragility of the Codex, none of the holders of the different portions was able to allow access to the whole manuscript. The BL together with Saint Catherine, the other holders of the manuscript, and leading international scholars, decided to reproduce the entire Codex in digital form by using cutting edge technology at that time and employing advanced scholarship to help in achieving a virtual re-unification of the different manuscript parts dispersed among several owners, including a new transcription of the text. Multi-spectral imaging was used, with a goal to enable differentiation of different scribes and correctors of the manuscript high-quality facsimile (cf. Brindley, 2008: 67–68).

At the early stage of digitization, there were two patterns of DL activities primarily used in Europe, one of which included almost all kinds of library collections and services over a network

[64] Manuscripts, paintings, textiles, and other artifacts dating from 100BC–AD1200, found in the Library Cave al Dunhuang and at numerous other ancient Silk Road cities in the late 19th/early 20th century, were jointly digitized by BL, and libraries in China, Russia, Japan, and France. The project started at the beginning of 1997 and its goal was to bring together collections of material dispersed to museum and library collections worldwide in virtual space, thus allowing scholars from around the world to access the collections easier (cf. Brindley, 2008: 68–69).

[65] The Göttingen State and University Library implemented the project Gutenberg Digital from 1999 to 2002 with a goal to make the *Gutenberg Bible* from 1450 freely available on the web. In addition, the British Library has also digitized its two copies of the *Gutenberg Bible,* so users could view and compare the two digital copies on the network (cf. Liu, 2005: 466).

[66] A collection of parchment leaves from 10th–15th century known as *Fragmenta Membranea,* which is kept at the National Library of Finland.

[67] Codice from 1047 with 28 miniatures, held in the National Library of Spain in Madrid.

[68] *Cosmographie universelle, selon les navigateurs tant anciens que modernes* by Guillaume Le Testu, dated in 1555, is the digitized atlas available in Gallica digital library.

[69] A digital library project of the National Library of Czech Republic.

decentralized in the library, and the other one set up an individual department within the library that was especially responsible for the DL activities. Today in Europe, both of the above types are very common.

In Milne's (2008) words, compared with the Google Library project, these early stage projects could be regarded as "boutique" activities, not only performed at Bodleian Library, but in many other institutions throughout Europe, focusing upon a particular subject, genre, or period. Efforts were made to identify areas where CH institutions experienced difficulties in adapting to the new social and technological conditions as well as to detect which areas of cooperative European actions would most contribute to the better use of all kinds of resources. Initiatives were taken either by national bodies that intended to stimulate digital activities in order to strengthen the position of a particular country in the digital environment, or by single institution. Examples of the former are: UK Electronic Libraries Program—eLib;[70] JISC Digitization Program; the German Digital Libraries Program Global-Info (Schmiede, 1999); The Memory of the Netherlands (cf. Savenije, 2009);[71] BIBSYS Digital Library in Norway (Gundersen, 1997);[72] National Electronic Library—FinELib and Finnish EVA, a joint project of libraries, publishers, and expert organizations (Häkli, 2002); the Danish Electronic Research Library—DEF (Thorhauge, 2000); Memory of Russia and Russian Digital Libraries (RDLP);[73] Memoria Hispanica; Scotish SCRAN; NEWSPLAN 2000; etc. Examples of the later projects, such as the virtual gallery of The State Hermitage Museum in St.

---

[70] In the UK, the eLib program had a goal to initiate and support the development and shaping of the electronic library (as the DL concept was preferably called) in the higher education community. Moreover, some activities covered subject areas (such as health, economics, or the humanities), others covered types of material (such as digitization of newspapers, musical items, or photography) and were the results of several projects (Dieper, Miracle, Memories, Easaier, Contrapunct, etc.).

[71] The Memory of the Netherlands (Het Geheugen van Nederland), a project of the Koninklijke Bibliotheek, had its first phase until the end of 2003.

[72] BIBSYS Digital Library (BDB) was a national DL initiative implemented in Norway as a three-year project started in 1998. The main goal of the project was to establish and integrate new and existing services for access to digital information resources for Norwegian users within the higher education community.

[73] With over 40 million volumes, the Russian State Library is the largest library in Europe and the second largest in the world, http://www.rsl.ru or http://www.rsl.ru/en. With the assistance of Unesco, the library underwent a modernization program called the Information Tacis Project, with an important component of this process being the implementation of information technology into everyday practice. The project in 1998–2000 had foreign partners (the British Council, the National Library of Scotland, and Jouve SA in France). Additional financing was provided under the EU for the New Independent States and Mongolia to foster the development of economic and political links between the EU and partner countries. At the same time, the creation and operation of the RDLP website (http://www.iis.ru/RDLP/) started, as did an open electronic discussion list for the experts interested in DL issues (el-bib@iis.ru) and the scientific electronic journal *Digital Libraries* (cf. http://www.elbib.ru; Syuntyurenko and Hohlov, 2000).

Petersburg,[74] Gallica—program of the èèque nationale de France (cf. Trunel, 2009); Scottish Documents project;[75] British Library Cooperation and Partnership Program (Brindley, 2008); Muisti project in Finland or Project Runeberg in Sweden; Bodleian Library's initiatives (cf. Liu, 2005);[76] European digital deposit library coordinated by the German National Library (Lehmann, 1998) or Saga Net in Island (Sigurdsson, 1998).[77] Faletar Tanacković (2005) positioned and described projects like MALVINE, CALIMERA, which included as partners several heritage institutions. A number of projects focused on only one field/discipline or type of document or object, for instance, projects of medieval manuscripts in Germany, *Codices palatini and Codices iconographici* (cf. Altenhöner et al., 2011; Fabian and Schreiber, 2013); the Database of Watermarks and Digital Historical Atlas in the Netherlands (cf. Savenije, 2009); Digital Image Archive of Austria (EC, 2002);[78] online guide to music collections in archives, libraries, and museums in the UK and Ireland—Cecilia (cf. Chapman, 2005), MALVINE—modern manuscripts and letters across Europe; CHILDE – Children's historical literature disseminated throughout Europe; EVA—European visual archive with historical photographic collections (cf. EC, 2002).

There were also a number of smaller projects that were driven by the intellectual inquisitiveness of those professionals who anticipated the potentials of digital products and services. The computing and library services of Tilburg University, for example, have set an international example in electronic library development since the late 1980s, with strong economic and political incentives. The support from university management throughout the project activities was considered to be very important, and there were strong links between the academic computing department and the university library (cf. van der Zwand, 1996; Raitt, 2000).

In fact, DLs from that period could have been present mostly as components of the isolated research initiatives taken by computer scientists, some "techically advanced" librarians, usually from national or university libraries, or information scientists. But during the 1990s, and even more by the start of the 2000s, research, practical developments, and general interest in DLs has exploded

---

[74] The Hermitage Museum Digital Collection was facilitated by a $2 million grant from IBM, which still demonstrates the high start-up costs associated with creating cultural assets for the digital domain. This collection won awards including the Best Overall Website award at the Museums and the Web, http://www.hermitagemuseum.org.

[75] Since 1999, the National Archives of Scotland (NAS), in conjunction with the Genealogical Society of Utah, has been digitizing Scottish historical records on a huge scale, in order to preserve the original records and to make digital surrogates more widely available (cf. . http://www.scottishdocuments.com).

[76] Oxford has been involved in digitization projects since 1993, starting with the digitization of motor car ephemera (sponsored by Toyota City) and continuing with a number of activities that led to developing special digitized collections of valuable holdings (Milne, 2008: 4).

[77] The project started in 1997 in cooperation with Cornell University and the Arnamagnean Institut in Island (cf. Sigurdsson, 1998).

[78] The project aimed to restructure the Collection of Portraits, Picture Archive, and Fidei Commissa Library, Austria's largest picture documentation center.

globally, as Saracevic and Dalbello (2001) noted. However, early developments were very much driven by the grade of the technological development and the desire to present the richness of a particular institution or country, rather than being user-oriented.

Also significant were the European-scale cooperation projects being pursued by many libraries, among them some prestigious national institutions, such as the NEDLIB (Networked Deposit Library) project, operating in the area of conservation of electronic documents (cf. Steenbakkers 2000; Giordano, 2001), or DigiCULT, which explored the technological landscape for the future potential of CH (EC, 2002).

In 2002 several European national libraries and the Internet Archive saw the potential in cooperative efforts in developing new tools for web archiving. Although the NEDLIB harvester worked reasonably well, its development was stopped due to the lack of further financial support. The negotiations between the Internet Archive and national libraries were successful, and, as a result, the International Internet Preservation Consortium—IIPC was established in 2003, consisting of the Internet Archive and 11 national libraries. IIPC had a goal to foster web archiving by implementing new standards, best practices, and tools,[79] to enable long-term access.

The period of experimenting with digitization, 1995–2005, was characterized by the attitude of cultural institutions to focus on digitization of unique items or attractive collections of treasures displayed in the form of online exhibitions. Such digitization projects focusing on single objects became a trend in elite institutions in the whole Western world, not merely in Europe, with a goal of highlighting national treasures. Later on, the second type of digitization initiative aimed to provide access to full-text editions through systematic digitization (e.g., Caxton's *Chaucer* at the British Library or *Codex Gigas Suecia antiqua et hodierna* at the National Library of Sweden); or through the cooperative projects at the European and inter-continental level (mostly with the U.S. and Australia), as well as the participation in projects in which the most experienced institutions offered assistance to smaller countries in their attempt to digitize unique heritage items—for example, the digitization project of oriental manuscripts run by VESTIGIA Manuscript Research Center in Graz (cf. Renhart, 2013). Cooperation among several disciplines soon become "a must," since the DL, being a very complex concept, called upon experts from various disciplines to join forces in new discoveries. On the other hand, a lot of cooperation has brought into closer relation content providers and information caretakers.

Aside from the previously mentioned "big" actors in early digitization efforts, there were other important players, such as national libraries of smaller countries, which also had and have an important role in ensuring that less obvious material is digitized and that globalized digital content meets local (national) needs. Some national libraries of smaller countries, such as Norway, have already committed themselves to digitizing the entire published record in their languages (the

---

[79] The consortium is led by the Bibliothèque Nationale de France, and participating libraries include the British Library and all Nordic national libraries (Hakkala, 2003).

initiative was first launched in 2006). In Scotland, digitization of unique material, such as out-of-copyright Scottish Gaelic material, had been the focus for the first "mass digitization" initiative by the National Library of Scotland and the not-for-profit organization, the Internet Archive (cf. Hunter and Brown, 2010). Similar approaches have been taken by museums and archives, which digitized the most valuable items from their collections to be visible and approachable to everyone.

In some countries, for example, in the UK, Germany, or the Netherlands, local academic libraries as well as interregional service providers started to offer, with different intensity, a multiplicity of digital services paying attention to comprehensiveness and quality of the digital resources and their accessibility. As for the coordinated activities at the national levels it was noticeable that digitization strategies would help in coordinating scarcely operated digitization projects and suggesting management activities. The concepts of the German Digital Libraries Program, Denmark's DEF, Electronic Russia, or Italian Digital Library (Biblioteca Digitale Italiana—BDI) were designed and managed in a way that could use much of the existing infrastructure and extend it, with different actors responsible for the programs.

In the late 1990s, as the cost of ICT technologies, especially of digital capture equipment, and the cost of processing information have continued to fall at the same time as access to resources was increasing, many organizations started a more large-scale digitization of their holdings, motivated either by their own visions or by the availability of funding from national bodies, or both. As Peacock et al. (2004) concluded, a decade of digitization created a sequence of cultural and historical information collections and services across the LAM sectors.

By the mid-2000s, European academic libraries offered many noteworthy services, such as virtual online catalogs, DL portals, subject gateways, electonic journal libraries, organized document delivery and online interlibrary loan, e-learning platforms, etc. (Lossau, 2008; Koch et al., 2001). Nevertheless, a number of obstacles that prevented the fulfillment of the core requirements in the comprehensive searching attempts of the students and researchers soon became obvious. This resulted in new projects aimed at more comprehensive, integrated indexing and searching of information sources, intuitive usability of search systems, information services structured by subject, and relevance filtering of search results, as well as new ways of direct access to full text and data (cf. Liu, 2005; Ball, 2009). According to Coyle (2004), the experience of academic libraries from the early phase of DL development spotlighted the importance of reasonable access control and showed that no limits on usage were successfully promoted as a viable rights paradigm for some categories of materials. However, it can be noticed that discussions about IPRs have been held for years now on political, professional, and economic levels with an aim to find the best possible models to solve the issue of "orphan works" in DL programs or referring to collective licensing. Discussions also cover issues of rights II as a key tool in assuring the availability of digital assets and protection of IPRs. P. Attanasio (2010) claimed that, in some key documents on copyright matters approved by the European Commission, there was explicit mention of the option based on Nordic experience with

Extended Collective Licenses—ECL,[80] but there were also references to systems with other types of Voluntary Stakeholders Agreements—VSA.

The involvement of commercial publishers and various funding bodies added to the complexity of the digital arena. Moreover, one of the significant impetuses was the announcement of the Google Print Library Project, which aimed to digitize huge quantities of books from some of the world's leading libraries. The initiative provoked public sector response and some new ideas and projects (cf. JISC, 2005: 3; Brindley, 2008).

One of the most visible results of these actions was the growing awareness that for small and regional cultural institutions the essential question is not technology, but the lack of staff, skills, training, and support, as well as coordinated national or European programs (cf. EC, 2001). For instance, the Federal Target-oriented Program Electronic Russia 2002–2010, the goals of which basically were in accordance with trends from other regions, did not consider digitization and development of cultural and scientific information resources as the program's priority.[81] Another federal program—Culture of Russia (2001–2005), implemented by the Ministry of Culture and the Federal Archive Service, albeit with extensive sections concerning digitization in the field of culture, did not clearly announce a national policy in the area of CH digitization, digital heritage preservation, and sustainable access (cf. Digitisation, 2004).

In many countries the number of bodies that had taken digitization under consideration was also growing, making coordination efforts more difficult. The structure of the coordination mechanisms for digitization activities varies between countries.[82] Most come under the ministries of culture and/or education (Czech Republic, Denmark, Finland, Greece, Italy, Latvia, Lithuania, Slovakia). Others function as working groups (Bulgaria, Luxembourg, Slovenia), foundations (Netherlands), councils and committees for digitization (France, Spain, Estonia), state agencies (Latvia), or competency centers (Poland, Germany). Their competencies include drawing up national digitization strategies, implementing digitization polices and projects, coordinating digitization activities through dialog with the main heritage institutions, developing common infrastructure and services, preparing quality guidelines, and, finally, monitoring the digitization process (cf. EC, 2010c: 6–7).

As the DL sector matured, it was widely recognized that equal access to the cultural and scientific heritage of mankind is every person's right and that DLs help promote learning and understanding of the richness and diversity of the world, not only for the present generation, but also

---

[80] For instance, Green Paper on Copyright in the Knowledge Economy from 2008, or Communication on Copyright in the Knowledge Economy from 2009.

[81] However, the program envisaged development of the united digital catalog for Russian libraries, but this project didn't receive any funds, and the Ministry of Culture was not involved in the program in the first stage (cf. Digitisation, 2004).

[82] In the UK, for instance, the digitized research library material was in the care of several bodies and institutions, including the JISC, the British Library, the National Archives, the Research Information Network (RIN), the Research Councils UK (RCUK), and the Museums, Libraries, and Archives Council (MLA).

for the generations to come (cf. IFLA/UNESCO, 2011). New projects focused more on access, introducing sophisticated browsing and retrieval tools, interoperability, and multilinguality. A multilingual approach to the digitized collections and services had an enormous influence on proposed models and research efforts. A spin-off project of the MINERVA initiative, known as MICHAEL, launched a multilingual service that was designed to enable people to find and explore European DCH held in museums, libraries, and archives from different European countries. Based upon an innovative open-source platform equipped with a search engine, the MICHAEL platform was capable in 2007—through a European-level portal linked to a network of national ones—to enable discovering digital collections that had been dispersed across Europe. Originally covering France, Italy, and the UK, the initiative was later extended to 11 other EU countries under a follow-up project, MICHAEL-Plus. The project aimed to reveal all the digitized resources within the CH sector up to the time of its running, as well as the coordination of future digitization projects and initiatives. In some countries, a clear need for a better mechanism for identifying relevant projects and collections at the national level was recognized with an aim to index and describe them as well as to make them easily discovered and used.

As the number of massive digitization projects opened up another phase in digitization across Europe, heritage institutions had to turn to externally funded initiatives, such as the European eContentplus program or the JISC's Content Digitization program. Under the eContentplus program, funded projects related to accessibility issues were: MILE, with a goal to investigate the metadata for digital images and set up an "Orphan Works Database," which should act as a repository for all orphan works; ARROW (Accessible Registries of Rights Information and Orphan Works), which delivered an infrastructure for the management of any type of rights information and strengthening interoperability between public and private collections; and EDLnet, a core project to Europeana, which brought together museums, libraries, and archives from 25 member states to work on an operational framework for interoperability between LAM sectors. Other projects aimed to bring collections from various cultural domains into Europeana, for example, VideoActive (television archives, radio archives), European Film Gateway (film archives), Internet Gateway for the Archives (national archives), and EDLocal (local and regional museums and other cultural organizations) (cf. EC, 2009b: 25).

A number of projects are presented in the DigiCULT Report (EC, 2002), which provided an in-depth analysis of state-of-the-art of technologies, organizational situations, cultural services, and applications. Furthermore, the report highlighted "the surrounding legal and policy framework that sets the conditions for technological developments, organizational changes, and economic opportunities in the CH sector as well as drew conclusions and gave recommendations on measures to be taken in order to exploit the opportunities and overcome current technological, organizational, and legal impediments" (EC, 2002: 13).

The second reporting period witnessed an increase in the number of countries supporting open CH data and promoting its re-use, by making the data available through API services, or, in some cases, as linked open data. A growing number of countries had already implemented comprehensive digital and long-term preservation strategies. For doing so, some countries funded the testing of the necessary digital infrastructure and the implementation of standards and protocols. From the data produced via the ENUMERATE questionnaire it was also apparent that digital legal deposit arrangements and provisions to enable the collection of digital cultural materials, such as web-harvesting, had progressed. As concluded in the report (EC, 2010c), in spite of a noticeable number of new countries reporting provisions of new digital legal deposit laws, this was an area where implementation of the recommendation still required further efforts in order to properly preserve European digital heritage for future generations.

A few years later (EC, 2014c), 14 member states reported that they were using structural funds for the digitization of cultural material and related services during the programming period 2007–2013 (Austria, the Czech Republic, Germany, Greece, Estonia, Finland, Italy, Latvia, Lithuania, Malta, Poland, Slovakia, Slovenia, and Sweden). Poland, Slovakia, Lithuania, Latvia, and Greece have used structural funds as the main funding source for implementing their digitization strategies and/or programs in addition to the allocation of budgets for the digitization of different types of material (such as, for instance, ecclesiastical registries and archives in Austria; cinematic heritage and historic photographs and documents in Austria and Poland; archaeological, museum, and archive collections in Greece; library collections in Italy and the Czeck Republic; and newspaper digitization in Sweden). These funds were used in the development of information systems and e-services in the field of culture, for which digitization was considered an important part (e.g., virtual museums, including exhibits digitized in the form of three-dimensional images, virtual libraries, educational projects), or for the development of a digitization strategy, the setup of regional digitization workplaces, or the supply of digitization equipment (cf. EC, 2014c: 19).

The latest report (EC, 2016a) stated that almost all member states had achieved good progress in the digitization of cultural material, reporting a continuity of plans that had been established or new developments, such as the inclusion of digitization in an ambitious national strategy for the digital agenda (for instance, in Romania). Different approaches in planning digitization were again reported, with schemes ranging from national strategies (in 10 member states) supported by national funding programs or implemented through domain-specific digitization plans, to domain-specific initiatives (in 6 member states) led by ministries or by national institutions, to regional schemes or even planning based on strategies of individual institutions.

Member states employ different methods of organizing their planning and monitoring of digitization that range from overarching national strategies and frameworks (Czeck Republik, Denmark, Estonia, Latvia, Lithvania, Slovenia, Sweden), national funding programs (Greece, Poland, Slovakia), domain-specific national initiatives by ministries (Spain, Italia, Hungary), and regional schemes (Belgium), to individual digitization strategies of institutions (Finland, Nether-lands, Luxemburg, Portugal). In some cases (Austria, UK, Germany) it is a combination of more than one of the above (EC, 2014c: 9).

As for the provision of services offered, it is evident that the predominant impetus was the public's desire to have access to the unique, rare, and valuable collections available in European cultural and heritage institutions. A few member states refer to previous studies from the period 2003–2006 (Austria, Belgium, Ireland, Italy). In Latvia, studies have been conducted to investigate the social and economic impact of cultural institutions. It is not suprising that the EC planned to overcome the knowledge gap by obtaining empirical evidence of the actual long-term effects of the digitization of CH (EC, 2010a: 7) by funding the projects that were expected to develop method-ologies for such studies. ENUMERATE was one of these projects. As part of Europeana it seeks to regularly (for two-year periods) collect the data about digitization of CH in relevant European institutions. As is clear from the national reports and statistical data provided by ENUMERATE statistic (cf. EC 2010c, 2014c, 2016a; Nauta and van den Heuvel, 2015) on the input side, CH or-ganizations have continued to digitize their collections and acquire new born-digital material. As a consequence, the nature of the holdings of CH institutions has fundamentally changed, especially in regard to the management and presentation of digital content. On the other hand, the quality, sustainability, efficiency, and availability of basic digitization infrastructure (equipment, skills, and space, as well as skilled personnel) have improved considerably.

Taking Nordic countries as an example of good practice, it is noticable that all the Nordic countries have been developing strategies for digitization and digital communication of CH based on a shared awareness of how digital media represent opportunities to better preserve CH and to make it accessible to a wide audience, including researchers, in a more efficient way. Each country has found different ways to fund, organize, and prioritize this digitization. The idea of the estab-lishment of strong competency centers was presented, not only with regard to the CH content, but also in terms of technological skills. In all the Nordic countries, the national libraries act as hubs for these efforts, in cooperation with public as well as research libraries.[83]

In her overwiew of the development of the DL in Europe, Liu (2005) concluded that most of the initial DL projects in Europe were focused on preserving CH in which field historical materials occupy important positions. But, according to the DigiCULT Report (EC, 2002), 95% of all cultural institutions in the EU are small cultural institutions with limited resources, and it is particularly difficult to position themselves on equal terms with big media houses and even big cultural institutions with rich resources and an established reputation. Still, those numerous small

---

[83] Thus, it came as no surprise that the Norwegian Minister of Culture hosted the meeting of Scandinavian min-istres of culture in 2012 that included a session devoted to the topic of digital libraries. It was an important step that demonstrated how the development of libraries in the digital age had climbed high on the Nordic political agenda (cf. Skarstein, 2012).

museums, archives, libraries, and other types of cultural institutions hold a significant amount of recorded knowledge about European heritage, especially of a local or regional nature. This provokes tension between "dominant/center" and "emergent/periphery" participants that plays an important role in the creation of heritage. (cf. Dalbello, 2011)

In line with a myriad of new digitalized items and born-digital material was the growing focus on preservation and digital curation. Starting from the early stage of DL development, the rising issues of the preservation of digital material was moving from the stage of uncertainty for the future of digital assets to the management models that sought to stress the importance of the whole lifecycle of digital documents and direct the field of digital curation. The Cedars project in the UK, for example, was dealing with the strategic, methodological, and practical issues involved in the long-term preservation of digital information resources with the aim to develop a national UK strategy for digital preservation. Another representation of early systems of preserving digital material originated from Europe, more precisely from Sweden—Kulturaw3, a system for archiving national web spaces that started to harvest national websites since 1996. Collaborative projects focused around frameworks for sharing information and experience among national initiatives and projects have been developing since 1997 (for instance, the Nordic Web Archive—from 2000 until 2008).

Among EU or nationally funded initiatives, activities, and research projects from the first half of the 2000s that focused on digital preservation in Europe, the most known are the Digital Curation Center (DCC) in the UK, DigitalPreservationEurope (DPE), CASPAR (Cultural, Artistic and Scientific knowledge for Preservation, Access, and Retrieval), PLANETS (Preservation and Long-term Access through NETworked Services), and the Digital Preservation Cluster of the DELOS Network of Excellence in Digital Libraries (DELOS-DPC).

The European investments for digital preservation in the first decade of the 21st century had been large and persistent but had not been able to fully support an accepted common vision, general services, and adequate infrastructures. The main innovative and challenging question became tightly connected to the fact that the global financial crisis had effected not only the research environment but also all other areas of human endeavor. The economic situation and financial crisis from 2009 onward influenced the understanding of the importance of CH and made the major responsibilities of universities and scientific centers to preserve cultural and scientific memory. In accordance with economic trends, Guercio (2012) pointed out that identification and analysis of the main obstacles weakening the relevant investments of the EC in the area of digitization and digital preservation should be investigated. Funded research programs, within the European academic environment, cultural institutions, and, in some cases, in cooperation with researchers outside Europe, have resulted in publications, software, demonstrator systems, archives, and DL services, training materials, and handbooks, and two types of guidelines: guidelines and high-level abstract models (e.g., OAIS), or very specific solutions tied to a particular format of material or institutional context (cf. Ross and Hedstrom, 2005).

However, making the resources from Europe's libraries and archives available online was not an easy nor straightforward task. The discussions about new approaches and research methods, as well as how to use innovative technology and imply new business models, are still vivid.[84]

Many initiatives focused on other issues and challenges surrounding DLs, such as intellectual property, digitization techniques, or management, were funded by the EU, starting from EU's FP3 and FP4 for Research and Technological Development and, more specifically, the Telematics Programs of which libraries have been a part. The lists of initiatives and specific activities in the DL field in European countries—either on a European level, or on a national or local level—is quite impressive and these are well documented in the literature (e.g., Raitt, 1999; Liu, 2005; EC, 2002; 2004; 2010c; 2014c; 2016a).

In 2007, the EC launched the Numeric Study, a two-year study that aimed to establish a framework of standardized methods for the collection and analysis of data on digitization in the EU. The regular issuing of the data that relate to the digitization strategies, projects, outcomes, and remaining challenges make provisions for better insights into what has been happening among EU member states, whereas numerous digitization projects taken by the end of the first decade of the 21st century were not coordinated, and collecting the data was a very time-consuming task.

In Greece, for instance, there were 180 digitization projects supported through the national Information Society Program, including efforts to achieve interoperability of all digitized collections and Europeana. In the UK, the Integrated Architecture Project was initiated with a goal to make a large number of digital items from 30 different institutions available to Europeana. In Germany, a German Digital Library was under development, bringing in content from institutions at the federal, state, and county levels (Länder). In Latvia, to encourage partnership and cooperation in the digitization process, a special program, Cooperation of Archives, Museums, and Libraries in the Digital Environment, was developed. (cf. EC, 2009b). In France, the French National Library's online portal Gallica reflected the results of the mass digitization programs; by late 2010, Gallica had also offered a full-text-based search engine and the possibility that users could create a personal space where they could save their documents and insert page markers. However, up to now, digitization centers have been established in quite a few member states—these are being linked to either a university (e.g., Germany), a national library (e.g., Finland, France, the Netherlands), a national archive (e.g., Sweden, France, Greece), a ministry (e.g., Italy), or a private company (e.g., Hungary). In Spain extra funding was made available for digitization training tools for archives to promote the use of standards required by Europeana.

---

[84] Among such projects, for example, was BRICKS, which dealt with new services for digital access to museum, libraries, and other organizations' collections, or ATHENA, a network of best practices within the eContent-plus Program.

From another perspective, digitization initiatives and models proposed became more and more user focused. To deal with these challenges, some projects (for example, DC-NET, INDI-CATE, and OpenAir) experimented in order to interlink datasets and publications across different disciplines by automatically inferring semantic relationships between them, by enabling end-users to construct enhanced publications, and by interoperating with existing infrastructures, e.g., DataCite, Mendeley, EUDAT (cf. Manghi et al., 2012).

Last but not least, activities related to the promotion of European DLs have been focused in particular on the role of social networking. That is why the most popular methods of promoting digital collections include managing DL profiles on Facebook (e.g., all major DLs in Poland have their accounts), introducing information on the most attractive digital content to Wikipedia, publication of selected scans and content from DLs in popular photo sites such as Flickr or Pinterest, and posting information about new products in DLs on Twitter, as well as undertaking activities popularizing DLs in online editions of local newspapers.

3.4   THE DEVELOPMENT AND FUTURE OF EUROPEANA

Co-funded by the EU, the Europeana portal was started in 2005 and launched in 2008 as an EDL. The initiative was part of the commission's DL initiative elaborated in i2010: Digital Libraries (EC, 2007c, 2005a), a document that contained the suggestion to create an EDL. For the general public, Europeana is the most visible result of the initiative that has aimed to collect, organize, and make publicly available the most beautiful, historic, or highly regarded items, content that users most often want to consult or view, and hidden treasures, for example little-known items that could be enormously attractive to users once digitized, since most of them are too fragile for users to consult, or to be displayed. To manage ever-growing content and services, an organizational structure was set up in order to support the further development of Europeana.[85]

Furthermore, following the recommendations (cf. EC, 2011b), the efforts were directed toward the development of appropriate mechanisms for coordination of many of Europeana's and its partners' activities to avoid digitizing the same objects from different collections twice and to see that related collections are digitized in a shared context. Such an approach led to the practice that Europeana makes Europe's collections of cultural and scientific heritage from libraries, museums, and archives accessible to everyone on the basis of cooperative activities and enriched information services. This also meant that several networks of CH organizations have been consolidated as

---

[85] The European Digital Library Foundation, established on November 8, 2007, has been overseeing the operations of Europeana, coordinating its activities in projects that aim to create useful tools and a pan-European infrastructure for information professionals and researchers (such as Enumerate, ARROW or Europeana Newspapers). On a day-to-day basis the site has been run by the Europeana office, hosted by the Dutch National Library (http://pro.europeana.eu).

networks of partners that integrated different types of digital content and made the information searchable through a common search engine.

The EC's policy target in 2005 was to have 10 million objects accessible through the site in 2010 and Europeana used to manage this goal well and even overcome it on the grounds that LAM and other institutions around Europe have been systematically adding the content.[86] By September 2009, France contributed 47% of the content, Germany and the Netherlands 16% each, followed by the UK (8%), Sweden (5%), and other countries that contributed altogether 8%. Already in 2010 the situation started to change, bringing in, for example, Spain (13%) and Norway (8%).

In 2016,[87] users could search over 54 million items, provided by a network of 3,521 institutions that share their digital items and collections, from 44 countries and by 50 aggregates, including 48 national libraries in Europe and an increasing number of research libraries, museums, archives, and other cultural and research institutions. Among the first national aggregators and portals for online access to CH contributing to Europeana were: Hispana, the Spanish Directory and harvester of digital resources, with 120 digital repositories and 439 projects; "epaveldas" (e-heritage) in Lithuania, which comprised a database of digitized manuscripts, books, posters, paintings, graphics, photographs, and other objects; Kulturpool in Austria, which aimed to stimulate closer cooperation between the arts, culture, education, and science sectors, offering cross-disciplinary access and contextual information; Culturaitalia (Italy); Culture.fr (France); Culture Grid (United Kingdom); Gallica (France); Letonica (Latvia); Czechiana (Czech Republic); Slovakiana (Slovakia); and Deutsche Digitale Bibliothek (Germany) (cf. EC 2010c).

Today, researchers can search within unique collections of works, for example, by approaching collections organized by certain themes or exibitions, e.g., Reading Europe: European Culture Through the Book, Treasures from the National Libraries of Europe, Manuscripts and Princes in Medieval and Renaissance Europe, Traveling through History and Europeana 1914–1918.

Using the technology of that time, Europeana 1.0 (cf. Gradmann, 2010) and Europeana 2.0, which resulted from the project Ev2 (2011-2013),[88] aimed to enchance content, increasing and facilitating the re-use of content, developing sustainable finance and provision models, creating centralized repositories of linguistic resources, releasing new versions and maintaining the service

---

[86] The French National Library helped the Europeana service move a step closer to the goal of a comprehensive collection of CH by raising funds for uploading thousands of items each year from the library's Gallica collection. The French National Library also provided a starting template for what will be used as the basic Europeana interface.

[87] Statistical data from http://statistics.europeana.eu/europeana show that Europeana has (as of March 5, 2017) 54,2008,951 items, out of which 55.2% are images and 41.3% are texts. It is registered that in 2014 there were a total of 7,042,603 views; in 2015 the number of total views increased by 14.93% to a total of 8,093,788.

[88] More information can be found at: http://pro.europeana.eu/get-involved/projects/project-list/europeana-v20.

and its APIs,[89] developing features and functionalities, improving user experience, and coordinating a network of contributing organizations. Europeana v3.0 (Hill et al., 2016), a project under the ICT PSP Work Program, aims to provide the majority of the funding required for the continued functioning and development of the Europeana central services and the Europeana Network.

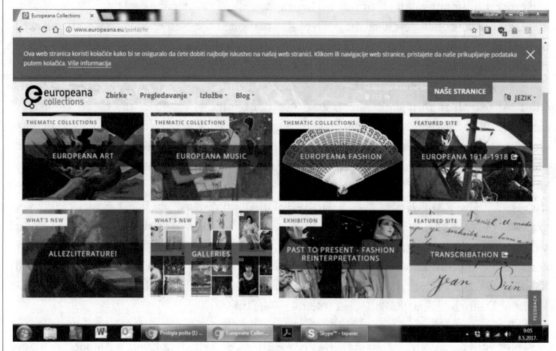

Figure 3.1: Europeana's paths to many collections (http://www.europeana.eu/portal/hr).

In the last few years, in regard to core technology/infrastructure projects, the EDL has been active in Europeana Creative, Europeana Cloud, Europeana Sounds, and Europeana Space projects. As far as delivering technology is concerned, the important projects are Europeana Inside, Europeana Awareness, and LoCloud. From the content side, among the most interesting have been APEx, Europeana Fashion, Digitized Manuscripts to Europeana (DM2E), EUScreenXL, Ambrosia, PartagePlus, and Europeana Photography.[90]

The European Library service is aimed at users worldwide, both professional and non-professional, who want a powerful and simple way of finding library materials. Thus, Europeana has been working on including social networks and putting badges of Facebook, Twitter, Pinterest, and

[89] The European Library Open Search API provides access to raw data describing the collections and catalogs of national and research libraries. The data is made available under the licensing terms of Creative Commons CC0 1.0, which allows the unrestricted use of the data for any purpose at all by anyone, including commercial use.

[90] The EDL also makes available a subset of the RLUK (Research Libraries UK) database comprising nearly 20 million bibliographic records from 34 UK libraries.

Google+ on its landing page as an invitation to share content. Users can recirculate the emblems of CH or reuse an image with their own interpretation (and "metadata").

As Poole (2010) pointed out, Europeana has the potential to make a significant contribution in opening up and democratizing access to and engagement with Europe's CH—both directly through its public portal and indirectly in its role as a broker to the media, broadcasting, publishing and other creative industries. In order for Europeana to fulfill this potential, however, it depends on the sector achieving a scalable and sustainable model for the creation, management, and distribution of new digital content.

There is no doubt that interoperability is at the heart of Europeana and has been one of its main challenges. Integrating format types across borders, across domains, and between institutions—LAMs and AV collections—is a challenging process connected with different traditions in contributing institutions, various user-groups, and a number of general or specific purposes, e.g., those that are reflected in diverse approaches to cataloging and the development of varying standards (cf. Purday, 2009).

Other features and services of Europeana include the creation of a central index of all harvested metadata that is searchable by the users. Search results are shown with a thumbnail image, sample, title page, or other representations. In such a way, users get an idea of the full digital object and then, if they want, they can go to the full object by clicking the appropriate URL, which takes them to the full-size file on the website of the holding institution. In such a way, Europeana avoids having a server space of its own. In fact, Europeana does not duplicate millions of large, high-resolution files from contributing institutions. The holding institutions have to deal with their hi-resolution files as well as with issues of copyright and ownership.

By the end of the first decade of the 2000s, the Europeana website was improved with new functionalities and services as well as an enhancement of those that already existed. Key issues still to be addressed are search features and interfaces, with special attention given to developing Web 3.0 services that are seen as a welcome tool for creating communities of interest and improving multilingual features. Driven by the awareness that users are crucial in evaluating developed features and services, the whole approach to the improvement of the Europeana portal started to be based on the results of a survey supported by the EC (EC, 2009a: 4).

One of Europeana's goals has been to find the right approach to IPR. The Europeana portal provides access to three sets of assets: the Open Source code base, the authority-controlled metadata, and the digitized content. Since Europeana has integrated metadata standards across the heritage domains, it has been licensing the metadata as a resource for the development of linked data and semantic web applications. However, the main rights issues concern the digitization of public domain content and orphan works. Digitization of out-of-copyright analog material does not create new rights and the Europeana Public Domain Charter (Europeana, 2010)[91] provided guidelines for the sector. The charter[92] acknowledged the dilemma in which heritage collections find themselves when they are striving to make public domain content accessible and preserved, following the legally based agreements with those who are willing and able to fund digitization programs, including the private sector. The charter sets out a number of principles that are essential to preserving a meaningful understanding of the public domain (e.g., the principle of the copyright's duration, the need to have in the public domain all items from the public domain, and the lawful use of a digital copy of a public domain, including its re-use, copying, and modifying). As it comes to DRM, a general requirement for DLs is that any rights management must not eliminate public, educational, and library user rights that copyright law allows, e.g., DLs should take into account the issue of fair use/fair dealing. Copyright and DRM regulations, and international, national, and local or institutional policies and practices with regard to digital products and services made the "digital arena" even more complex and often unpredictable.

An inhibitor to digitization is the problem of orphan works, which has been under review by the EC. The project ARROW, closely connected to Europeana, had objectives that led to the creation of a distributed network of sources for information on copyright status, gathering data about European literary works for the identification of rights-holders, and provision of guidelines for the identification of the status of a work, as well as to the creation of an European Registry of Orphan Works known as ROW (cf. Purday, 2010: 179).

Since Europeana offers only 10% of the many facets of European culture captured in books, paintings, letters, photographs, sound, and moving image, it is obvious that only one third of the European cultural facets are currently available online, and barely 3% of that works for real creative re-use (for example, in social media, via APIs, for mash-ups, etc.).

Having this in mind, the EU initiated a new plan, Europeana: strategy 2015–2020, with a goal to make as much of this material available online, preferably in open formats, and by developing standards, embracing new technology, changing copyright, and developing new business models (cf. Europeana Strategy, 2014; Hill et al., 2016). This new strategy listed several challenges, such as Europeana platform advanced features and the role of national aggregators or users' expectations. The EC was aware of the fact that the tension between the intense focus on individual objects as traditionally characteristic of LAM institutions and Europeana's status as a truly mass aggregator existed. In fact, national aggregators and portals for online access to CH started to offer their services and coordinate digitization activities at the national base and act as mediators toward Euro-

---

[91] In the context of further development of copyright protection in Europe, member states were asked to adopt legal provisions that are as uniform and comprehensive as possible, and designed to ensure that digitization processes be executed smoothly.

[92] The charter can be found in several EU languages at: http://pro.europeana.eu/publication/the-europeana-public-domain-charter.

peana (EC, 2010c). Europeana works with three types of aggregators covering the national/regional level (e.g., SEE Cult—cultural portal of SEE), domain-level (e.g., LAM, etc.), and theme-focused (e.g., music, architecture).

Figure 3.2: Europeana: strategy 2015–2020 http://strategy2020.europeana.eu.

In professional literature and through some research projects (more in Chapter 4), the tensions within users' needs and expectations in relation to Europeana content and services have been observed and commented on. With its large corpus of digitized and born-digital items that is constantly growing, Europeana is capable of providing more depth of understanding, through provision of greater context, than any other single organization. But, having such a large corpus, the user expectations are getting higher. Europeana has been determined to improve searching facilities through projects/experiments with varying success. On the other hand, Europeana is not just a portal or DL exposing a great amount of CH information to the public, it is also an open services platform. Europeana enables users, partners, and other institutions to access and manage a large collection of surrogate digital objects and content via APIs. It is obvious that, with the right data structure, Europeana seeks to slip into new and different dress. It is not focused only on providing optimal tools for finding particular cultural artifacts, but seeks to find a way of engaging with and understanding culture (cf. Hill et al., 2016: 10).

When it comes to openness and accessibility, Europeana strives to integrate all available digital content from LAMs and audiovisual collections and make it available and easily approachable. Following some suggestions (for instance, LIBER, 2009),[93] Europeana should aspire to find ways to be better embedded in research and educational infrastructures. There are also suggestions that Open Access and Creative Commons should be the guidelines for accessibility and that Europeana should work as a catalyst for further mass digitization projects. In regard to financial matters, Europeana should also aim to encourage the efficient use of digitization funds, through the avoidance of duplication, the adoption of appropriate standards, and a concentrated effort by contributors to adopt a unified standard for metadata (more re-use of bibliographical data). One of the most interesting side effects of digitizing and making content freely available in many languages is that this will result in large bodies of material that can be used to teach search engines to translate in the blink of an aye. When it comes to long-term access, Europeana should play a major role in preserving European materials available via Europeana and in guaranteeing perpetual access to that content for the European user. As suggested by LIBER group (cf. LIBER, 2009), Europeana should seek strategic alliances with those involved in long-term curation.

In the document Europeana—Next Steps (EC, 2009a: 2) the main challenges for the coming years were set, emphasizing the need to constantly enrich Europeana's content with both the public domain and in copyright material of the highest quality and relevance to users, through a sustainable financing and governance model. The objective was to ensure that Europeana and the underlying policies for digitization, online accessibility, and digital preservation give European culture a lasting visibility on the internet and turn its common and diverse heritage into an integral part of Europe's II for the future.

The digital agenda for Europe also takes Europeana as its focus in regard to rights harmonzation. There is no doubt that fragmentation and complexity in the current licensing system also hinder the digitization of a large part of Europe's recent CH, and Europeana should aim to contribute to the improvements of rights clearance, e.g., by offering more in-copyright works, particularly out-of-print and orphan works, taking a sector-by-sector approach, while complying with laws governing intellectual property and preserving the legitimate interests of rights-holders.

Europeana is managing its resources by a series of organizational systems that are built into the architecture, such as vocabularies, thesauri, taxonomies, or other classification schemes (cf. Hazan, 2010: 67). Searching throughout a huge number of digital objects in many languages

---

93 As founding members of the EDL Foundation, and active members of the EDL Thematic Network, which was engaged in developing Europeana, LIBER, CERL (Consortium of European Research Libraries), and CENL took active parts in an open discussion about the future of Europeana and came out with some worthy suggestions (LIBER, 2009).

has been and still is a difficult activity for users who want to locate what they are looking for in an easy and not too complicated way. In the document Europeana Search Strategy (Hill et al., 2016), which was prepared by the working group of the Europeana Foundation R&D, several improvements were called upon in relation to search strategies, especially related to the improvement of known-item search, the launch of Europeana Collections, the replacement of the Europeana Portal, or necessary changes in UI and UX that aim to affect users' interactions with the site. The Europeana platform's functionality has been expanded with the further development of the API, in particular when it comes to the possibilities for users to annotate Europeana records in a variety of ways, including freetext and semantic tagging, as well as object-to-object linking. The background semantic layer is, in fact, the key to true interoperability and this is what makes Europeana's content accessible, useable, and exploitable. In the case of Europeana, the platform uses the SKOS (Simple Knowledge Organization System) standard as a common data model that shares and links knowledge via the Semantic Web by capturing the internal rules, making them explicit, and sharing them across the whole platform. Once discovered, users can log into Europeana to save their selections in "My Europeana," where items, searches, and tags are saved for future reference (Hazan, 2010: 67).

The most significant change to the platform, however, is the creation of the Entity Collection and associated Entity API7, which was released in January 2017. The entities in the collection consist of approximately 200,000 agents (people), 100,000 concepts (topics), and 50,000 places.[94] Currently, the Europeana corpus is fundamentally a document store searchable by keywords in a wide range of languages. After completing the "entityfication" procedure, the user is directed toward a network of entities defined in large part by their connections to each other, instead of navigating through the offered content and services.

As to economic issues, the EC has contributed financially to the creation of Europeana. According to Arnold and Gezer (2008: 40), in the period 2005–2008, €60 million of the total budget of €149 million were made available for leveraging the access to a critical mass of digitized cultural and scientific content across borders. Through the EDL-net project, co-funded under the eContentplus program (which ended at the beginning of 2009) only Europeana was supported with a budget of €1.3 million (cf. EC, 2009a).

For the period from 2009 to mid-2011, the development of Europeana was co-funded with €6.2 million through the Europeana 1.0 project, selected under the eContentplus program, and the contribution of several member states, as well as a few individual cultural institutions. Nevertheless, after 2013 when funding through the Competitiveness and Innovation Program ended, it was agreed that Europeana should seek other ways to fund its activities and further development, including complementary sources of financing through public-private partnerships (PPP) or through a more structural contribution by the member states.[95] Thus, for the period after 2013,

[94] The latest information can be found at: http://labs.europeana.eu/api/entities-collection.

[95] www.europeanlibrary.org.

additional ways of financing Europeana were considered, taking into account the need to strike the right balance between EC's funding and other resources, and deliberately moving away from the existing project-based financing toward complementary sources of financing provided through PPP or through a more structural contribution by the member states. In this regard, a number of recommendations were directed toward re-shaping the PPP model for Europeana at EU and national levels by including a model of private sponsoring, as Europeana develops further and attracts more users, or by introducing payment for the links provided by Europeana. However, all the initiatives didn't work and in July 2016 the European Council made the decision to assure financing (under procurement) to halfway through 2020 and possibly until the next multi-annual framework and beyond. The EC is asked to carry out an independent evaluation and member states to increase the quality and openness of material that is made available, as well as to improve user friendliness on Europeana Collections.[96]

3.5   CONCLUDING REMARKS

As was obvious from the cited literature, there were several moments of special importance for the development of DLs at a general European level, in particular when it comes to the constantly improving IIs and providing an appropriate legal framework. As related to the support for the development of DLs, a rising awareness about the need to build an appropriate II, flexible enough to be constantly improved in order to support the ingestion of multiple digital formats as well as to find the best possible solutions for their accessibility over time, has been considered by various acters in the field.

As was clear from the short overview of DL development in Europe, DLs passed through three phases: the early phase (until 1999) with a model of a young DL; the mature phase when DLs became an object of planned research (2000–2008); and the phase in which advanced features of DL content and services have started to be visible and the consideration for social elements of DLs became more evident.

Most of the initial DL projects in Europe were focused on preserving CH in those fields where historical materials occupy an important position. From the beginning of the 2000s the most spoken-of strategy was, no doubt, mass digitization. It aimed to digitize massive numbers of documents (thus an all-inclusive strategy) using automated means, in a relatively short period of time, such as Google Book Search, Internet Archive, Europeana, the Norwegian digital national library, or the late Microsoft Book Search. Mass digitization has been contributing systematically to the increasing number of large collections, document by document, with no particular means of discrimination. Despite many critical remarks, there are strengths and positive effects of mass digitization projects that have been in progress all over Europe (as well as in the rest of the world).

[96] http://pro.europeana.eu/blogpost/owning-our-position.

The creation of Europeana as the unique access point to European CH is a relevant achievement. Europeana's digital content and services slowly but surely increased public awareness about the power of digital media. There is no doubt that the digitization of European CH has significantly improved the accessibility of heritage material for research, education, culture, and enjoyment. It is evident that Europeana continues to point at the richness of European culture, and is, at the same time, aware of the need to constantly improve its performances in order to make Europeana more sustainable and user-oriented.

There is another issue that concerns the digital cultural community, and this relates to the need to maintain all digitized as well as "born-digital" material in order to be available for use and select for preservation. Digital assets are at constant risk of getting lost or becoming inaccessible because of the deterioration in the quality of the recording or storage media. Technical obsolescence in hardware and software is also a noticeable obstacle and there are many other threats to the future use. The basic challenges for digital preservation are similar to those for digitization, and they have been approached from several perspectives (technical, economic, and human-resources management, for example).

Of increasing importance and interest therefore is the manner in which heritage institutions and other stakeholders digitize and subsequently publish digital reproductions—in terms of, for example, selection, exhaustiveness, level of detail, transparency, and authenticity. Indeed, during the last decades, libraries have been experimenting with different levels, sample sizes, and strategies when digitizing collections and artifacts on their own, as well as in various forms of public, private, or public-private partnerships. There is no doubt that the web space provides a basis for the optimal paths to transfer mankind's knowledge and experience. The transfer of information and generation of human knowledge is an indispensable feature of the digital heritage sector, which brings the digital heritage library to the central position of the educational proccess at all levels, starting from nursery school to the variety of programs offered as a part of lifelong education.

CHAPTER 4

Research into the Digital Library: Problems Researched, Outcomes of Research Projects, and New Challenges

4.1 INTRODUCTION

In this chapter we intend to offer an overview of the research activities in the domain of DLs in Europe, based upon articles published in mainstream peer-reviewed LIS/IS journals, recent books, and official publications published by the EU and some national funding bodies.

Over the past twenty years there have been some useful research and development activities related to various digitization issues conducted not only by world-known institutions (like BL, BNF, Deutsche Bibliotkek—DB, Koninklijke Bibliotheek, Netherland—KB),which were among the first ones to perform research and development projects, but also by research institutions and experts around Europe that have been determined to enrich DLs for CH with research data, reliable conclusions, and useful recommendations. Research is ongoing into many advanced digitization capture practices, users and use problems, evaluation of digital content and services, preservation, economic topics, etc.

It could be said that the first research attempts related to DLs in Europe were more technically oriented, but there were also attempts to research conceptual and contextual issues recognized by the LAM and CS communities as well as by digital humanists. Partly stimulated by U.S. activities, the DL field started to emerge as a clearly identifiable area of research with the funding of some important national initiatives (e.g., the eLib program in the UK and the MeDoc project in Germany).[97]

In the mid-1990s, Dempsey (1996) reported a number of metadata and resource discovery initiatives in the UK in the eLib program and the EU's FP4 program for research and technological development. These projects—focused on quality-controlled, subject-based information gateways within eLib (e.g., ROADS project and the large-scale Desire project)—had shared some common features and development strands. Important steps were made at that time in preparing the Dublin

---

[97] There are a number of articles, books, chapters, and reports on e-Lib (cf. MacColl, 1996; Raitt, 2000; Hamilton, 2016). MeDoc is described by T. Baker (1996).

Core Metadata Element Set to be used in describing digitized items and in identifying the need for a higher-level container architecture and the Warwick Framework for the aggregation of metadata information objects.

The ERPANET project—a network of excellence active in the period 1999–2003—was run by four partners, some of which later collaborated in the DELOS project. To proceed, there were projects such as PLANETS and DPE. Other domains, CH in particular, were able to develop their influence and assume a strategic role in cooperation initiatives such as the projects MINERVA and MICHAEL, ATHENA, or Linked Heritage.

At the beginning of the 2000s there was also some effort to provide national and/or international coordination and collaboration between a number of scattered initiatives. In the UK, one example of national coordination was the Digital Preservation Coalition—DPC. There were also two valuable JISC's initiatives. One was related to the promotion of the use of the broad understandings and concepts embodied in the Reference Model for Open Archival Information Systems (OAIS) as a conceptual model for construction and management of digital archives (cf. Beagrie, 2004). The other was JISC's Continuing Access and Digital Preservation Strategy for the Joint Information Systems Committee 2002–2005, which argued the case for the creation of a Digital Curation Center to provide generic curation and preservation services as well as new research and development.[98] In 2004 a multidisciplinary Digital Curation Center (DCC)[99] in the UK was established. The *International Journal of Digital Curation* started to publish the increasing number of research and professional papers on the topic of digital curation.

From another perspective, as the research environment for many disciplines in the sciences, arts, and humanities involves widespread creation, collection, organization, storage, and sharing of huge volumes of digital data, the development of altogether new, analytical, comparative, and interpretive frameworks has emerged. In the CH sector the use of ICT grew very quickly in the first decade of the 21st century as part of the explosion in digital arts and humanities research driven by both public interest in CH and the opportunity to enhance intellectual inquiry in the digital humanities sector. It was more and more discernible that research in digital humanities "had reached the stage, which not only led to novel techniques in art and humanities but in computer science as well" (cf. Derr and Arnold, 2011: 10). DLs are more intensively viewed as essential to enhance

---

[98] In mid-2006, for example, JISC requested that the DCC undertake a small-scale study to synthesize and help disseminate the results of projects funded under the Supporting Digital Preservation and Asset Management in Institutions (SPAM) program. The report, written by Pennock (2008), provided the final outcome of that exercise.

[99] Over the past ten years, the DCC has been involved in numerous international initiatives to help improve the quality and consistency of research data management and curation training and education. This has included participation in working groups to define digital curation curricula and leading several research projects to define, assess, and benchmark skills required for research data management (RDM), curation, and open science (cf. Davison, 2016: 64).

research activities in all fields by offering valuable objects for research, research data for re-use, and all kinds of new services.

The role played by the EC in the recognition of DL as a research discipline was of great importance as the EC had funded a large number of DL-directed projects.[100] FP6 supported a number of projects' activities (cf. EC, 2008d), mostly organized within large-scale projects that were seen as having the potential to integrate Europe's research landscape based upon common endeavor and scientific excellence. Already in the first IST call for proposals in FP6 the access to CH was recognized as one strategic objective. Among eight proposals selected for funding, six were Research and Technological Development (RTD) projects covering research in the field of DL services (BRICKS, DELOS), the digitization and restoration of audio-visual and film heritage (PRESTOSPACE), and research into new virtual representations or reconstructions of cultural and archaeological objects and sites (AGAMEMNON, TNT).

The fifth call for the IST priority within FP6 included the strategic objective "Access to and Preservation of Cultural and Scientific Resources" and funding was assured for two large-scale projects that aimed to test OAIS-based systems and tools: CASPAR, which looked into how to support the longer-term availability and accessibility of multi-sourced and multi-formatted resources; and Planets, which was investigating how to integrate preservation functions and services into organizational workflows and processes (cf. Giaretta, 2006). The DPE—DigitalPreservationEurope project started to work toward coordination of national activities in preservation, focusing on advocacy, certified repositories, and mobilizing centers or networks of competency.

It was obvious that the EU intended to fund diverse types of projects, such as integrated projects and specific targeted research projects.[101] Networks of Excellence supported by the EU have been playing a special role in strengthening scientific and technological excellence on a particular research topic with the goal to foster European leadership and overcome fragmentation of existing research capacities in the long term. Two other approaches taken by the EU in funding research and development activities that were expected to intensify cooperation or networking of research and innovation projects were coordination actions and specific support actions, which also contributed to the implementation of the FP6 and FP7 programs.

Under FP7, projects aimed to investigate key aspects of CH, such as cultural interactions, museum challenges, cultural identities, and linguistic diversity. A number of projects were dedicated to research in infrastructures and developing materials for the protection, conservation, and res-

---

[100]FP6 had an overall budget of €17.5 billion until the end of 2006. One of the 7 thematic priorities was Information Society Technologies (IST), with an indicative budget of €3.6 billion for the 5-year period. In relation to the technical content, there was an FP6 program, focused on specific themes that are strategically important to Europe's future (cf. EC, 2008a: 4).

[101]Integrated projects, expected to assemble the necessary critical mass of activities, expertise, and resources to achieve ambitious goals, are known as program approaches; specific targeted research projects, known as STREPs, took an attitude to "single problem approach" and more focused objectives.

toration of CH assets, etc. (cf. EC, 2010b). One stream led toward technology-enhanced learning (EC, 2009d). In order to strengthen collaboration and cooperation between member states and non-EU countries, FP7 made available a budget of €54.6 billion as EU's main instrument for funding research and development and fostering growth and integration of the European Research Area (ERA) in the period from 2007 to 2013.[102] In particular, the EC recognized the need to stimulate the creation of an integrated European DL research community and for this reason has supported the DELOS Network of Excellence on Digital Libraries, the EPOCH Network of Excellence, or ATHENA, which were focused on processing open CH since their very beginnings.

According to Liew's (2009) review article, significant research streams could be recognized until 2007 and are more or less the same ones that are still prevelant. DL use and usability, organizational and economical issues, as well as legal issues, especially issues related to the IRM and digital curation, and evaluation of DLs, are certainly the most dominant topics. *Ariadne, D-Lib Magazine, The Electronic Library, ERCIM New, Information Technology and Libraries, International Journal on Digital Libraries, Journal of Documentation, LIBER Quarterly, Library Review, Library Hi-Tech, Online Information Review, Program,* and several other journals have a number of published articles on research in DLs in Europe. The journals also mirror an overall upward trend for journal publications in research areas, in particular in the brisk period of the middle of the first decade of the 21st century.

The European conferences on digital libraries (ECDL; later becoming International Conference on Theory and Practice of Digital Libraries—TPDL),[103] LIDA,[104] and a number of nationally based conferences on DLs, also serve as testimony of the high interest of researchers from different fields—mostly from LIS, CS, and Digital Humanities—for the problems of the DLs in CH. Organization of conferences at national and international level not entirely devoted to the CH, but

[102]In fact, it comprises four programs "Cooperation," "Ideas," "People," and "Capacity." "Cooperation" (collaborative research projects) with €32.3 billion has the largest budget and the ICT theme with €9.12 billion the largest share in this budget. To add, from 2007–2013, out of a total of €347 billion for cohesion policy, the European Regional Development Fund allocated €3.2 billion for the protection and preservation of CH, €2.2 billion for the development of cultural infrastructure, and €553 million for cultural services, which also benefited CH (EC, 2014a: 10).

[103]The first European Conference on Digital Library (ECDL) was held in 1996. In the past 20 years ECDL has become the major European forum focusing on DLs and associated technical, organizational, and social issues, as well as for the presentation and sharing of the research results. The involvement of researchers and practitioners from CS and IS disciplines is well established at ECDL (see more at: http://www.tpdl.eu).

[104]LIDA stands for Libraries in the Digital Age and has been run annually since 2000. In 2010 LIDA became a biannual conference. It is an international conference that aims to address the changing and challenging environment for libraries and information systems and services in the digital age, with an emphasis on examining contemporary problems, advances, and solutions. Its particularity lies in the organizers' intention to enable students to interact and learn from well-known experts from around the world during official and social programs (see more at http://ozk.unizd.hr/lida) .

covering the area from many angles, also formed an important foundation for future developments, especially for building networks of professionals interested in various issues that tackle DLs.

Starting from the statement that the DL concept is of enormous social and economic significance for its potential "to transform the way that services are delivered to the public" and to "redefine the nature of the relationships between information users, providers, and intermediaries," Bawden and Rowlands (1999) studied the literature on DLs. Their conclusions warned that the DL research efforts by the end of the 1990s were highly fragmented and characterized by a wide diversity of assumptions, definitions, and views. They also identified a set of 20 assumptions from the diverse literature on DLs, which still seems an interesting base for comparative analysis, at least some of these, from today's point of view and experience. Of particular interest to this chapter is their view on the possibilities to do research on DLs and evaluate their effectiveness.

According to Liew's research (2009), there were several dominant research topics in the period 1997–2007; DL research that would address ethical and socio-cultural issues was almost not present. She also came up with data about the geographical and socio-political regional distribution of the authors, which revealed the fact that most of the research and studies are from North America, namely the U.S., closely followed by the UK and European (non-UK) contributors.

A myriad of research projects were devoted to specific targets with expectations that the outcomes could have a great impact on the development of the IIs and ICT. Many new technologies, tools, and standards for digitization of different kinds of digital objects and artifacts were presented in the literature and used later in CH information projects (cf. Ruthven and Chowdhury, 2015). In a special issue of *ERCIM News* (July 2006) devoted to European DL, the authors discussed some new tools and standards, such as a portable spectral imaging system for digitizing special types of CH objects, including paintings, encrusted stonework and ceramics, speech recognition and IR techniques, fast synthesis of dynamic color textures, logistics performance of SMEs in the automotive sector, or dependability evaluation methods for IP networks.

Another example are the projects based on data sets from the available DCH collections, such as the international project Diggicore co-funded by the European Library and the Digging into Data Challenge.[105]

In the context of the TEL-ME-MOR project, a survey of the national libraries members of the CENL was performed (cf. Manžuch and Knoll, 2007). The main objective of the survey was to create a European panorama of CH and ICT activities, achievements, and challenges in the national libraries by collecting and analyzing data that could explain a strategic approach to management of CH in the digital environment (e.g., the strategic commitment of the national libraries

---

[105]The project (started in 2012) was allowed to use the European Library's dataset of full-text articles as a base from which to identify patterns in the behavior of research communities with a goal to detect trends in research disciplines (http://core-project.kmi.open.ac.uk/about-diggicore-project).

in the domain of CH and ICT and the availability of long-term strategies, major strategic priorities, and statistics of participation in relevant international projects). Their research also addressed the issue of the availability of appropriate technological infrastructure and activities related to building DLs and digitization—in particular, the experience of national libraries in running and maintaining DLs, their capacity to produce digitized materials, and the quality of DCH services the respondents provide. The results showed a high commitment to manage CH in the digital environment of European national libraries, which was reflected in their strategic documents.

Another important research area was the use of leading-edge technologies (e.g., for knowledge management systems, or semantic tools, graphics, and interfaces) in empowering applications that improve the visualization of complex objects and enrich the experience users get from cultural resources. Under the Competitiveness and Innovation Program, three large-scale demonstrations were launched to test and demonstrate better support for sustainable tourism in rural areas, where innovative mobile solutions could be used to facilitate access to CH sites (cf. EC, 2010b).

Also, the CS community claimed that DL research in mid-2000 was seen as strongly based on SC and engineering research and informed by domain research across disciplines. Griffin et al. (2005) stated that this kind of research was applicable to a broad set of scientific and nonscientific problem domains, and characterized by novel collaborative efforts focused on the creation, collection, organization, use, and preservation of large volumes of digital information in a rapidly changing, globally linked knowledge environment.

Horizon 2020 is the new EU FP for Research and Innovation, with €80 billion for the 2014–2020 period. Support for heritage-related research is available through the three pillars of the program: excellent science, industrial leadership, and societal challenges. In the latter, one of the challenges stressed is Europe in a changing world: inclusive, innovative, and reflective societies, which mainly focuses on the transmission of European CH, identity formation, heritage of European wars, European collections of archives, museums, and libraries, and digital opportunities. Inside the Horizon 2020, relevant funding strands include several projects in the area of European CH.[106]

All these efforts and funding have been dedicated to the vision of the EU as a leader in the field of CH preservation, restoration, usage, and valorization. DL features, the problems detached, and research outcomes have been assessed in a number of expert surveys focusing on technologies, access and impact, preservation and sustainability, and economy of DLs (cf., for instance, Agosti et

---

[106]The funded CH programs are, for example: ERA-NET on the uses of the past; social platform on reflective societies; emergence and transmission of European CH and Europeanization; European cohesion, regional and urban policies, and the perceptions of Europe; Cultural opposition in former socialist countries; the CH of war in contemporary Europe; advanced 3D modeling for accessing and understanding European cultural assets; innovation ecosystems of digital cultural assets; materials-based solutions for the protection or preservation of European CH; and European research infrastructures for restoration and conservation of CH (EC, 2014a). It is estimated that the digitization cost of CH information in Europe could be €100 billon (EC, 2016a: 7).

al., 2007d; JISC, 2010; Athanasopoulos et al., 2010; Tsakonas and Papatheodorou, 2011; Tanner, 2012, 2016; Ross, 2012; Orgel et al., 2015).

4.2 PRINCIPLES, MODELS, AND FRAMEWORKS FOR DIGITAL LIBRARIES

In developing and managing DLs there are a number of basic principles (such as content quality, interface usability, service quality, system performance, or user satisfaction) which depend upon the use and sustainability of the content and service they offer. These principles comprise a starting point of the various research investigations, leading toward a proposal of models and frameworks that could serve as test-beds and bases for future developments, and by all means they apply to the research into digital heritage features and outcomes.

At the turn of the century, Rowlands and Bawden (1999) and Oppenheim and Smithson (1999) produced theoretical models for DLs, taking into consideration the changing nature of communication in the digital environment, which had a profound effect on pondering new models for knowledge transmission, usage, and preservation. It was obvious that existing models of LAM institutions would have to square with DLs that entered their "territory" and provoked them to include digital content and services as part of their mission and tasks. The Digital Library Manifesto[107]—the aim of which was to set the foundations and identify the cornerstone concepts within the universe of DLs—was engaged in facilitating the integration of research results and proposing better ways of developing appropriate systems. The manifesto envisioned a DL as a tool at the center of intellectual activity, having no logical, conceptual, physical, temporal, or personal borders or barriers to information (cf. Candella et al., 2007b).

As for different approaches to the research in DLs, following the fact that a DL represents textual and non-textual environments, the research could have been framed by the macrosocial theory or strictly technical point of view. For the former approach, researchers generally take into account the frameworks for analysis provided in the literature on the study of cultural memory and identity and history as cultural invention (cf. Dalbello, 2004), and, for the latter, several frameworks were proposed to enable holistically based interpretations of rising technical challenges (cf. for instance, Agosti et al., 2007a; Thanos et al., 2007; Darányi et al., 2010; Fox et al., 2012).

---

[107]The document came out of the collaborative work of members of the EU-co-funded DELOS Network of Excellence on Digital Libraries. The manifesto discussed and summarized the collective understanding that had been acquired, over more than a decade, on DLs by European research groups active in the DL field, both within DELOS and outside, as well as by other groups around the world (cf. Candella et al., 2007b).

Technology-driven projects[108] were directed toward developing expert models based on advanced technologies and coordinated actions, including expertise in attempting to identify long-term research needs through a wide ranging foresight activity, one of these being DLs for science.

Although there have been more than 15 years of intense research regarding the solidification of the domain of DLs, these systems continue to be challenging in terms of modeling, management, and sustainability, which often call for dependency on technologies and a strong association with the social context. Indeed, as Tsakonas and Papatheodorou (cf. 2011) stated, DLs are complex sociotechnical systems and their operation is subject to many interactions, either internal—in the sub-system level—or external—in the organization or the general environment level.[109] In their research Tsakonas and Papatheodorou evaluated different approaches and ontologies for the evaluation of DLs and offered their views on ontology.

Because of constant DL transformations and developments, one of the most challenging tasks in this field is to find a comprehensive way of modeling the main constituent parts and the relationships between them. Studies using classifications for the description of DLs seem to be very useful in reducing ambiguity. They also support attempts that tend to structure more specific perceptions of DLs or their specific parts/elements. The terms "formal models," "conceptual models," "reference models," and "frameworks" have been interchangeably used to describe initiatives of modeling the DL space. For instance, the Joint Working Group between DELOS and the National Science Foundation in the U.S. (NSF) preferred the notion of "conceptual model." This can be seen from their approach to conceptualization of the DLs itself, and its particular features or entities. When discussing the "digital imagery" for significant cultural and historical materials, the members of the group defined three interacting entities, i.e., the user, the technologies, and the content (cultural in their case) that communicate together in several stages, from the creation and preservation of content to its usable provision and its retrieval through technologies (cf. Hughes, 2011b: 10). Similarly, these entities are discussed in other DELOS models.

For example, the 5S model—one of the most comprehensive models of DLs, proposed by Gonçalves et al. (2004) and elaborated in several other articles and conference presentations—encompassed the process of data streaming inside spaces and structures that are taken as a base for describing how these serve the scenarios of use of a given society. The model also presented the classification of recorded concepts and practices into self-excluded and compact categories (such as, for example, active agents, processes, activities, constituent parts, socioeconomic, legal contexts,

---

[108]The ERCIM (European Research Consortium for Informatics and Mathematics) experts' network initiated the Beyond-The-Horizon Project, a European coordination action to identify ICT-related research trends and strategic areas that required support (https://www.ercim.eu/about/objectives).

[109]In their attempt they also proposed "a set of formal statements to declaratively express instances of DLs" (Tsakonas and Papatheodorou, 2011: 1578).

and environment). In describing the 5S model the authors put to maximum use the existing terminological basis of the DL domain and aspired to sort the mined concepts.

Another kind of modeling is the development of reference models, which aim to describe a system or a phenomenon free from the conditions imposed by the environment. In the case of the DL reference model, some suggestions of the development and application were offered, focusing on specific parts of a kind of "hypersystem"—such as human agents—to understand the networking and the interaction of the streams of the DL. The DELOS Reference Model considers the content, functionalities, architecture, quality, and policy as integral components of DLs. The model was developed to cover existing and planned DL systems and activities and to serve as a reference base to guide future R&D in the EU and more broadly. The model was elaborated further in the Digital Libraries Manifesto (Candella et al., 2007b). In the DELOS model the components of the DL correspond to different conceptual constructs, such as the DL, the DL system, and the DL management system. In such a way, the conceptual convergence between the different approaches, which all originate from the different communities' backgrounds, was expected to support various activities in order to contribute to the advancement of common and coordinated action. In its latest version, the Digital Library Reference Model (cf. Athanasopoulos et al., 2010) presented the relationship between six main concepts—namely, DL resource, user, content, functionality, policy, and quality. The concept of quality represents all activities that have the goal of judging and evaluating the meaning of the DL systems with respect to specific facets that reflect the main concepts of the reference model. The reference model has been used in the DL domain for many reasons, for instance, in a proposal to revisit the goals of DL and to suggest a movement of the field from research to practice (cf. Tsakonas and Papatheodorou, 2011: 1578).

In modeling the DELOS Digital Library Management System (DLMS) the overall research goal was the implementation of a prototype of a next-generation DL management system, based upon a combination of text and audio-visual searching. The model respects the idea of personalized browsing that used new information visualization and relevance feedback tools. Furthermore, the DLMS model "provides novel interfaces, allows retrieved information to be annotated and processed, integrates and processes sensor data streams, and, finally, from a systems engineering point of view, is easily configured and adapted while being reliable and scalable"[110] (Agosti et al., 2007b: 1).

Two of the above-mentioned modeling schemes—5S and DELOS RM—have been widely articulated and have been worked together to synthesize a new reference model in regard to the concept of quality, which is associated with the evaluation of interaction in the various stages of information processing, for instance, in search and dissemination (cf. Agosti et al., 2007c).

[110]The prototype was built by integrating DL functionality provided by the DELOS partners into the OSIRIS/ISIS platform, a middleware environment developed by ETH Zürich and later on expanded at the University of Basel.

A conceptual model to describe the main activities of users in creating and interacting with specific paths was developed by Clouah et al. (2015). This model captures the main activities that users follow as they construct paths for use by others and captures key activities when interacting with paths (e.g., developing a concept, collecting relevant materials, creating a path, communicating and sharing the path and its content, and consuming paths created by other users). Following the specification of functional requirements, they develeloped both low- and high-fidelity prototypes that were used to investigate approaches for supporting users with exploration of the digital collection. Through the PATHS project four generic user profiles for the PATHS system were identified: expert path creator (e.g., curator of researcher); non-expert path creator (e.g., family historian or student); path facilitator (e.g., teacher or museum educator); and path consumer (e.g., student, visitor, or casual user). Specific behavior profiles (i.e., details of typical user profiles, activities, tasks, and processes) and use cases were then developed for each type of user and were used to define the functional requirements and inform user evaluation, which allowed them to observe differences in user behavior with varying degrees of functionality. Testing of individual components and the whole prototype system, as well as the evaluation of users' preferences, were carried out with a range of users of Europeana.

From the perspective of the federated nature of resources and their very large size in terms not only of the volume of digital objects but their numbers as well, the concept of content as defined by DLRM was refined further to address not only single objects but also their characteristics and the appropriate issue of size. Here one could argue that this had already been done in the 5S model that introduced the basic notions of Streams, Structures, Spaces, Scenarios, and Societies (cf. Fox et al., 2012). The model was found very useful in formalizing the representation of objects in DL, but again the context within the DL remained unaddressed. This motivated researchers to suggest a new model, called 5M (Multicultural, Multilingual, Multimodal, Multivariate, and Modeling), which looks with more detail into the specific characteristics of DL, crystallizing a point of view that helps to position the notion of context (cf. Darányi et al., 2010). As for DLRM, multicultural and multilingual aspects of digital objects fall under Content, e.g., multimodal content expressed and processed by multivariate methods. This approach connects Content and its modeling under Functionality. The implications of diverse information needs are covered by Users. In the 5S model, although it is considered that Streams cover multimodality, Structures imply document classifications, Spaces include multivariate methods and their use to process cross-language documents in vector space, Societies represent users, and Scenarios are seen as sequences of events with the specific parameters allowed for modeling (cf. Fox et al., 2012).

As related to digital curation, DCC's Curation Lifecycle Model provided a graphical, high-level overview of the stages required for successful curation and preservation of data from initial conceptualization or receipt through the iterative curation cycle. Being offered as a theorethical model, it is rather an ideal that serves as a base for its users for entering at any stage of the lifecycle depending on their current area of need. The model enables granular functionality to be mapped against it—to define roles and responsibilities and build a framework of standards and technologies to implement. It can be used to help identify additional steps that may be required—or actions not required by certain situations or disciplines—and to ensure that processes and policies are adequately documented.

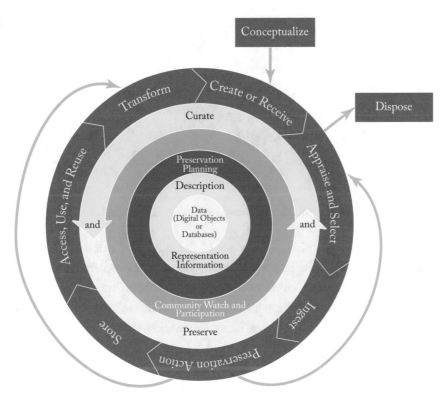

Figure 4.1: The DDC Curation Lifecycle Model based on http://www.dcc.ac.uk/resources/curation-lifecycle-model.

In response to the challenge of providing a focused and more exacting measure of impact, Tanner (2012: 12) developed a Balanced Value Impact (BVI) model as a framework in which to consider, plan, and implement impact assessment for a digital presence. In the extended BVI Model, impact is defined as the measurable outcomes arising from the existence of a digital resource that demonstrate a change in the life or life opportunities of the community. The BVI Model was designed to provide a balanced approach to assess impact, and it reflects this within its Balanced Scorecard approach. The core perspectives headings were implemented in the model (social and audience impacts, economic impacts, innovation impacts, and internal process impacts).

Figure 4.2: The Balance Value Impact Model. Based on Simon Tanner (2012).

Moreover, the model establishes a new set of five modes of cultural value for digital resources (named as "five values"). The first one is "utility value" (e.g., people value the utility afforded through the use of digital resources, current ones or those used sometime in the future). This value is followed by "existence and/or prestige value" (e.g., people derive value and benefit from knowing that a digital resource is cherished by persons living inside and outside their community and exists whether the resource is personally used or not). And "education value" (e.g., people are aware that digital resources contribute to their own or to other people's sense of culture, education, knowledge, and heritage and therefore value it). The last two values from the BVI model are "community value" (e.g., people benefit from the experience of being part of a community that is afforded by the digital resource) and "inheritance/bequest value" (e.g., people derive benefit from the inheritance passed down to them and satisfaction from the fact that their descendants and other members of the community will, in the future, be able to enjoy a digital resource if they choose to). It seems that the BVI model could be used on the ground that respects several attributes of context for the DL. Tanner presents four balancing perspectives (e.g., internal/innovation/economic/social) to allow a faceted view of impact. Together with five value drivers (e.g., utility/existence/education/community/bequest) this ensures that priorities are matched to perspectives and that DL stakeholders understand and set priorities appropriately (Tanner, 2016: 10–13), which could also be applied to CH. There are no reports of the usage of the model up to now.

4.3   ACCESS AND USE OF DIGITAL LIBRARIES

User-centered solutions, collaboration with users, and raising their awareness about the potential benefits of CH services through DLs should become important criteria for all those who provide funding and/or participate in digitization projects. Active participation of users during all stages of the development of DL and its services should by all means contribute to multiple benefits. On the other hand, as stated by Manžuch (2007), such an approach could bring DL services much closer to actual user needs.

Investigating users, access, and usability of information systems and services in DLs has been an ever-expanding area for researchers. As for the digital heritage and digital culture in general, the research began in the late 1990s. Since then, although certain efforts have been noticed, there are still relatively few projects and publications in this area.

As the proportion of digital documents and services has been growing exponentially, it was a challenge (and still seems to be) for researchers to attend to Buckland's (2003) observation about the approach to the building of DLs. His claim that all DLs have been designed backward, from the available data to the users they serve, rather than from actual user needs to data, is increasing the motivation for researchers interested in DL use and its evaluation issues. As Bearman (2006) suggested, new approaches were worth investigating in order to design a DL that is more responsive to a universal clientele. In doing so, it is important to have in mind the theoretical base of the information organization, traditional values of heritage institutions, and new challenges of the digital environment (e.g., availability at the global level, multilingual approaches, multicultural dialog, etc.).

As Europe is especially rich in languages, and many European DLs are accessible in several languages, one of the main issues is to meet the users' expectations concerning their language skills. A variety of programs and tools for multilingual DL development were available through the Cross-Language Evaluation Forum (CLEF) at DELOS, and projects such as Cross-language Information Retrieval (CLIR) aimed to overcome language barriers with respect to the user's query and its representation, as well as the document collection. Researchers are combining IR techniques with methods from machine translation and natural language processing, taking into account the multilingual and crosslingual IR. The crosslingual approach is directed toward the best solutions that allow users to enter their query in one language and get results in other language/s (for instance, as described in Görtz et al., 2012).

Concerning multilingual access to CH, several projects were started in order to enable users to explore and interact with online CH content, across media types and language boundaries. Examples are: the project MultiMATCH, which had developed a multilingual search engine specifically designed to access, organize, and personalize the presentation of CH information from websites with multiple languages; MEMORIES, which designed an audio semantic indexation system allowing information retrieval for access to archive content; and MOSAICA, which produced a technology toolbox for intelligent presentation, knowledge-based discovery, and interactive and creative educational experience of CH resources.

In an attempt to investigate usage of digital content and DL services, human information behavior is indispensable. Having in mind that human information behavior is complex and highly context dependent, in particular when it comes to the constantly evolving DL's concept and technologies, researchers approached these issues carefully. Examples can be found in theoretical approaches, for instance, in Ingwersen and Järvelin's book (2005), in the Tuominen, Talja, and Savolainen (2003) study on multiperspective DL, or in studies that employed a special perspective, as in Steinerová's (2003) ethnographic studies of academic and research library users in Slovakia. In the first half of the 2000s, significant progress was made in the field of human-computer interaction and the notion of sustainable interaction design.

G. Chowdhury (2010) presented several projects that dealt with time and space as essential concepts in CH applications having users in focus. He claimed that such concepts are used for the annotation of cultural objects and also for querying datasets containing information about these objects. Researchers applied ontological knowledge in representation and visualization of different kinds of georeferenced data, and in enabling spatio-temporal searches (e.g., searches based on spatio-temporal ontologies and visualization of historical content on maps), and agreed that temporal and spatial dimensions and the context of information are extremely important in the retrieval as well as the preservation of CH information.

Additionally, a number of in-depth usability studies have been conducted focusing on specific features of DLs when using, for instance, music library tools, childrens online material and services, etc. A range of activities were discernible in the mid-2000s, including user research undertaken by projects in the UK.[111] The result of this research pointed to an interest in online cultural content, but a notable lack of interest in multimedia or interactive content forms, which was caused by the technical limitations of communication at the time of investigations (cf. Miller et al., 2003).

In the first ICT Work Program, which defined the research priorities for 2007–2008,[112] a myriad of projects dealing with cultural and scientific multi-format and multi-source digital objects were supported, including those that investigated how to assist communities with practice in the creative use of content in multilingual and multidisciplinary contexts (EC, 2007a). Through FP projects, ICT was looked at in relation to various services that needed scalable and interoperable platforms that could support online access to heterogeneous digital content, from distributed collections and across languages. Another track focused on information retrieval and use. In particular,

---

[111]Projects were funded under the New Opportunities Fund's non-digi program know as the Omnibus Survey, and a survey of cultural websites undertaken by McKinsey and Co. (2013) for the Department of Culture, Media, and Sport.

[112]DL research was part of Challenge 4: Digital Libraries and Content, under the heading "Digital libraries and technology-enhanced learning."

funding support was offered to researchers who investigated how digital libraries and archives had been exploring methods and tools for (semi-)automatic indexing and semantic description of textual and non-textual objects. It was also felt that research was needed in relation to how to enhance information and knowledge retrieval through efficient search engines that are able to deliver results from complex multimedia and multilingual resources (cf. EC, 2010b).

One of the major objectives of user-studies research in general has been to identify new trends and patterns in the seeking, access, and use of digital information, since the way people access CH information services has been rapidly changing. Today, for instance, many CH information services can be accessed through what is known as referrals, where the users are referred to them by search engines.

A number of projects and individually taken research dealt with usage issues of Europeana. The PATHS study, for instance, started from the state-of-the-art natural language processing to enrich the content and enable rich user interface features that support a range of users in carrying out different tasks. Evaluation results indicated that the system was capable of fullfilling its goals of supporting users with accessing CH content from Europeana and creating paths that can act as subject guides for other users. The suggestions were also directed toward improvements in access to Europeana by indicating that information access to DCH information had to be constanly challenged in order to find the best solutions for unlocking the rich information contained within CH collections that was often hidden from end-users, particularly inexperienced ones.

While studying mobile-user behavior of Europeana, Nicholas and Clark (2013) and Nicholas et al. (2013) noted that search engines, and predominantly Google, are the key drivers, sending as much as 80% of Europeana's traffic. They also noted that fixed and mobile users do not differ much in terms of their referral patterns for the Europeana service. This indicated that search engines are the first port of call and users are referred to the respective digital information services by the search engines in response to a query.

Based on the analysis of some research projects and literature, some emerging patterns of user behavior and usage of CH information have arisen, such as access patterns via mobile devices and search engine referrals. It was also noted that mobile devices are a very fast-growing market segment for Europeana (cf. Nicholas and Clark, 2013).

The topics that need to be studied in depth were identified by the Europeana team itself (cf. Hill et al., 2016). These are: users' mental models, user interface and user experience changes, and diversification of search results. Moreover, Europeana started funding projects through its Research Grants program to stimulate scholars to become actively engaged in research that makes use of the Europeana collections for digital humanities research.

Other trends in access and usage have been crowdsourcing, user-generated content, and collaborations in digital culture. Warwick et al. (2012) stressed that social networks, blogs, podcasts, and crowdsourcing had become central for digital humanities as well, because these technologies facilitate information sharing, collaboration, participation, and community engagement.

Stiller and Petras (2015) studied the assessment of interactions in one type of CH information system, the aggregators. Aggregators accumulate DCH material across languages or domains. A special focus lies on Europeana, the single access point for digital cultural material in Europe. Twelve aggregators that cover a single domain or aggregate content across domains were included in the analysis. Aggregators measure their success by the size of their collection and often display this on the home page. Size and number of records differ considerably across the different systems. This is due to the different missions of the aggregators and their goals.

Managing DCH information to be easily accessed and used also involves a number of social, legal, and policy issues, especially when related to the availability and accessibility of digitized objects. There is a general consensus that CH information should be made available to everyone for the social good. However, there are a number of intellectual property and DRM issues that are, by their nature, complex and challenging.

The Blue Ribbon Task Force Report (BRTF, 2010) noted that the interests of future users are poorly represented in selecting materials to preserve, which is another research question that needs to be investigated more than it has been up to now. It also pointed out that LAM, professional heritage organizations, and others can play important roles in identifying the demands of their stakeholders. Every study of users and usage should pay attention to the goals of the DL investigated, in particular, how the DL defines its value proposition (e.g., to whom it is assigned, for what purpose, and what will be the benefits of such use, etc.), and which are its incentives to preserve in the public interest.

When discussing the issue of free access to digital content, one of the main goals of The European Library (TEL), which used to offer free access to the resources of the 47 European national libraries,[113] was to empower not only core DL services, like search and browse, but also to support user interaction with functionalities that enhanced the information life-cycle, such as connection with other information systems. With such aims, TEL initiated, for example, a cooperative relationship with the DELOS Network of Excellence, in order to improve TEL services with the help of DELOS expertise.[114]

The trend of user-centered research in archives and libraries around the middle of 2000 had been to focus on two general issues: typologies of users, or user groups; and search strategies and techniques, essentially linked to user behavior. In general, the research was provoked by the fact

---

[113]TEL started in 2004 and ended on December 31, 2016 (cf. http://www.theeuropeanlibrary.org/tel4/history).

[114]Under the fourth task, the DELOS WorkPackage 7, the research team has undergone an evaluation campaign in order to provide the areas of design, navigation, and visualization. The initiative had four tasks which included: the validation and refinement of the DL reference model through interaction with TEL; the assessment of multi-lingual information access in TEL; the exploration of the personalization functionalities of TEL; and the improvement of user interface design (cf. Klas et al, 2007).

that public sector organizations in Europe were under increasing pressure to demonstrate that they were used and valued by an appropriate audience. Indeed, freely accessible cultural organizations, such as museums that do not require any kind of registration, often do not know exactly who their audiences are. According to Quirk et al. (2008) these organizations have worked on the assumption that they should make available artifacts, information, and education according to the Reithian principles,[115] which include an equal consideration of all viewpoints, probity, universality, and a commitment to public service. The assumption was, indeed, that projects and services must be delivered to the widest possible range of audiences. However, with the advent of digital content and services, audiences became ever larger and more widespread. For the DL concept and design of its services to be offered to such a large and varied user population it is crucial to rely upon research into needs, expectations, and satisfaction of the audiences. In this sense, the research methodology, focus, and goals need to be exact and accurate.

Moreover, understanding the user needs in a specific context, in particular the context of CH information, and building this into the information access systems are challenging tasks. The Digital Agenda (EC, 2014b) pointed out that access to and use of digitized cultural material in the public domain needed to be improved. It was considered that support in developing new tools helps research and innovation for content creation, access, and preservation for future use. From the point of view of the development of digital services in European countries and their collaboration at the international level, there were various actions taken to improve, for example, interoperability and standards, security, and fast and ultra-fast internet access, in order to improve access and usability of digital content and services. For these tasks the underpinning technologies included "computer vision, advanced graphics, simulation and visualization tools, 3D immersive environments, cognitive systems, multi-sensorial interactions, and semantic-based content search" (Rouhana, 2011: 3).

NUMERIC investigation[116] into digitization in Europe covered issues of digital collections, digitization activities, digital access, digital preservation strategies, and digitization expenditure. As for the users and use, the study highlighted in 2015 that, in relation to digital collections, 90% of the respondents were memory institutions with collections to be kept for future generations, 84% of these institutions had a digital collection, and 60% of the institutions had born-digital items in their collections.[117]

---

[115]Reithian principles stay at the bottom of the independent public service broadcasting in the UK proclaiming its duties: inform, educate, entertain.

[116]The ENUMERATE surveys started in 2008 and were followed by reports in 2011, 2013, and 2015. The 2012 report was prepared by Stroeker and Vogels (2012), in 2014 by Stroeker and Vogels (2014), and for 2015 by Nauta and Heuvel (2015). The ENUMERATE efforts continued under Europeana CEF in 2015–2016.

[117]It is also interesting that the most-mentioned object type as part of the heritage collection of the institutions is text based (83%) and visual 2D (81%) followed by time-based material (56%) and 3D man-made material (46%).

Overall institutions reported that they had 45% of their descriptive metadata online for general use, libraries being at the high end of this indicator, whereas museums had the lowest score. Also, overall institutions claimed that they had 32% of their digitally reproduced and born-digital heritage collections online for general use, with libraries being again at the high end for this indicator (48%), whereas archives and other records offices had the lowest score (32%). Interesting data relates to the reasons to provide digital access to the collection: academic research is perceived as the most important reason, followed by educational use of the collection, with the least important being sales and commercial licensing. Moreover, LAM institutions showed that they measure the use of digital collections (over half of them), by using web statistics or social media statistics. For the digital objects that are available online, the most popular channel used to approach them were institutional websites. Data that refer to future use is particularly interesting since respondents foresee a decrease (-5%) in the number of digital objects that will be available through institutional websites in two years. Channels for which substantial growth is expected over the next two years are Europeana (+7%), national aggregators (+6%), and institutional APIs (+6%) (cf. Nauta and Heuvel, 2015: 4–5).

4.4   PRESERVATION AND CURATION ISSUES

Digital preservation research enters into the problems of keeping, preserving, and managing sustainability of digital content and services, focusing on new models and tools for preserving digitized as well as born-digital content. The research principles stemmed from the preservation of analog material basic principles. Thus, the research reflects a kind of continuation of previous research in preservation, and seeks to propose models that are based upon a vision of the necessity to connect the analog and digital material for future use. As new digital formats and new communication pathways inside the digital environment have been bringing a number of new challenges to the digital arena, the answers have been looked for by using new approaches, methodologies, and research techniques.

As early as the mid-1990s the EC recognized that preservation of new digital material was an emerging and important issue and started funding pioneering research projects in digital preservation. At that time the challenge of managing digital content so that it could be accessed and used reliably in the future was being confronted mainly by national libraries and archives, the key institutions with the mandate to keep publications and records for the future. They were "at the sharp end of facing the problems posed by the new shifts toward electronic journals and toward electronic records" (Manson, 2010: 1).

From the early Swedish initiative to harvest all their websites, many heritage institutions joined in with similar projects.[118] Bbut the question was how to make these archived data sustainable over time and digital space, knowing that the average lifespan of a web page is less than the blink of an eye. Similar problems arose from the need to capture and manage scientific data (e.g., earth observation data, medical data, or archeological sites data), which require not only efficient and cost-effective preservation systems that can handle significantly large amounts of objects and their metadata, but curation models that could assure usability and combinability of these research data for future uses. Moreover, there are not only digital objects that are increasingly complex as a combination of text, image, sound, metadata, and embedded software, but also constantly emerging software has a great impact on the use of digital content and services in the future. Having in mind all these features and the problems they cause, it is comprehensible that research could and should support various needs of heritage organizations that are involved in digital preservation.

From the time when N. Beagrie (2003) published a report on national digital preservation initiatives in Australia, France, the Netherlands, and the UK, as well as in the U.S., and Harvey (2005) described the landscape of preservation based on his comprehensive survey, the preservation approaches appeared to be best characterized as handicraft and needed to be approved in a dedicated research environment. However, as digital preservation in general aims to ensure the value of digital entities and their maintenance over time, there has been a constant preoccupation with possible solutions.

One of the earliest examples of the awareness that research in digital preservation needed a more holistic approach was the NSF and DELOS working group, established in 2002, to define a research agenda for digital archiving and preservation (DAP-WG) within the context of DLs. The report of this group—Invest to Save (2003)—laid out a range of research challenges that needed to be addressed. Researchers involved in the study also suggested that research in the domain of digital preservation could benefit from being expanded and refocused by including new research communities, making the research more rigorous, and taking a significant shift in what was being researched (Ross and Hedstrom, 2005).

Later on, through the FP6 and FP7 projects, the objectives for research have moved from a library/archive-centric view to one that has been increasingly focused on understanding the challenges posed by the nature of the digital content itself, including the awareness of the need to in-

---

[118]It is worth mentioning some of the worldwide known projects, such as PADI, established in 1996, a comprehensive archive of information on the topic of digital preservation from the National Library of Australia; LOCKSS (Lots Of Copies Keep Stuff Safe), established in 1998 at the University of Stanford; National Digital Heritage Archive, a program that is a partnership between the National Library of New Zealand, Ex Libris Group, and Sun Microsystems to develop "Rosetta," a digital archive and preservation management system, established in 2004; and the U.S. National Digital Information Infrastructure and Preservation Program, established in 2000 and run by the Library of Congress.

vestigate new methods for web archiving. The focus was on ensuring the authenticity and integrity of the archived content.[119]

Projects such as CASPAR, PLANETS, SHAMAN, SHERPA, Covax, and PrestoSpace, were collaborative and directed toward theoretical or pragmatical issues, highlighting, for example, truthworthiness, audiovisual preservation, preservation and digital archiving of audiovisual documents, or the need for end-to-end support across the preservation lifecycle (cf. Bordoni and Poggi, 2004; Tuck, 2008; Macevičiūtė and Wilson, 2010).

PLANETS, a digital preservation research and development project co-funded under the FP6 by the EU, delivered a framework for the long-term preservation of digital content. As part of the project, the usage model and user field studies work packages were also observed in order to develop an understanding of usage and communication over time. The research was seen as a way to help in deep understanding and appreciation of digital object creation and use as well as how these processes may impact digital preservation (Snow et al., 2008: 3).

SHAMAN focused its research on integrating the data grid, DL, and persistent archive technology, developing support for context representation and annotation, with deep linguistic analysis and corresponding semantics, and modeling of preservation processes. The project aimed to deliver a reference architecture for the design and development of solutions for digital preservation in distributed scenarios (Borbinha, 2010; Wilson and Macevičiūtė, 2012).

Another focus was on methodologies, tools, and services that could allow users to analyze digital objects in order to establish significant properties that would then—based on innovative preservation solutions—ensure that object properties were saved and maintained during appearance. Investigations into preservation issues looked at advanced ICTs as a support for DLs in order to allow them to act on high volumes of dynamic and unsteady digital content as well as on safeguarding integrity, authenticity, and accessibility over time.[120] Among challenges was the need to keep track of the context (evolving meaning and usage) and development of automatic and self-organizing preservation.[121]

Some of the obstacles were recognized at the early stage of research efforts related to digital preservation. According to Ross (2012: 47), ERPANET case studies from the first half of the 2000s reported different levels of awareness of the importance of digital preservation across organizations,

[119]As known from the archival theory, the material that is archived in any of the heritage institutions usually is characterized as being distributed and dynamic and it can disappear if not captured at the right point in time and managed in the best possible manner. Digital assets on which DL depends are fragile and easily changeable and their preservation is costly.

[120]Authenticity, in its many faces, has indeed become a 21st-century challenge that reaches into every corner of modern life (Duranti, 1995, 2001; Ross, 2012: 53).

[121]In the digital preservation community, known projects from the second half of the 2000s were: InterPARES; a study done by Verheul that investigated the state-of-the-art in 15 national libraries; the DigitalPreservationEurope that also brought in a list of Competence Centres in 2007; a survey of archives and libraries in the EU Member States; Digital Preservation Coalition UK survey from 2006; etc.

and even across different divisions of the same organization; lack of long-term strategies for digital preservation at institutional, national, and international levels; a general recognition that preservation and storage problems were aggravated by the complexity, diversity of types or formats, and size of the digital entities; low level of cost understanding as well as of investments; and dependence upon solutions to be delivered by technology developers, researchers, and service providers.

In their article on preservation research and sustainable DLs, Ross and Hedstrom (2005) offered an overview of the thinking in the area of digital preservation and discussed projects that promoted research and raised awareness in this area, such as CEDARS, CAMiLEON, ERPANET, InterPARES, and PADI. It was evident that different funding bodies supported research in the digital preservation issue (in Europe, for example, the EU, JISC, and German Research Society—DFG). In their opinion, two decades of research had done much to raise awareness of the digital preservation challenges and encouraged some organizations to adopt policies and procedures to improve the longevity of their digital resources, as well as to contribute to improvements in practice, including enhancing metadata creation, and increasing the use of standards. The researchers also put effort into establishing widespread recognition that all necessary interventions need to come early in the life of digital entities (if not before they are even created), which was quite a worthy observation.[122]

On the other hand, as the volumes of information, diversity of formats, and types of digital object increase, digital preservation becomes a more pervasive issue and one that cannot be handled by uncoordinated approaches. In Manson's words (2010: 1), research into digital preservation issues called for the acceleration of the "move from human monitoring and decision making to embedding reasoning and intelligence into the systems themselves."

It could be said that research projects in digital preservation have been of various kinds and research focus (e.g., from general digital preservation theory and its technological implementation, to focusing on certain domain areas, such as culture, art, heritage, research and education, industry, engineering, or publishing; or choosing to investigate the digital preservation strategies and activities in certain types of memory institutions, producers of databases, large scientific organizations, private companies, or public departments facing the need to preserve data and documents (cf. Macevičiūtė and Wilson, 2010)). For the research community that is involved in preservation issues, the challenge is also to build new cross-disciplinary teams that integrate CS with LIS and archival science, and even with social and historical sciences (cf. Manson, 2010).

According to Beaudoin (2012), research and publications on preservation were primarily concerned with technical issues, such as content issues of hardware and software, emulation and migration, formatting, translation, and the use of Dublin Core elements to preserve details about

---

[122]The InterPARES Task Force on Authenticity (Authenticity, s.a.: 1) was engaged with the development of two sets of requirements. One set includes the requirements "that support the presumption of the authenticity of electronic records before they are transferred to the preserver's custody." The other set includes requirements "that support the production of authentic copies of electronic records *after* they have been transferred to the preserver's custody."

the technical context of digital materials. However, context was also seen as especially important in discussions of digital preservation. Contextual information surrounding digital content has been varied, but eight major preservation topics could be identified: technological aspects, utilization, physical, intangible, curatorial, authentication, authorization, and intellectual aspects. All of these elements need to be studied carefully and comprehensively, which is not only time-consuming, but also an expensive enterprise. On the other hand, a survey of proceedings from ECDL and JCDL conferences between 2002 and 2006 showed that most DL research tended to focus on the issues that needed fast solutions.

Some studies produced important data about the attitude and activities related to the preservation of digital assets, such as the study by Nauta and van den Heuvel (2015).[123]

The other problem addressed concerned socio-economic aspects affecting the creation of a critical mass of digital preservation solutions and services. One example of such studies is DPimpact, which analyzed the drivers for digital preservation development, the potential socio-economic impact of the preservation of born-digital content, and the technological, organizational, and economical conditions required for further progress of digital-preservation-related disciplines. The outcomes of the study pointed out that there was a general lack of awareness about the risks of losing digital information, to a great extent based on social misconceptions about digital resources (e.g., "digital is forever," or "digital content can easily be retrieved from the web"). The organizational barriers were elaborated: in particular the lack of interdisciplinary collaboration and cooperation among institutional and business-oriented stakeholders; the lack of organizational readiness to change existing inner structures; and the absence of policies aimed to secure long-term preservation and future access to and re-usability of digital assets. Technological gaps, legal constraints (e.g., IPR legislation, conflicts between creativity protection, and the needs of the preservation processes), and resourcing problems that relate to the lack of an adequate skilled workforce or to funding in general as well as funding for special pilot projects were also noted. The need to invest in the development of technologies for long-term preservation of digital content was recognized in the early phase of the digitization, but there was another problem—a continuous lack of knowledge about the economic impact of such developments (cf. DPimpact, 2009).

The number of papers investigating digital preservation has begun to grow. The addition of a digital preservation cluster to the DELOS Network of Excellence was an important step forward, but the research did not provide the framework that would incorporate preservation functionality and capabilities into the robust DELOS framework for DLs. As Ross (2012: 55) concluded, the research in preservation, although innovative in some instances, has been "far from sufficient to

---

[123]Twenty-six percent of the institutions that participated in the survey are reported to have a written digital preservation strategy that is endorsed by the management; 47% of the institutions do not have a solution yet for long-term preservation based on international standards for digital preservation. National libraries and other types of institutions are "front runners" in using digital archives that meet the international criteria for long-term preservation.

underpin projected DL developments and the increasing complexity and interrelatedness of the digital entities they will contain."

Indeed, despite all the discussion in recent years about what kinds of research are needed in the area of digital preservation, no concise and well-developed strategy representing the views of a broad community has yet emerged. There is no doubt that the DL community has much to offer the preservation community through its research into the GRID and its collaborative initiatives in the domain of eScience. However, digital preservation is not only about technology. It is about how to "maintain the semantic meaning of the digital object and its content, its provenance and authenticity, retaining its 'interrelatedness', and how to secure information about the context of its creation and use" (Ross, 2012: 44).

There is no doubt that the development of the preservation and curation of DLs and research into the related issues proved that theoretical, methodological, and technological issues had to be reconsidered and fine-tuned if the principal goal remains the same: allow DLs to remain sustainable, authentic, accessible, and efficent in offering content that is approachable and understandable over time. With the inclusion of archivists and archival science's main principles, the whole sector of preservation and digital curation gained new dimensions that enriched the existing theoretical framework provided primarily by LIS and CS communities.

Basically, one should agree with Ross (2004) when he states that preservation risk is constantly present at all stages of the longevity pathway, with its technological, social, organizational, and cultural challenges. Ross pointed out two classic statements of the digital preservation challenges, Roberts's from 1994 and Tibbo's from 2003, which precisely indicated that the approaches that intend to overcome obstacles in preservation remain limited, regardless of the fact that overall understanding of the challenges surrounding digital preservation had become richer and more sophisticated. Moreover, research into their long-term viability and the easy and satisfactory accessibility of their contents still remains "in its infancy."

4.5   DEVELOPING AND TESTING THE EVALUATION CRITERIA

As Saracevic (2001: 351) wisely concluded, it was too early to evaluate DLs in any formal way during the 1990s since "the conceptual state-of-the-art of digital library evaluation was not sufficiently developed" at that time. It was not surprising that the first evaluation attempts related to technical issues. However, the evaluation of DLs could serve many purposes as Marchionini et al. (2003) suggested—ranging from the understanding of basic phenomena (e.g., human information-seeking behavior) to assessing the effectiveness of a specific design that would measure return on investment. In an attempt to classify evaluation studies in the DL domain, Saracevic (2004) followed a procedural approach by identifying four main classes of entities and posing several questions that needed answers in order to be able to fully explore the nature and properties of DLs. Taking Saracevic's (2001) evaluation criteria and measures for DL (content, technology, interface, service, user, and context), Tsakonas and Papatheodorou (2011: 1579) proposed classes of constructs, context, criteria, and methodology that could give a substantial reflection of the digital evaluation domain.

There are a number of evaluation criteria identified in the literature (such as interface usability, collection quality, service quality, system performance, and user satisfaction) that were the object of various research investigations. Within these categories one can find a number of finer-grained variables. Ioannidis (2005) discussed the methods and metrics used for the evaluation of DLs and concluded that they vary according to different perspectives one may have on DLs. Macevičiūtė and Wilson (2010) suggested that under collection quality, for instance, there should be scope, authority, accuracy, completeness, currency, and copyright, all of which would apply to various systems. When evaluating a long-term preservation system, the added criteria should be integrity—as digital resources migrate between different technologies they might loose some of their valuable properties.

According to Tsakonas and Papatheodorou (2011: 1577), DL evaluation constitutes a significant part of the domain, not only for the obvious reasons, such as the contribution of critical information systems, but also for the provision of a discourse field for the understanding of their nature.

Evaluation of digital resources starts from the presumption that these are valuable to different audiences for different reasons, and some values may not be realized immediately. Information resources in general include the intellectual nature of collections that can be seen from different perspectives, according to search and use purposes. Deegan and Tanner (2006b) studied the value and impact of digitized collections and concluded that there was a lack of adequate means to assess the impact of digitized resources and services on the creative, cultural, and academic sector (CCA). Later on, a document published by Tanner (2016) spotlighted the research interest and social demand to investigate the impact assessment of DLs. Namely, Tanner was interested in finding out how the recently developed BVI model could contribute to the measurement of a digital resource by balancing both internal organizational and external community perspectives with social and economic considerations, based upon research case studies from the Wellcome Library digitization program and Europeana Impact Taskforce. As was already mentioned, the value of the collection and each item within is a subjective category; it changes over time and has different meanings that are contingent on external factors (cf., for instance, Hughes, 2011b). In response to this issue, Tanner (2016) suggested five different modes of value in digitized resources in order to provide an impact assessment of the often intangible benefits of digitization. Tanner's modes of value are a useful taxonomy for those attempting to frame the discussion of the potential—or known—impact of their digitization project, to show the benefits that it could possibly have to a range of users, and perhaps persuade funding sources of the necessity for digitization.

The evaluation of DL—from the perspective of users' information needs, their characteristics, and contexts in which they are engaging with digital resources and services—has been in focus since the first practical examples digital environment had to offer. In particular, research into human-centered DL design became challenging as early as the late 1990s, with two important aspects: assessing human information needs and the tasks that arise from those needs, and evaluating how the DL affects subsequent human information behaviors.

The DELOS team worked on the development of the evaluation model that was based on three dimensions: data/collection; system/technology; and users/use. The model was strengthened with a quality dimension, elaborated extensively inside the 5S model (cf. Candella et al., 2007b). Following six domains of the DELOS Reference Model, the EU-funded project DL.org investigated and identified several solutions for interoperability as one of the most important elements of DLs.

Furthermore, evaluation is different if a DL is viewed as an institution, as an information system, as a new technology, or as a combination of new services. Nicholson, for example, focused on the organizational context of evaluation in regard to library services. However, his approach did not result in the explanation of the possible combination or even integration of different viewpoints or measures related to libraries he investigated.

From research in evaluation theory and methodology, some projects examined methods to evaluate how DLs were valued by their users, others explored the consequences and means of allocating resources to user-identified needs. For example, the British Library[124] has tried to use impact assessment and evaluation as a means of justifying its expenditure, thus showing a significant return on investment. Various projects have been looking in detail at the evaluation of DL services and systems, but the economic consequences of choices remain an area that deserves much more exploration. Since it is commonly understood that DCH information can contribute to economy and business in a number of ways, it is important to develop measures for evaluation of the economic impact of DLs. Digitizing and providing wider access to cultural resources offers enormous economic opportunity and is an essential condition for the further development of Europe's cultural and creative capacities and its industrial presence in this field.[125]

Parallel to the development and testing of different evaluation models in Europe—such as DELOS, DL.org, or Tanner's proposal and attempts to establish evaluation criteria and useful metrics (for instance, Nicholson's criteria or EQUINOX) that would allow a holistic approach in evaluation processes—there were theoretical and methodological outcomes developed in the U.S. that influenced further studies in Europe as well (e.g., Saracevic's and Marchionini's approaches, Zhang's model, DIGIQUAL, and LIBQUAL). It should be noted that research on comprehensive

---

[124] The figures produced by the BL were based almost entirely upon the time saved and travel costs mitigated by the online user with an added element of consumer surplus value (cf. Tanner, 2016: 6).

[125] An average of 8 people are involved on a full-time basis in digital collection activities and about 52% of the costs are qualified as being incidental and 47% are structural costs. Digital collection activities are funded by internal budgets (88% of the institutions). National public grants are available to 35% of the respondents; 21% receive regional or local public grants (Nauta and van den Heuvel, 2015: 5).

models, albeit highlighted as desirable, is quite limited by their nature and thus, evidently, did not attract enough attention.

Investigating mass digitization and its features and results, in particular over the last 20 years, showed that LAMs have created, collected, purchased, or otherwise obtained a huge quantity of digital resources and delivered these online to a range of users worldwide. A myriad of activities related to the design, building, organizing, using, preserving, and funding of DLs need to be constantly evaluated from as many different perspectives as possible using reliable criteria and specially designed models or frameworks.

4.6   CONCLUDING REMARKS

During the last decades, libraries and other cultural organizations have been experimenting with different levels, sample sizes, and strategies when digitizing collections and artifacts, on their own as well as in various forms of public or private partnerships. To be able to manage an ever-growing number of digital assets and services, DL needed research-based models, infrastructure, guidelines, and tools for various purposes. However, it is clear that much of the experimental work has used empirical testbeds consisting of precisely such digital artifacts that come out of LAM and archeological institutions, as well as from local history collection societies' digitization and DL initiatives.

On the one hand, research is approached and conducted by information and computer specialists who are interested in finding new ways to empower DL infrastructure, design, management, access, or preservation. On the other hand, humanities scholars are focused on critical analysis of the interpretative dimension of digital reproductions and the ways in which digital artifacts are represented. These approaches and uncertainities, which emerged from the complexity of DL, called for collaboration between well-bounded disciplines in search of new methodologies that could be used in the research of common phenomena. Although a number of models and theories have appeared over the past few decades in Europe, it still seems too early to conclude whether they influenced the practice of DLs, in particular when it comes to DCH, since the absence of a critical mass of the digitized CH content on the European level to be used for testing and evaluating purposes is noticeable. Then again, the research in DL has been pointing out the myriad themes that have been considered worthy of investigation and still attract researchers as well as funding bodies, whose growing role is to support investigations of DLs from many perspectives.

From the studied literature, one could conclude that a common awareness of perspectives, priorities, constraints, and capabilities across the DCH and e-infrastructure communities in Europe has been established. Research shows that known approaches to information needs, information seeking and retrieval, and information use and interactions are significantly influenced by the culture and context of users, as well as the nature of the digital domain and digital information itself. As noted in some research initiatives, search engines, predominantiy Google, are still key drivers, of the majority of Europeana's traffic. They also noted that fixed and mobile users do not differ much in terms of their referral patterns for the Europeana service. However, these results gave an impetus for the improvement of Europeana search facilities.

Research also shows that issues related to DL use and usability and organizational and economical issues, as well as issues that cover IRM and digital curation, and evaluation of DL, have been the most dominant topics. However, it should be noted that the situation is anything but satisfactory when it comes to research interest in ethical and social-cultural issues. Obviously, DL research has been creating scalable and interoperable platforms in order to support the digitization, retrieval, use, and preservation of heterogeneous content in various multimedia formats, from distributed collections and across many languages. Although appreciable efforts and financial resources have been invested in digitization activities across Europe, the EC cautions that these activities were, and to some extent still are, highly fragmented. Additionally, a number of technical and organizational obstacles jeopardize their success and economic sustainability.

There have been many efforts, projects, and proposals (both conceptual and technical in nature) over the 20 years of research in digital curation and preservation. The fundamental issues of digital entity interpretability and trustworthiness have not yet been given generic solutions and remain startlingly limited.

Moreover, the target for the economic sustainability of digital information systems and services—to ensure cheaper, easier, and better access to information—also brings in various economic issues that could point out how successful, if so, digital processes and services are, by measuring them according to the level of reduction in direct costs, the savings created from sharing resources for digitization and delivery of information services, or through better design of systems and services that can reduce user time and effort required for information access and use.

CHAPTER 5

Education for Digital Libraries: Roots, Approaches, and New Directions

5.1 INTRODUCTION

In the digital age, the ability to "access and exploit both indigenous and extra-territorial knowledge stocks" (Cronin, 1998: 37) depends on several key components—the quality of a telecommunications infrastructure being one of the basic prerequisites, and the extent to which information and media literacy in general and processing and analysis skills in particular have been diffused throughout the work-force. The changes that have been occurring in Europe during the last 25 years were driven by the awareness of the Higher Education Institutions' (HEI) administrations and teaching/ researching staff of the need to re-envision the approach to education. Appropriate and qualitative education of today's and the future's information professionals is a highly demanding task. Existing HEIs in the wide area of information studies—which are mostly known as LIS/IS departments or i-schools in the U.S. and Europe—seek new approaches that will enable them to focus on old and new tasks and efficiently prepare competent information professionals. Required competencies should enable information professionals to not only act as librarians, archivists, and museologists in fulfilling their mission—to bring these institutions and their patrons to the center of the mediation of information—but also to work as team members who design and maintain information architecture, analyze and administer big data, develop web, ontologies, and strategies for social media, perform usability testing, data curation, etc., in an ever-changing environment.

Since the early 1990s a huge amount of money has been invested in DL research, including on how DLs can support education processes at all levels, but there has been no parallel investment to support teaching and learning about DLs or on how to find the most suitable approaches and teaching methods to prepare future professionals. Thus, the future of the educational programs—regardless of their situational place inside the university (e.g., being affiliated to a certain school, faculty, or department), or their program and institutional title—seems to be unpredictable and very challenging.

In this chapter we intend to offer insight into the main trends in the European HEI field, with special focus on the development of institutional structures, programs, and challenges that lay behind the concept of the DL. The concept itself is a "vogue, if deliquescent, construct" (Cronin,

1998: 43), and learning outcomes needs to be well pondered, meaningful, and accomplishable in such a diversified arena.

At the policy-making and funding level, since the 1990s several action programs had a significant impact on collaboration between HEIs in Europe, including the attempts to modernize education in CEE countries (e.g., Tempus, Phare, and Leonardo da Vinci). Several EU programs have been promoting the use of ICT in education (e.g., within the eEurope 2002, eLearning Program 2004–2006, projects containing e-learning elements supported within MINERVA, Leonardo da Vinci, Grundtvig, Lingua, Comenius, and Erasmus).[126] The EC's higher-education programs (Socrates, Tempus, and Erasmus) also provided financing for LIS schools networks (e.g., for research or particular agreement on competencies required for digital librarians) and joint courses (within the Erasmus Mundus).

Inspired by the idea of mobility and offering collegial help to LIS institutions from Eastern Europe after the fall of the Berlin Wall, several European LIS schools started to organize annual student-teacher conferences known as BOBCATSSS.[127]

The overall goal of the ERASMUS Mundus program—focused on cooperation and mobility in graduate and post-graduate HEIs—is to promote the EU as a center of excellence in learning around the world, by attracting high-quality students from countries outside the EU to register for joint masters degrees, supporting the development of European modules and European Intensive Programs, thematic networks, etc. The program was extended later to include many other activities (e.g., teacher mobility, joint curriculum development, international intensive programs, thematic networks, language courses, European Credit Transfer System—ECTS). Thousands of partnerships have been created between universities and departments, and hundreds of networks and associations have been established globally (EC, 2007b).

For Scandinavian and Baltic countries there is NORDPLUS, a scheme for HEIs in the region that supports cooperation and innovation. In the UK, the Netherlands, France, Croatia, Germany, and Slovenia, for instance, there are national research foundations and billateral funds that help in promoting and building up the cooperative networks of HEIs.

Harmonization and modernization issues in European HEIs were intensified by the introduction of the Bologna Process.

Although some universities in Europe and elsewhere could claim to have earlier origins, the first degree-granting university in Europe was the University of Bologna, founded in 1088 A.D. Its historic significance led to its selection as the venue for the meeting of

---

[126]In 1995 Erasmus became a part of the broader Socrates Program, which covered education from school level and university to lifelong learning, including actions such as Comenius (addressed to schools), Grundtvig (adult education), Lingua (language learning), and Minerva (e-learning and the use of ICT).

[127]BOBCATSSS stands for the first letter of towns from which the LIS schools originated: Budapest, Oslo, Barcelona, Copenhagen, Amsterdam, Tampere, Stuttgart, Szombathely, and Sheffield.

the European Ministers of Education, from which the Bologna Declaration was issued in June 1999 (cf. Johnson, 2013), after being signed by the Ministers of Education of 29 countries in Europe. The Bologna Process is seen as the political support offered by European governments for globalization of higher education, underpinning promotion of employability and competitiveness as a priority. The goal was the creation, by the year 2010, of the EHEA in order to enhance the employability and mobility of citizens and to increase the international competitiveness of European HEIs. The Bologna Process has grown from 29 countries in 1999 to 46 countries in less than 10 years and has extended beyond the geographic borders of Europe. Cooperation with other continents is very much a part of the Bologna Declaration and is supported through a series of bilateral programs as well.

Keeping in mind that the Bologna Process is about transparency, comparability, compatibility, and cooperation in HEIs, the Bologna Declaration (Bologna, 1999) was not taken as a starting point that could lead toward "standardization" or "uniformization," but as a path toward empowering discussions about cooperation, joint programs, and mobility. European HEIs were seen as common spaces that should be achieved within the framework of the diversity of cultures, languages, and educational systems. Principles of autonomy and diversity have been highly respected in the Bologna Process, albeit the Bologna Declaration recognized the value of coordinated reforms, compatible systems, and common actions.

The action program set out in the declaration was based on a clearly defined common goal, a deadline, and a set of specified objectives. These objectives included: adoption of a system of easily readable and comparable degrees; implementation of a system based on two main cycles, undergraduate and graduate; establishment of a system of credits (such as ECTS); promotion of the mobility of students, teachers, and researchers;[128] promotion of European cooperation in quality assurance; and promotion of the European dimension in HEIs. Thus, the declaration is accepted as a key document that marked a turning point in the development of European HEIs.

In 2007 London Comunique expressed the commonly accepted opinion that European higher education "should play a strong role in fostering social cohesion, reducing inequalities, and raising the level of knowledge, skills, and competences in society" (EHEA, 2007: 5).

As the 2010 deadline was set for the realization of the EHEA, there has been enormous change in European HEIs. To follow up all developments, the European University Association (EUA) regularly publishes a series of documents entitled EU Trends Reports (from 1999[129]). The Trends V Report contained significant findings on the implementation of Bologna reforms and

---

[128]In Europe, the tradition of mobility from one university to another, following the idea of being able to listen to the experts in a particular area of study, has a long tradition dating far back to the early days of HEIs at Bologna, Oxford, Cambridge, Padova, Göttingen, Paris, Praha, and other famous medieval universities.

[129]The last report was published in 2015 (EHEA, 2015) and covered issues related to the main reforms implemented on the grounds of Bologna and other declarations relevant for the EHEA.

also on the attitudinal shift that had taken place across the HE sector. The authors gave clear evidence of the progress that was going on in relation to the implementation of structural reforms, with 82% of institutions in 2007 answering that they had the three cycles in place, compared to 53% in 2003. Across Europe, there was no longer any question of whether or not reform of degree structures would take place, but rather a shift to considering whether the conditions and support were adequate to enable the process to be successful. In line with these doubts, it was realized that the national understanding of reforms became crucial, in particular with regard to different national interpretations of the nature and purposes of the three cycles, and whether these different national interpretations would prove to be compatible within Europe (cf. Croisier et al., 2007). In 2010 the report covered a decade of changes in European HEIs (cf. Sursock and Smidt, 2010). Published in the year of the official launch of the EHEA, it examined a decade of Bologna reforms in the context of other changes that have affected HEIs—whether through international, European, or national developments—and set an agenda of priority actions for the next decade, building on previous achievements.

In 2015 the document "Learning and Teaching in European Universities" (cf. Sursock, 2015) placed greater focus on learning and teaching, including e-learning and Massive Open Online Courses (MOOC).

After a period of 15 years of major reforms across Europe as part of the Bologna Process, it is evident that the implementation of these reforms is not yet entirely completed. Nevertheless, it is evident that improved quality appeared to be increasingly linked to the information society, digitalization, internationalization, research and innovation capacity, and, to varying degrees, the impact of the economic and financial crisis. EHEA was seen as an opportunity to reaffirm the EU's commitment to higher education as a key element in making HEIs sustainable in Europe and its member countries. Having offered an insight into future trends, Sursock (2015: 15) highlighted the context of technological developments and the need to link (digital) libraries, centers for learning and teaching, and overall data management facilities that collect and analyze data in each university.

In Europe there has been longstanding cooperation in all academic disciplines that seek the development of "zones of mutual trust" (Abdullahi and Kajberg, 2004), stimulating quality enhancement in the EHEA. The European experiences of globalization have emphasized the concept of individual mobility and curricular harmonization despite the scepticism expressed in the writings of some leading educators, based upon the evidence of many different educational traditions on one side, and attitudes of governing bodies at European universities on the other side. The administration often tends to be submissive to beaurocratic decisions that sometimes result in ad hoc decisions about departmental mergers, cutting of funding, and lack of vision. As Tammaro (2011) observed, EC's higher-education programs (such as Socrates, Tempus, and Erasmus) have contributed to stimulating mobility experiences, financing scholars' and students' exchange, and, more recently, supporting joint degree courses (within the program Erasmus Mundus).

Looking at the educational challenges in the field of DLs and acquiring ICT knowledge and skills in general, a packet of measures—such as the recognition of non-formal learning; the development of flexible curricula to accommodate student and staff mobility; and enhanced university-employer collaboration in innovation and knowledge transfer (cf. EC, 2008a)—opened up the space for academic programs to include entrepreneurship as the best way to combine theory and practice, in particular related to the new sets of competencies that could be tested and practiced in a myriad different institutions that needed digitally skilled people. In many countries (especially in CEE countries) this was a big step forward in connecting theory and practice, since, in traditionally based university environments, the theory was predominant and entrepreneurship was limited to a low number of study hours.[130] To make a success of the Lisbon strategy (cf. EC, 2006b), Europe also stimulated the entrepreneurial mindsets of young people and challenged European HEIs with their capacities in promoting the idea of entrepreneurial education, designing appropriate curricula models, and establishing closer relationships between education and business in general.

Furthermore, the Europe 2020 Strategy acknowledges a need for a fundamental transformation of education and training in order to address the new skills and competencies that will be required if Europe is to remain competitive. Innovation in education and training became a key priority in several flagship initiatives of the Europe 2020 Strategy (e.g., in Agenda for New Skills and Jobs, Youth on the Move, and Digital Agenda), where the contribution of ICT to achieving these targets was recognized (cf. Kampylis et al., 2012).

It should be pointed out, especially for the non-European audience, that HEIs are recognized as important players in the Europe 2020 strategy, although their potential to contribute to Europe's prosperity remains underexploited and too few European HEIs are recognized as world class in global university rankings (cf. EC, 2011a: 2). Therefore, the EC document "Opening up Education: Innovative Teaching and Learning for All through New Technologies and Open Educational Resources"[131] sets out a European agenda for stimulating high-quality, innovative ways of learning and teaching through new technologies and digital content building. Such an approach—based upon the recent initiatives Rethinking Education and European Higher Education in the World, as well as the initiative Digital Agenda—contributed to the EU headline targets for reducing early school

---

[130]For instance, in some countries, such as in the former Yugoslavia, up to the late 1900s, students training in academic institutions used to not exceed 60 hours all together during the studying years.

[131]The document proposes actions toward more open-learning environments in order to deliver education of higher quality and efficacy, thus contributing to the Europe 2020 goals of boosting EU competitiveness and growth through a better-skilled workforce and more employment (EC 2013: 2).

leaving and increasing tertiary or equivalent attainment, and focusing on innovation, new skills and jobs, digitalization, resource efficiency, and poverty reduction.[132]

According to Sursock (2015), it is more than clear that demographic trends and the financial and economic crises are having a profound effect on European HE systems. The weak economic outlook has been accompanied by an increase in youth unemployment in many parts of Europe. The other visible trend is the growing strategic importance of internationalization, which contributes, among other things, to better university rankings and institutional positioning. A number of publications gave evidence of technological advances as one of the most important future change drivers in HEIs. In 2014, the Horizon Report on Higher Education (NMC, 2014) identified six emerging technologies that were likely to have an impact on HEIs in the next five years.[133] The Horizon Report also indicated the key trends that were seen as most likely to impact changes in HEIs globally over the coming five years. These trends are sorted into three time-related categories: fast trends, that will realize their impact in the next one to two years; and two categories of slower trends (mid-range and long-range trends), that will realize their impact within three to five or more years. The key trends mentioned in the 2014 report are: the growing importance of social media; the integration of online, hybrid, and collaborative learning; the rise of data-driven learning and assessment; the shift from students as consumers to students as creators; and the agile approaches to the change and evolution of online learning (cf. Johnson et al., 2015). In the 2015 report, the key trends are: increasing the use of blended learning; redesigning learning spaces; growing focus on measuring learning; proliferation of Open Educational Resources (OER); advancing cultures of change and innovation; and increasing cross-institution collaboration. Each of these trends has numerous implications for teaching and learning practices. Further, blending formal and informal learning and improving digital literacy are perceived as solvable challenges. Among these challenges, personalization of learning and teaching and complex thinking are considered difficult tasks, and competing models of education and rewarding teaching are defined as wicked challenges (cf. Virkus, 2015: 4; Johnson et al., 2015).

There is no doubt that traditional educational models are so challenged by the increasing number of online courses, OERs, and MOOCs, that the world of formalized degrees is challenged (van Rij, 2015: 33) and focused attention on a range of issues related to learning pedagogies and the use of ICT-based learning is growing (Sursock, 2015: 33; Rajabi and Virkus, 2013).

---

[132]In its report (House of Lords, 2015), the authors highlighted that the process of digitization generates new jobs and estimated that 35% of current jobs in the UK could become automated. The committee recommended that the government should establish a single and cohesive digital agenda to enable the UK to be a competitive player and leader in technological innovations.

[133]These are: flipped classroom and learning analytics; 3D printing and games and gamification; quantified self and virtual assistants; Bring Your Own Device (BYOD) and flipped classroom; makerspaces and wearable technology; adaptive learning technologies and the Internet of Things (cf. Johnson et al., 2015; Virkus, 2015).

Although the Europe 2020 Strategy acknowledges the need for a fundamental transformation of education and training, it is obvious from published reports that the full potential of ICT is not being realized in formal education settings and that only a few innovative projects manage to survive beyond the early adopter stage and become fully embedded in educational practice (cf. Kampylis et al., 2012). Other open questions relate to the sustainability of known and lately developed educational models that bring to the educational arena innovative teaching methods—new ways of acquiring necessary knowledge and skills that will enable todays' students to work in tomorrow's world. Some thoughts about how to educate information professionals of different kinds for the digital environment, what are the main triggers that motivate innovative approaches and teaching methodologies, and the potential strength of joint programs will be discussed in the following sections, focusing on European educational spaces.

5.2   EDUCATION OF INFORMATION SPECIALISTS IN EUROPE: TRADITION AND MODERNITY

Education for the digital environment today concerns every academic discipline, even the primary and secondary school educators and those who are involved in lifelong learning activities. In the 1990s, though, these kinds of educational needs were seen as belonging to, first of all, LIS, including archival and museology studies, and the computer science field. Cronin (1998: 43–44) stated that the DL functions could be interpreted "as a zone of convergence where librarians, computer scientists, electrical engineers, cognitive scientists, cultural anthropologists, organizational theorists, and sundry others are forging a *lingua franca* for better understanding the nature of distributed information systems and knowledge access." He saw that the DL paradigm could be "a useful lens through which to apprehend some of the defining contours of tomorrow's information landscape" (Cronin, 1998). DL education indeed was seen by some LIS experts as a vehicle for strengthening the position of LIS/IS education inside the university system, which was (and still is) jeopardized not only by a number of factors—such as cultural differences; staff unprepared to take risks and leadership; beaurocracy; the low level of qualification required by the labor market (cf. Audunson, Shuva, 2016: 4)—but also by a lack of cooperation between different departments on new information professionals' profiles and the predominance of "today's utilitarian concerns" to embrace technology in order to improve productivity (cf. Marchionini and Moran, 2012: III).

In order to fully understand the education for DLs, it is neccessary to shed some light upon the development of LIS/IS and CS education since these two fields were the environments within which the education for DLs was "born" and started to blossom.

In general, LIS/IS and CS fields in Europe have been characterized by a great diversity and complexity that are bound to different traditions, approaches, models, program structures, levels, placements, duration of courses, thematic profiles of curricula, content of courses, ways of teaching and assessment, and other factors. As to LIS education, in Kajberg's (2008:184) opinion, differences in Europe arose from historical, cultural, social, economic, and political factors as well as from educational traditions, epistemological frameworks, and a patchwork of national traditions. Audunson (2005) believed that the pluralism was a strength upon which future scientific and professional development should be built, and Kajberg (2003a) was concerned that the diversity might have hampered transparency and student mobility, which presented obvious difficulties to the intentions of working together and organizing joint programs. Later on, Kajberg (2007: 69) concluded that such a diversity "definitely has its charm, while at the same time a valuable asset." The practices and regulatory systems in a particular country still make the diversity both a positive and negative issue, while at the same time representing a valuable resource in international cooperation. As to CS education, it could be said that not all of the CS departments had found a new digital area of special interest in the direction of educating for digital information, but some continued to focus upon technical matters or acted closer with mathematics departments.

As different approaches of HEIs could be found at the organizational and managerial level, so it counts for approaches to teaching. European countries have different traditions in teaching, which is evident not only from the approach (professional vs. academic education), profiles offered, structure of the schools, and their connections with partnering departments/schools, but also in principles upon which educational processes are based and teaching/learning methodology is used. There are a number of articles that describe the status of LIS and CS education in particular in individual European countries, and several overviews offer in-depth analysis of the educational developments in a particular country or region, e.g., different age of birth or structure of chairs, departments, or schools and their educational programs.

In the post-Bologna era, many educational institutions have been granted degree-awarding powers, including the right to teach master's degrees. While retaining their traditional names, many (e.g., the Dutch Hogeschool and the German Fachhochschule) now present their institutional title in English as "University of Applied Sciences." A majority of LIS or CS HEIs function either as a department within a specific faculty (e.g., the former within the faculty of philosophy, economy, pedagogy, arts and humanities, or social sciences; the latter within the faculties of electronic engeneering, mathematics, or science) or as a program within a specific department (e.g., the former, in IS, cultural history, communication and media, or computer science; the later, in computer science, history, or archeology) and only a few institutions function as an independent faculty/department inside a university, or as an independent academic institution.

According to Borrego's (2015) findings, the combination of centers and degrees specializing in information and communication is quite common, especially in France, where centers and degrees in Information ét Communication are frequent. In fact, a majority of undergraduate LIS-related degrees identified in French universities combine the terms "information" and "communication" in their titles.[134] In Italy, the Education for Information professionals are highly divided between departments of history (for instance, programs in DH), literature, or comptuter science, which usually do not have any kind of connections, except in some rare cases (such as at the University of Pisa, where digital humanities, situated at the department of CS, cooperates with some other departments inside the university; or a new approach by Växjo, Sweden, where LIS department initiated a joint program in digital humanities jointly offered by several departments). Some CS departments have been developing programs in IR, HIB, or IL by themsleves or in partnership with departments other than LIS/IS (for instance, in Germany, Austria, or Spain).

When the organizational and managerial patterns are considered, it can be noticed that these patterns emerged from the different interpretations of conceptual definitions of the related field (including what is core and what is innovative in a curriculum), from different learning and teaching styles (ex-cathedra vs. the student-centered approach), and from the perceptions of expected learning outcomes (that ensure a student's active role in the achievement of appropriate knowledge and skills).

Different approaches to LIS/IS and CS education focused on information processing also caused procedural complications in coordination efforts when it came to the issues of joint programs or research projects. Adding to these, other factors, such as a different understanding of the LIS/IS paradigms, different learning and teaching approaches, and skills-based or knowledge-based outcomes, contributed to the feeling that academicians need to discuss harmonization issues and cooperative programs.

Collaborative activities in the area of Education for Information specialists have been focussing on the role of associations and networks, EU projects and support schemes, joint international programs or courses, including CH and ICT, and joint doctoral programs. There are also many institutional case studies and several overviews that cover two or more of these aspects or focus on collaborative activities in a specific region (for instance, Virkus and Harbo, 2002, refering to collaborative efforts in Nordic and Baltic countries, and Dixon and Tammaro, 2003, describing the cooperation between Northumbria and Parma). In some countries, cooperative efforts were directed toward enabling staff in LAM institutions to undertake digitization activities by offering courses related to the use of new ICT and digital technologies. Centers for lifelong learning have been organizing seminars, workshops, and webinars jointly with computer specialists, managers, and specialists for the organization, use, and preservation of information. Some of these types of education became seed-plots for joint development and research activities and innovative approaches.

There has been wide discussion at the European level about the core content of educational programs for future information specialists who were expected to encompass areas of knowledge

---

[134]In France, undergraduate degrees (licenses) last three years. However, universities also offer DUTs (diplôme universitaire de technologie) and DEUSTs (diplôme d'études universitaires scientifiques et techniques), both lasting two years. These degrees can be supplemented with a one-year degree (license professionnelle).

and skills needed, including those based in social science, cultural studies, computer science, etc., and be included in curricula. Wilson (2001) suggested that "information studies" may be seen as resulting from interactions among four fields: information content; information systems; people; and organizations. Audunson (2005) suggested that profound ICT-competency and a profound understanding of the librarians' role in a multicultural context is the *sine qua non* of every educational program in LIS.

The development of curricula for CS has also been challenging, considering the speedy evolution and expansion of the field. The attempts had brought in a growing diversity of topics potentially relevant to the field, as well as to the increasing integration of computing with other disciplines. On the other hand, globalization implicitly affected the content of curricula, teaching, learning and delivery methods, staff competencies, and quality. New courses, such as IPRs, information and computer ethics, the digital divide, information assurance and security, and graphics and visualization, to name but few, attracted students regardless of their preference in choosing the program, e.g., CS- or IS-oriented. The growing need to adapt to the digital information environment demands considerable re-education and changes in teaching/learning attitudes. Having seen the diversification in the professional prospects of graduates, and being challenged by the growth of IS programs in other schools of the university, LIS schools started to seek to redefine their roles and their curricula to become flexible enough to support many different career tracks, not only the library or LAM alone.[135] Education paradigms have been shifting—with varying intensity—to include more online learning, blended and hybrid learning, and collaborative models (Johnson et al., 2015).

From a CS perspective, a myriad of programs offered had to deal with well-equipped labs and highly competitive curricula in some non-European countries. With the development of open education philosophies that focus on open content, open data, and OERs, together with the rise of MOOCs during the last decade, the courses, programs, learning objects, providers, and practices (Rajabi and S. Virkus, 2013; Virkus, 2015) have moved increasingly across the borders of a single university and even beyond national boundaries.

Although many EU-funded and bilateral programs have been supportive of cooperation and harmonization with a goal to help LIS/IS HEIs in overcoming the challenges of the digital age and visible differences, there are still many different approaches to the education of information specialists, which create problems not only for students (e.g., in establishing the equivalence of specific course elements and having recognized the study periods carried out in other schools), but for teachers as well. In particular, this relates to the focus of their teaching and research as the field has been changing and with the growth of new topics and methodologies.

---

[135]A recent book by Myburgh and Tammaro (2013) discusses various areas in education for digital librarians including curriculum design, pedagogies, and the future role of information professionals.

Another trend relates to the growing number of i-schools. As Dillon (2012) stated, i-schools are distinctive from other LIS programs less for their subject emphasis or methodological approaches than for their orientation to the study of information beyond agencies, their commitment to multidisciplinary work, and their formal emphasis on research productivity. These distinctions are more than labels or a re-badging of a degree title, they represent tangible and formal commitments to creating a distinct type of academic environment that presents challenges as well as opportunities. According to G. Chowdbury (2015a),[136] i-schools in Europe, the majority of which sprang from LIS/IS schools, vary in size and capacity and the focus of their educational and research interests goes from library, records, and archives management to information and knowledge management to data science. Chowdbury raised some (old) questions related to information education and research, such as: What is the core of the discipline? What is the key strength of graduates? What can be offered that others can't offer? What is the impact of research in the field? What is the field's contribution to knowledge, economy, and society? and What is the future: information science, data science, knowledge science?

However, in Kyriaki-Manessi's opinion (2003: 22), "the revolution of forms created a revolution in approach." Many schools have changed their names to schools of IS, schools of management, or some other name, while some others have kept their traditional names, prefering LIS. Streams were developed within the schools, such as IS, library science, informatics, arhchival studies, digital humanities, data science, information economics, and even encyclopedistic and lexicology, etc. It is also worth noting that some of the schools have adopted a more "holistic" approach toward information organization and management. Information was seen as a mere commodity that in today's world needs organization, retrieval, and quality of services.

5.3   OVERVIEW OF THE DEVELOPMENTS IN DIGITAL LIBRARIES EDUCATION

Spink and Cool (1999a; 1999b) observed that the shortage of librarians and information professionals with the expertise to fulfill the technological demands of libraries would be exacerbated by the future demand for digital librarians. From the 20 schools approached in their study that had offered some DL courses or related content, only one was from Europe—Loughborough University. The number augmented to 42 in 2003 as viewed by Liu (2005). Today, according to the studies of Borrego (2015) and Auduson and Suva (2016), a majority of European LIS/IS schools have already implemented DL topics or offered DL-related educational programs. However, since its early stage, education for DLs has been twofolded: developing inside the LIS/IS schools from one side, and inside CS schools, from the other side. Professional conferences also were organized by one or

---

[136]In his presentation at the International Conference in Barcelona, G. Chowdbury listed 65 current members of the iSchools movement (22 members from Europe, 6 members from the UK) and stressed their unity in diversity.

another community starting from the different definitions of the DL concept, as Borgman (2000) claimed. Thus, it is necessary to follow these two, until recently, almost separate tracks.

At the birth of DL education, most LIS programs seemed to start with courses that usually covered definitions of the DL, its history, development, organization issues, preservation and access, technology and maintenance, and intellectual property. Computer science departments were focused on technology, metadata, retrieval, and databases. On the other hand, there were several initiatives to prepare practicing librarians for the new environments (such as summer schools, workshops, and seminars). The TICER summer school at Tilburg University in the Netherlands aimed to update the skills of experienced librarians and offered programs from 1998 until 2012 (cf. van der Zwand, 1996). Open Society was focused on librarians and information specialists in ex-communist countries, offering programs related to the management of change, digitization, etc.

Summer schools and workshops have been organized throughout Europe as part of the research and development projects funded by the EU or through national funds. For example, NESTOR, a transnational partnership of academic institutions in Germany, Switzerland, and Austria,[137] offering a comprehensive qualification program based on e-learning tutorials, schools, seminars, and publications, has been established to meet this demand (Strathmann and Osswald, 2012: 13). Other research projects included seminars as part of the projects' activities and organized education around special themes, such as the use of new media to communicate heritage and culture (cf. Kolbmüller, 2006). A number of summer schools focused on DL issues that have been organized at the national level in many European countries, or jointly by two or more universities or professional societies. In the 1990s, JSTOR organized workshops related to the emerging DL (such as, automation, new software and technology, and online journal content). Later on, the number of workshops grew and topics focused on themes related to DL diversification. Besides content regarding information technology, other "digital" issues have steadily emerged: legal aspects, evaluation and performance measures, and questions concerning formats and norms (cf. Schöpfel, 2004: 246–247).

A number of national libraries that recognized their potential role as leaders in specific areas of innovation (e.g., digital preservation, provision of joined-up access to CH, and establishing and sharing best practices and expertise in metadata standards), had offered the expert knowledge of their staff through various modes of education (cf. Hunter and Brown, 2010). Since the 1990s, in-house training initiatives in CH digitization have been offered by LAM institutions in Sweden for their employees (Justrell, 2002; 2003). These were supported in 1997 by the funding of the national

---

[137]Early on, in 2006, WG's agenda was shaped by the results of a survey on the coverage of digital preservation topics in bachelor- and master's programs provided and planned by LIS departments in Germany, Austria, and Switzerland. WG's objective was to stimulate and promote qualification in the field of digital preservation and to prepare course materials, mutually accept credit points of courses regarding digital preservation, and seek to establish a cooperative and distributed master's degree program in digital curation as a long-term objective (cf. Strathmann and Osswald, 2012: 13).

Knowledge Foundation (KK-stiftelsen), and even more, these efforts were intensified in 2004 with the establishment of the coordinating Office for Archives, Libraries, and Museums (ABM-centrum), which quickly became a major national educational agent within the LAM community with the trainee programs Future in Access and Future in Access Plus.

According to Tammaro (2007a), there were four broad models of DL courses: technology as a tool for the building of DL and the courses' focus on technological infrastructure and processes; DLs as environments concerned with the social and cultural contexts that DLs reside in; the DL as composed of objects with the main focus on the management of the life-cycle of documents and artifacts in the digital environment; and a combined model that includes different perspectives on the subject.

As the American Institute of Museum and Library Services (IMLS) funded a collaborative DL education project in 2004, led by Virginia Tech and North Carolina SLIS (Pomerantz et al., 2006), some European teachers became involved or closly followed its outcomes. Recurring themes included the balance between theory and practice in the DL curriculum, the relationship between computer science and LIS in the education of digital librarians, and the importance of providing internships in working DL programs. From a computer science perspective, five topical areas were recognized: integrating and analyzing networked information sources; ingesting, digitizing, and organizing content; designing interfaces; creating and evaluating search strategies; and guiding and training users. However, it was agreed by the project's participants that a proper balance of computer science and librarianship knowledge should perhaps be required for digital librarians to be able to deal with DL systems and manage them properly (cf. Brancolini, Mostafa, 2006).

The rising influence of ICT and the development of the digital society clearly became an important "European theme," although there are no uniquely "European values" associated with them. How to approach them varies in practice, resources, and perception in different parts of Europe and influences curriculum content and development (cf. Bates et al., 2005: 84).

As digitization became a prerequisite for closer cooperation among LAM institutions, which have been increasingly treated collectively as memory and cultural institutions, their common functions and roles were highlighted. From the theoretical and educational point of view, the convergence of memory institutions is problematic as, for historical reasons, these cultural institutions have developed their own disciplines and could only look for a common theoretical framework and focus on similarities between them (e.g., communicational, curational, managerial, or access and usage aspects).[138]

Casarosa, Castelli, and Tammaro (2011b) argued for information professionals, given the increased use of web technologies for knowledge dissemination and for collaboration, to be in-

---

[138]Manžuch et al. (2005), considering the complex and multilateral nature of studies in CH, use the term "communication of memory" for the LAM approach as a conceptual background to contextualize the development of digitization courses and integrate them into the general body of LIS knowledge.

volved much more in the usage (and development) of interactive tools and services to facilitate their activities as information professionals. They pointed out that it is still unclear how and where to draw the line between increased education in CS and increased education in the usage of advanced applications and tools available for memory institutions.

It could be argued that the LAM conceptual framework is based on the traditional role of cultural institutions in society, including digital society, and their role as mediators of heritage, as well as their extended roles in today's learning society (for instance, becoming facilitators and educators). A more traditional library-oriented approach to ICT has gradually embraced themes related to knowledge creation and ICT-supported processes in libraries.

According to Bates et al. (2005: 97), "embedding digital library education into existing courses instead of labelling courses as 'digital library' (DL) can be seen as a strength, as this allows for a gradual and incremental development to meet new needs, and avoids the danger that relevant traditional skills and perspectives will be ignored." On the other hand it may lead to a piecemeal and partial approach where some students may fail to gain an overall appreciation of the topic. Koltay and Boda (2008) argued that DL educational programs need to be constantly improved, and that attempts to stay in line with societal changes are part of the normal process of the redesign of programs.

In order to strengthen the value of the DL educational programs, European HEIs started to join forces, resulting in a growing number of collaborative or joint programs. DILL has been one such program, a two-year master program organized in cooperation with Oslo University College (Norway), Tallinn University (Estonia), and Parma University (Italy).[139]

The DILL curriculum was based on the discussion outcomes and agreements about the core content, which was basically related to knowledge creation (e.g., research procedures as well as creative and innovative insights); knowledge representations (e.g., in language and other forms) and knowledge recording (e.g., in documents of all kinds); and knowledge of various communities, and the discursive and communication activities of such communities.

Looking at the education for digitization of CH as an emerging field, Manžuch et al. (2005) have identified two approaches in digitization in Europe that are also mirrored in educational programs: a library-oriented approach, which focuses on the evolution of the system of knowledge about concepts, processes, procedures, and tools related to the creation and maintenance of DLs; and a CH-oriented approach that provides an "umbrella" approach to fields that were previously developing independently, i.e., LIS, archival science, and museology. Tammaro added the third

---

[139] The curriculum was organized in such a way that students spend at least one semester in each partner institution. Depending on the subject of a student's master's thesis and the location of the student's main supervisor, the last semester was spent at one of these three institutions, which included one month of internship at a European institution that offers DL services in order to gain the technical and practical skills needed for their future career (cf. Gardašević, 2010).

approach taken by technologists, in which the subject "digital library" has been included in many computer science curricula.(Tammaro, 2007a)

According to Weech (2007), two different trends for DL education at the beginning of the 2000s can be recognized in Europe: the isolation of IT from library fields; and the programs offered to the converging sector of libraries, archives, and museums. It was noticeable that the content of digital librarianship education in Europe was more technically oriented than in North America. However, the problem of IT in profiles and curricula was common to the broader humanistic area and the discussion was not limited to librarians but included the specific needs of other communities (e.g., humanities or STEM), which all claim the need for highly skilled professionals equipped with knowledge and digital skills. Surely, IT profiles are at different levels of qualifications and they require an in-depth rethinking of the role and competencies of the digital librarian, such as those related to the profiles of, for instance, system librarian, library manager, and digital librarian.[140] However, it is necessary to envision the DL not only in terms of a technological infrastructure but also as a set of services (e.g., educational, services for communities of interest, support for scholarly activities, etc.) that build on certain managerial decisions and economic models and are intended for specific user communities (e.g., occupation-related, age-related, culture-related, etc.) and offered in specific institutional settings (e.g., museums, archives, libraries, and their networks) (cf. Manžuch et al., 2005).

In the EPOCH study (2008), several articles summarized the state of the art in the UK, Spain, France, and Greece, highlighting the different approaches in defining optimum programs for various studies tangential to the field of IST and CH. The last chapter of this report summarized the proposal for a curriculum, based on an extensive survey of related programs, mainly in the EU and the U.S., and the following successful meetings and workshops focused on this theme. In the proposed syllabus, at BA, MA, and Ph.D. levels of courses in Cultural Digital Heritage, the modules were grouped in order to reflect "the research pipeline in humanities and social sciences" (EPOCH, 2008: 65). The curriculum also sought to define a new discipline—Digital Approaches to Cultural Heritage Studies. Several joint programs came out as a result of international cooperation.[141]

[140]With the 2006 European Recommendation on Key Competencies, digital competency has been acknowledged by the EU as one of the eight key competencies for lifelong learning (cf. http://ec.europa.eu/education/policy/school/competences_en).

[141]For instance, programs in Cultural Heritage Studies—EuroMACHS, implemented at the Universities of Coimbra, Cologne, Turku, and Salento; Master of Archival Science, Cultural Heritage and Records with Vrije Universiteit Brussel as coordinator and Universiteit Antwerpen, Universiteit Gent, KU Leuven, as partners; Master in Digital Content Management with Universitat de Barcelona as coordinator and Universitat Pompeu Fabra as partner; and Master in School Libraries and the Promotion of Reading with Universitat de Barcelona as coordinator and Universitat Autònoma de Barcelona as partner; Joint Study Profile on Information Science and Cultural Communication offered by the Berlin School of LIS and the Royal School of Library and Information Science (RSLIS), Copenhagen, and the Joint Study Profile on Digital Curation offered by the Berlin School of LIS in cooperation with Kings College, London (EuroMACHS, s.a; Niccolucci, 2006; Borrego, 2015).

At national levels there are examples of joint programs funded by national science founda-tions, such as the Croatian graduate program Written Heritage in the Digital Environment (cf. Aparac-Jelušić, 2007), approved in 2008 and launched the same year.

The Swedish School of Library and Information Science (SSLIS) started to offer distance courses in digitization of CH in bachelor's or master's level programs since 2004, based upon pre-vious experience in offering two kinds of courses: extensive courses in electronic publishing and XML/HTML text encoding; and digitization education within an academic LIS context for the members of the Swedish LAM community (cf. Dahlström and Doracic, 2009).

Niccolucci (2006: 50) listed the data on educational efforts to introduce ICT to those professionals who are responsible for CH across Europe, concluding that the data showed that a significant number of the next generation of culture professionals will not have any computer skills taught in their courses at a university. He warned about the lack of these skills as a possible result of the traditional approach to culture as humanistic discipline *par exellance* and concluded that without changing this attitude, the academy would remain in perpetual struggle.

The situation in Spain reflects other trends. Although DL is a common term in many LIS lectures, it is mostly ignored as a topic in need of careful attention until very advanced stages of higher-education training. As García-Marco reported (2009), there were no formal degree pro-grams in digital librarianship, but the certificates offered by a few LIS and CS programs focused on specific courses on DLs. By 2010 a small number of LIS programs began offering certificate programs in digital librarianship. There is still, however, little agreement as to the content and scope of these courses and programs, and little coordination between institutions. Nevertheless, "a danger persists that DL education could get lost between two separated paradigms—the one of the tech-nology and the one of libraries—so that the students of each paradigm will be unable to integrate the different contributions to a unique problem: preserving and accessing digital content in the global quest for human knowledge preservation and use" (García-Marco, 2009: 146). However, this challenge could also be one of the great opportunities for the LIS/IS community.

5.4   RESEARCH OUTCOMES AND CHALLENGES IN EDUCATION FOR DIGITAL LIBRARIES

Although an increasing interest in internationalization of LIS/IS education during the last three decades has been evident—starting from harmonization issues that were in focus from the 1990s—at the beginning of the 2000s, however, an expansion of efforts and intensification of collabora-tive initiatives was mostly connected with projects funded by the EU. One of the main reasons for stronger collaborative programs in which European LIS schools started to participate more actively was the need to find the best possible solutions to many challenges of globalization and to improve, innovate, and strengthen the LIS curricula (cf. Virkus, 2008), by adding new themes, profiles, and teaching methods, in order to meet the international standards of quality in teaching, research, and services.

In the research article about DL education in Europe, Auduson and Suva (2016) discussed issues related to research in DLs. They noticed that the research had gained a lot of interest across the globe and that most funding related to DLs had been available for building them, rather than investigating the needs for the development and design methodology of new curricula as well as finding the main trends and educational changes that might influence future information professionals.[142]

Research trends have also changed, from topics that used to be linked either with practical matters concerning library operations or purely theoretical approaches, to bibliometrics and scientometrics, information architecture, semantic web, linked data, and digital environments, which called for team work and an interdisciplinary approach (cf. Ortiz-Repiso, 2015). In her article, Ortiz-Repiso discussed some other issues, such as the employment of LIS professionals (e.g., primarily found within traditional sectors, with rapidly emerging new jobs related to portals design, DLs, management, etc., which include other degrees). One of her findings referred to the need for many hybrid profiles with roles and responsibilities that often go beyond the field covered only by LIS.

Other research was done on the competencies and skills of digital librarians. Rowlands and Bawden (1999) saw the main differences between digital libraries and "traditional," or pre-digital, libraries as related to the change from ownership to access; a change from known item access and physical browsing to search and navigation; and a change in users' expectations. Bawden et al. (2005) conducted a comparative study with a goal to analyze the contents of education and training offered in the UK and Slovenia. They identified the DL content in the curricula and derived from these the competencies for DLs in accordance with Borgman's three-part model of knowledge and skills. They argued that competencies were wide-ranging and included creating search strategies, evaluating websites, guiding and training users, integrating networked sources, analyzing and interpreting information, creating metadata, imaging and digitizing, designing interfaces and portals, and project management. The authors affirmed that these competencies can be acquired in traditional LIS courses.

Južnič and Badovinac (2005) stated that the long period of traditional library education offered by schools in the new EU member countries does not make a great barrier to adjusting to new professional and political standards. They demonstrated that LIS schools in these countries have generally changed their curricula toward those of mainstream institutions in the field, and schools have also embraced the principles and guidelines of the Bologna Declaration. When it comes to curricular content, disparity does not seem to be a major problem. One thing that stands out from this research is the degree of homogeneity that exists across the analyzed LIS schools. This

---

[142]Based on online surveys, their article investigates the status of DL education/courses in Europe, in particular, the curriculum content of DL courses and the future direction of LIS curricula in the digital age: they also identify the competitors of LIS schools in the digital world.

homogeneity exists despite some differences which can be explained in the framework of historical, education policy and the social dimensions of individual LIS programs or countries.

While some diversity is visible, the desire for a higher degree of comparability, as introduced by EU instruments, provided an opportunity to work toward this European LIS common standard. Throughout Kajberg's study (2008), some general obstacles were identified that have been ubiquitous but tacitly present even today: language obstacles, historical/traditional reluctance to openness, not enough human resources (small LIS departments), financial resources, cultural/political differences, etc.

Two other examples shed more light on desirable content and skills as well as on potential collaboration between different departments. Moniarou-Papaconstantinou et al. (2008: 124) conducted a small-scale survey to assess the needs in LIS education. The aim of the survey was to explore students' and employers' perceptions of the existing curriculum and their demands for a new program of study. The majority of the students espressed their desire to have more courses on electronic organization and diffusion of information, on digitization, and on DLs and electronic information. The Science and Technology in Archaeology Research Center (STARC) of the Cyprus Institute, devoted to the development, introduction, and use of advanced science and technologies in the field of archaeology, CH, and history of the region, has been researching new perspectives on archaeology and CH in the region, concerning, in particular, topics such as digital heritage, ICT, digital documentation and semantics, scientific visualization and virtual reality methods, digital libraries and digital humanities, or diagnostics for CH conservation.[143]

In order to acquire an overview of educational initiatives related to DH in the Nordic LIS academic community at the undergraduate and graduate levels, Dahlström and Doracic (2009) conducted a brief survey of 12 LIS departments (4 in Sweden, 3 in Finland, 1 in Iceland, 1 in Denmark, and 3 in Norway), and, in addition, online course descriptions and syllabi. They found out that hardly any of the departments offered specific courses on the topic of CH digitization, at least not explicitly connecting digitization and CH. Nevertheless, several departments offered theoretical lectures on the topic as part of larger courses. One department started to incorporate the digital topics within a new master's program, others offered a number of courses related to digitization and electronic publishing in general, but none of the CH digitization courses were a mandatory part of LIS educational programs. Legal aspects (such as IPR, privacy, and access issues) and preservation aspects used to be the most common theoretical approaches, while socio-cultural and institutional issues, and project management and economic issues were considered by only a few of the institutions approached.

While some previous studies (e.g., Manžuch et al., 2005; Pomerantz et al., 2006) have identified an international trend toward more technical approaches in digitization education, the

---

[143]The center was established as part of the EC-funded project Ariadne through the FP7 program in 2013. http://www.ariadne-infrastructure.eu/About/Consortium/CYI-STARC.

results of the Tammaro (2007a) and Dahlstrom and Doračić (2009) studies suggest a dominance of non-technical approaches and the teaching of principles and theory.

The biggest project, in terms of the number of reseachers and institutions involved, was the LIS Education in Europe: Joint Curriculum Development and Bologna Perspectives, led by the Royal School of LIS in Copenhagen.[144] From today's perspective, joint curriculum development and cooperation among LIS schools in Europe revealed how the LIS research and teaching community approached the need to bite the bullet introduced by the Bologna Declaration and the new digital environmet. The project, supported by the EUCLID and EU Socrates Erasmus programs, analyzed 11 curricular themes within the LIS curricula in Europe,[145] some of them already addressed at several other joint seminars and conferences[146] (Kajberg, 2007; 2008). Starting with an overview of the LIS curriculum from a European perspective, team members presented their views on 11 themes (digitization of cultural heritage; information literacy and learning; information seeking and information retrieval; the information society; knowledge management/information management; knowledge organization; the library in the multi-cultural information society; information and libraries in a historical perspective; mediation of culture in a European context; practice and theory; and library management). Although some of them overlapped, to some extent these themes reflected the situation not only in the LIS field but also opened up discussions toward new themes that were in search of accomodation inside academia.

In the same e-book, Borup Larsen (2005: 234–235) offered an insight into the core subjects in LIS curricula of studied schools. From the data collected it was evident that subject areas followed pretty much the same order as that in which priority subject areas were given by respondents, with information seeking and information retrieval appearing as a core subject area in all institutions' LIS course offerings. Following were information literacy and learning and the information society, and CH and digitization of the CH. However, the culture-specific subject areas were represented in

---

[144]Six partner institutions were involved in the planning and running of the project: the University of Barcelona, Faculty of Librarianship and Documentation, Spain; Hanzehogeschool Gröningen, School for Information and Communication, Gröningen, the Netherlands; City University London, Department of Information Science, UK; Oslo University College, Faculty of Journalism, LIS, Norway; Potsdam University of Applied Sciences, Department of Information Sciences, Germany; and the University of Vilnius, Faculty of Communication, Institute of LIS, Lithuania (Kajberg, 2007: 71).

[145]The results of the expert-based analysis of a range of LIS school subjects are documented in the chapters of an e-book entitled *European Curriculum Reflections on Library and Information Science Education* (Kajberg and Lörring, 2005).

[146]EUCLID organized the first of its seminars in Parma, in 2002. The focus was on globalization in LIS. The idea behind the project on curriculum development in 2004–2005 goes back to the EUCLID conference Restructuring and Adapting LIS Education to European Standards in Thessaloniki in 2002, when the need to implement the intentions of the Bologna Declaration in the field of LIS education was highlighted. The follow-up conference, Coping with Continual Change—Change Management in Schools of Library and Information Science, was organized in Potsdam in 2003. The conference was jointly organized by EUCLID and ALISE. The conference proceedings, *Coping with Continual Change-Change Management in SLIS*, appeared in 2005.

a much more marginal way. Discussing the organizational patterns, the author found out that 59% of the LIS schools functioned as a department within a specific faculty, 25% of the schools operated as a program within a specific department, whereas 10% of the institutions had the status as an independent faculty/department, and only 6% indicated that they were an independent academic institution. In other words, the major trend or pattern for the organizational place of LIS schools in Europe was that they formed an integral part of larger educational frameworks/institutional environments. The LIS educational units are in no way exclusive to one academic superstructure, although arts and humanities seem to be the most common academic umbrella for LIS schools (35%). The others were listed as social sciences (15%), communication and media (13%), business and management (9), computer science (4%), and 24% in other various environments (cf. Borup Larsen 2005: 236–237).

Borrego's data—collected some 10 years later—are certainly very useful for getting a clear picture of today's organization and content researched at EU HEIs in the field of LIS/IS with regard to DL education. He brought up the data about the number of schools and departments that deliver LIS education in Europe,[147] tried to establish in which disciplines these schools and departments were positioned, how big they were, if they had any experience of collaboration with other LIS schools and departments, and what were the characteristics of the programs that these schools and departments delivered.

From his study results it is obvious that most European LIS-related educational programs are delivered by schools and departments that can be classified under the heading of "Humanities."[148] Disciplines under which LIS schools are listed include: communication (15.5%), LIS (28.2%), computing (9.1%), management and policy (2.1%), education (1.4%), science and engineering (1.8%), humanities (31.8%), and social and behavioral (1.4%), and 8.2% of HEIs had no classification data. Although Borrego's study was directed to EU LIS schools, the data collected indicate the changing environment in which these schools are been situated today.

The last "big survey" conducted by Auduson and Shuva (2016) presented data[149] that clearly showed that the majority of LIS schools had already integrated digital librarianship in their regular bachelor's and master's degree programs. The authors argued for the "Europe-wide unique LIS curriculum" for which the top subject areas, based on their importance as reported by the participants, should be taken into consideration before designing curricula for DLs.

---

[147]The research focused on LIS education in the 28 member states of the EU as of June 2015.

[148]However, this figure could be misleading, as among 70 schools and departments, most of them (49) are faculties of language, philosophy, and related disciplines based in Italian universities that offer degrees in CH (*beni culturali*). Others are bound to history when it comes to library and archival studies (cf. Borrego, 2015).

[149]This study received responses from 54 LIS schools/departments in 27 European countries.

According to the study done by S. Virkus (2015),[150] the main innovations that have been introduced in the last five years include structural changes at the departmental, institutional, or university level, including the merger of disciplinary institutes into focused interdisciplinary fields, such as educational innovation, cultural competencies, digital and media culture, healthy and sustainable lifestyle, and open society and governance. Moreover, research participants referred to changes and innovation related to ICT, including the use of learning management systems, teleconference systems, ICT-based learning objects, OERs, the integration of social media into learning and teaching, exploring the use of learning analytics and MOOCs, experimenting with BOYD, using cross-country teaching and learning with the help of ICT, transferring the curriculum to the online and blended mode, and the implementation of the new system of booking business travels and accounting. The third main area where innovation became common was the development of new programs, courses, and teaching methods, including online programs.

5.5   CONCLUDING REMARKS

During the past 20 years some of the key challenges and future action lines have been discussed in research groups and at conferences and seminars not exclusively related to Europe but to the world LIS/IS community as well. A number of key issues resulted in research papers and books covering education for DLs and DCH, as well as new profiles of LAM and other information professionals. It could be concluded that many European LIS/IS, CS, and other fields have been trying to clarify their mission and collaboration for future scenarios—strategic objectives of the ever-growing and multifocused discipline that deals with information and CH. LIS/IS and emerging i-schools in Europe have been looking at the disciplinary/ies core and addressing the peripheries, rebuilding and pursuing the interdisciplinary dimension of information and CH studies, and planning the educational levels within the framework of lifelong education. New position titles such as Director of Digital Curation, Chair of Digital Special Collections, Digitization Librarian, Director of Management of Digital Services, and Digital Museum Curator, also reflect emerging trends in DLs.

In the last two decades, a high degree of interest and activity in international DL education and cooperation between the U.S., Canada, and European departments is mainly motivated by a strong desire to improve and strengthen their curricula, to understand the nature of the LIS/IS profession, teaching, and research and to explore ways and means by which international as well as global cooperative schemes can best be utilized.

---

[150]The contribution of LIS institutions to innovation and change in Europe is examined through five institutional case studies: The Institute of Information Science and Information Systems, University of Graz, Austria; Institute of Information Studies of Tallinn University, Estonia; Department of Library Science and Information Systems, Alexander Technological Educational Institute of Thessaloniki, Greece; Faculty of Communication of Vilnius University, Lithuania; and the Swedish School of Library and Information Science, University of Borås, Sweden (Virkus, 2015, p. 2).

In line with collaborative efforts, BOBCATSS stands out as a successful, innovative, and very visible example of long-lasting cooperation in European LIS education. Other kinds of LIS collaboration efforts in Europe, such as joint curriculum development projects and offering of joint courses and modules, appear less spectacular and fewer in number. Actually, very little is written about bilateral partnerships and networking between individual European LIS schools.

As new information technologies have been widely introduced in different public sectors, there is an increasing demand for specialists well grounded in the former's information searching, utilization, and management functions, as well as in their new knowledge-generation potential. The reforms under the Bologna recommendations have, however, not been without controversy, for example in countries where the new structure did not map easily onto the traditional employment structures, and in others where efforts to introduce higher-level qualifications were not appreciated nor fully supported by employers. The EC's failure to address LIS/IS education could be seen as a consequence of the economic and political challenges that confront the EU, as well as the EC's lack of capacity to oversee the detailed implementation of EU policies that are directed toward a strong and innovative information society. In the case of European LIS/IS education, which is today increasingly inclined to follow i-school ideas and goals, there is a need for leading professional educational associations to work toward strengthening connections between LIS/IS HEI and ED, similar to the pattern used by EBLIDA for European libraries, information centers, and archivres. Unfortunately, EUCLID, the only association that connects LIS/IS schools in Europe, is not strong enough and until now it didn't accept such a role as was hoped for at the time of its establishment.

It has also been evident that a new teaching/learning methodology provoked by the use of digital resources and digital technology has been influencing the future of HEIs, and the ability to cope with these changes will depend on a significant expansion of information infrastructure, including skilled and competent information professionals.

If European LIS/IS education intends to keep up with the expansion of new teaching/learning approaches and models, they have to be designed around clearly defined learning goals and objectives for various degrees, certificates, or other programs of study in the wider area of information content and services delivered in analog and digital form (for LAM, digital humanistics, etc.). There is no doubt that HEIs should make a move toward an open approach to teaching that facilitates learning from multiple, alternative paths. It seems that European HEIs in the LIS/IS field are well aware of changing surrounding, challenges, and threats, as they already have been leading a number of innovative approaches to teaching/learning at the level of the whole HEIs they belong to (e.g., by, acting as innovators in implementing online learning programs, integrating technology into the classroom, and stimulating and taking an active role in cross-disciplinary collaboration).

As was already stressed, education for digital librarians in Europe is affected by the main trends in relevant research for DLs, which are moving from the stage of the isolation of IT from

LIS schools, to a transition with a purely technological approach, toward a better appreciation of social and human aspects in studies of CH and information processing.

As the financial and economic crises have had a profound effect on many HEIs, the visible consequences were the merging and loss of staff, countered by the introduction of innovation in education to deal with the growing need to use shared resources and infrastructure and keep education in LIS/IS field relevant, competitive, and proactive in terms of attracting more students. The changed environment offers new jobs and also requires new competencies and digital skills from the employees.

CHAPTER 6

Conclusions and Predictable Future Trends

Since the birth of the *International Journal on Digital Libraries* in 1997 and the start of the annual European conferences on digital libraries (ECDL), with growing participation of professionals from Europe and other parts of the globe, the scene for DLs and for bilateral and multilateral European research and development projects in DL has changed enormously.

In this book we discussed the birth and development of DLs in Europe and presented three phases of these developments: the early phase (till 1999); the mature phase when DL became an object of planned research (2000–2008), and the phase in which advanced features of DL content and services started to be visible. Most of the initial DL projects in Europe were focused on preserving CH, in particular on digitization of treasures from world-known institutions, such as European national libraries or museums. In other words, these objects were representative and a kind of proof of the rich socio-political and cultural rise of Europe over centuries.

The digitization of European CH had significantly improved the accessibility of heritage material for research, education, culture, and enjoyment, which continues to be one of the most important goals. The major digitization projects are well-known and well-documented in professional literature. However, projects initiated and carried out by individual CH and scientific organizations were, in many cases, uncoordinated and mostly unnoticed by the larger public. One of the challenges for the professional communities and funding bodies was how to identify those projects and register them in a national digitization inventory on the web. At the European and country levels, several reports identified a clear need for digitization plans referring to three levels—digitization, research, and business platform—and urging connection with these as much as possible.

Although some member states and the EU as a whole have taken some encouraging policy steps (e.g., a bolder regulatory reform, cooperation, and mobility shemes), there are still doubts about how to keep up with the growing need to make Europe competitive in the global economy, as well as how to foster its cultural, educational, and research role and power, keeping in mind recent socio-political and economic crises that could shake the future of the EU in particular.

Considering that telecommunication networks worldwide face growing pressure to increase their capacity, and that telecommunication players in other parts of the globe have already made massive investments to upgrade network technologies, the EU and other European countries seek to improve their positions, which are jeopardized by slower processes than hoped. At the same time, revenue and profitability growth in European industry are falling. Europe's telecommunication industry now lags behind the rest of the developed world in many measures, and there is a constant fear that the region may fall behind many developing countries that are rapidly leap-frogging older technologies.

In such an environment, the expectations from the cultural sector, the digital cultural sector in particular, are considerable. To achieve full exploitation of its CH, the EC identified three key areas for action: digitization of analog collections for their wider use in the information society, aiming to uplift the potential of European tourism and cultural industries; online accessibility, which is a precondition for maximizing the benefits that citizens, researchers, and companies can draw from the information; and preservation and storage to ensure that future generations can access the rich digital material and to prevent the loss of precious content.

From the mid-1990s—prompted by the Bangemann Report—the EC had launched a stimulating and encouraging program to give impetus to the use of ICT in the emerging information society, and anticipated the economic growth, a growing employment market, and an overall increase in quality in all aspects of everyday life. It soon become obvious that the information infrastructure was a necessary framework for future activities in the digital environment, and that the legal basis for its creation and development had to be prepared on national and EU levels. Some countries, in particular those from CEE or South Europe, were slower than others who provided, at a fast rate, a number of laws affecting the field of information, informatization and protection of information, science development, education, LAM services, copyright, licensing models, orphan works, preservation, etc. Various strategic documents in the field of culture, education, science, ICT, etc., have been governing the relationships between the participants in information processes and defining working principles for the whole information infrastructure, digitization activities and building of a national digital collection, and Europeana in particular. Furthermore, a number of guidelines, handbooks, and presentations of best practices has been published. In all these developments and plans the role of the ECo and EC have been of utmost importance, especially when it comes to cultural policy activities and funding. Even so, the goal of enabling and developing a Europe-wide virtual research community dedicated to DCH remains a high priority. One reason for constantly improving access to European heritage by digitizing objects and collections from many stackholders is its widely scattered nature caused by the involvement of multiple ministries in some countries, by different funding models, by different economic growth rates, etc.

The legal basis, in particular the documents accepted by the EU, laid the foundation for active involvement in the international information exchange and the mobility of students and members of educational institutions, and enabled the growth of expert networks, joint projects, and educational programs. Above all, this was important for countries that were behind the Iron Curtain, as the new legal regulations secured citizens' rights to free access to information and reinforced international cooperation and participation in a Global Information Infrastructure (GII) movement.

Between 1996 and 2001, the EC and national governments managed to create regulatory frameworks that aimed to remove some of the noticeable obstacles, such as national telecommunication monopolies or obsolete educational systems. The Council of the EU and the EC presented the e-Europe initiative, expecting that new funded programs should develop advanced systems and services in order to improve visibility and access to Europe's scientific, cultural, and educational resources. The vision of the "new Europe" included digitization, accessibility, and digital preservation of CH and scientific knowledge and highlighted the role of DLs. In building and developing the digital culture framework of Europe's rich heritage, the policy documents have respected the principles of multiculturalism and multilingualism.

The purpose of the EDL, and Europeana in particular—which was seen as one of the most important European goals in fostering democracy, equality, and social justice—was to increase access to information, disseminate culture and knowledge, and contribute to the quality of meaningful and informative leisure time. To realize these goals, Europe put a tremendous effort into making cultural, educational, and scientific resources publicly available for use worldwide. The collections and services are based on national or thematic aggregators and enriched with semantic web features, with the availability of LOD resources growing exponentially. However, the potential of all digital resources still remains largely untapped, especially in regard to CH collections, which are hidden from the mainstream hubs.

At a general European level there were several moments of special importance for the development of DLs, in particular when it comes to constantly improving IIs and providing an appropriate legal framework. Undoubtedly, the awareness of the need to build appropriate IIs to support the development and ingestion of multiple digital formats has been rising. The financial support for researching information systems, retrieval tools, or preservation strategies and methods helped the efforts directed at finding the best possible solutions for the accessibility of digital assets over time. Contrary to the first attempts and early digitization projects taken mostly by growing awareness of the DLs' potential among computer, library, and some other professionals, new approaches in the digitization of heritage items and collections en masse have been aspiring to make the rich European heritage available through fast and capable search engines and standardized protocols, as well as protecting and preserving them for the future.

Moreover, the growing awareness of the need to fully consider the issues of economic sustainability of digital information systems and services could be seen. Besides cooperative efforts, joint projects, and the sharing of digital resources, the search for new cooperative models and cost-effective approaches continued in order to ensure cheaper, easier, and better access to digital content and services. Evaluation of existing services was felt neccessary to claim successful investment or savings made by sharing resources for digitization and delivery of information services.

Another issue of concern to the digital cultural community around Europe is the preservation and long-term availability of digital content and services. How to best conduct digitization processes and preserve digital content attracts the attention of policy makers, LAM, and other heritage professionals and researchers from a growing number of disciplines.

After the wave of mass digitization activities—aimed at enriching the amount of digital documents, for Europeana and at levels of a particular nation—a number of obstacles were recognized, especially those that prevent adding too much metadata and information about the source document that accompanies the digital representation, because of the high expense and lack of skilled personnel. The creation of Europeana as the unique access point to European CH is indeed a very relevant achievement. More than 54 million items expressing European cultural richness are currently accessible through Europeana, and this number is constantly growing. Europeana continues its efforts to include as much content as possible and offers the best services. In line with this, Europeana seeks to collaborate with partners not only in Europe but worldwide, especially in regard to research and development projects, and to engage in the exchange of expertise.

As for the educational arena, Europe's cultural diversity and variety of national educational traditions, program structures, and curricula represent a valuable resource in European and international cooperation, albeit the influence of the EC on LIS education in Europe has been indirect and limited. However, the reforms under the Bologna Declaration have not been without controversy. It looks as if the EC also failed to address fully and properly the DL education, which could be seen as the consequence of the economic and political challenges that have confronted the EU, as well as the lack of the EC's capacity to oversee the detailed implementation of EU policies related to the building of a strong and innovative information society. Some optimists see that maybe the new documents, such as Horizon 2020, could bring new impetus and stimulatation to HEIs to take a much more active part in educational research projects funded by the EC.

The appearance and development of DLs showed that during the last 15 years DLs have been looked at as a new educational perspective and that related content and learning/teaching methodology have been included gradually in single courses and curricula. In some cases this led to degrees with the word "digital" in their titles, but the programs offered came under various HEI frameworks. These changes certainly require significant expansion of II, including skilled and competent teachers. It is not easy to foresee the directions of higher education in general, but it is already clear that one of the most profound and far-reaching changes in education could be the move from a mass production model focused on teaching to an individualized model focused on learning, as in many other parts of the world.

Having in mind the need for various digital profile vacancies in Europe, HEIs should be more aware of the need for change and take responsibility for well-thought-out and designed curricula, cooperation, and exchange of expertise and experience. As the noted isolation of IT-related disciplines from education and research themes has resulted in internal fragmentation of DL topics within the LIS/IS domain and the lack of communication with computer scientists, it is a "must" to carefully consider what content and skills to include, which new profiles to offer, and how to combine technical and socio-cultural issues in study programs. Indeed, concentration on narrow, purely technological issues in the LIS/IS curricula and the production of applications or services that do not meet the real needs of society may lead toward gaps within users' expectations from todays' and future professionals dealing with information products and services. Examples of expressed doubts relate to situations in which, for example, digitized collections on the web are accessible to all but at the same time not usable because of an inconsistency with users' needs or skill levels; or, sophisticated CH applications that do not consider the social, economic, cultural factors of real-life situations, etc. On the other hand, many of the technical or business-related profiles within the digital content industry are transversal and may be a great opportunity for information specialists to expand their knowledge and skills and take responsibility for jobs they didn't consider possible when enrolling in their academic programs. By all means, the changed environment offers new jobs and requires new competencies and digital skills from the employees. Successful educational programs for the digital age should be based on assumptions that there exist diverse perspectives and the need for interaction between disciplines and sub-fields. In an attempt to develop and offer qualitative and innovative educational discourse, this assumption should be one of the starting points for program designers.

However, one of the main triggers leading to the introduction of innovations in teaching/learning and digital market environments is the economic crisis and inadequate financial resources that give impetus to re-thinking all challenges and new possibilities for information professionals in the digital age. But there is also a fear connected with budgets and cuts in resources, e.g., they have already had a profound effect on many HEIs with one visible consequence being the merging (often not well planned or not planned at all) and loss of staff.

As for the research perspective, it is obvious that, during the last decades, LAM and other CH organizations have been experimenting with different levels, sample sizes, and strategies when digitizing collections and artifacts on their own, as well as in various forms of public or private partnerships. To be able to manage an ever-growing number of digital assets and services, DLs needed research-based models, infrastructure, guidelines, and tools for various purposes.

On one hand, research is approached and conducted by information and computer specialists who are interested in finding new ways to empower DL infrastructure, access, or preservation. On the other hand, LIS/IS and humanities scholars have been focused on the organization and management of metadata, critical analysis of the interpretative dimension of digital reproduction, and ways in which digital artifacts are represented. These approaches and uncertainties emerged from the complexity of DLs and called for collaboration between various disciplines in order to strengthen their potential while researching common phenomena, new structures in academia, and new competencies needed for jobs in the digital environment.

Research shows that known approaches to information needs, information seeking and retrieval, and information use and interactions are significantly influenced by the culture and context of users, as well as the nature of the digital domain and digital information itself. Over the past few decades in Europe, a large number of models and theories have appeared that cover these issues.

The dominant research topics relate to use and usability, organizational and economic issues, and issues covering IRM and digital curation. The research into the evaluation of DLs has also been growing in the last decade. However, the need to research in more detail social-cultural issues of DLs, especially DLs for CH, remains a big challenge.

It is obvious that, since early initiatives in building up DLs, "digital pioneers" failed to anticipate the extent to which digital systems and services might come to be consolidated under the auspices of a few large players. This is not only a European issue. In such an environment the efforts to build up Europeana as the main aggregator and first access point to the rich European digitized and digital heritage have reflected the determination of Europe to be among the leaders of the new trends. Indeed, through institutional or cooperative digititzation activities, in particular in the last 20 years, DLs have created, purchased, or otherwise obtained a mass of digital resources and delivered these online to a range of users worldwide.

The research in DLs has pointed out the myriad of themes that have been considered worthy of investigation and attractive to researchers as well as funding bodies, whose growing role is to support the investigation of DL from many perspectives. As digitization activities related to CH are very resource-intensive, as well as strongly dependent upon the relationship between different stakeholders, a holistic lifecycle approach for digitization initiatives was needed, not only in order to develop sustainable and successful digitization projects, but also to provide models and frameworks that could form a base for research into user satisfaction and the sustainability of DL of CH.

During the past 20 years, some of the key challenges and future action lines have been discussed in several research groups and at digital libraries conferences. Outcomes of these discussions and individual attempts are presented in research papers and books covering various topics, but there are still many open questions that need to be taken into account in future research and development projects.

Appendix: List of Projects Mentioned in the Book (with Useful Links)

AGAMEMNON: Pictures from the Past: Agamemnon is a wireless network of magic digital cameras and palmtops for archaeological travels through the time. The project strove to research how to exploit 3G mobile phones equipped with embedded cameras for enhancing visits of open-air archaeological sites and museums. This was done by testing devices that provide visitors with enriched and personalized multimedia (pictures, video, audio, text) information on monuments.

> http://cordis.europa.eu/ist/digicult/agamemnon.htm

ARROW (Accessible Registries of Rights Information and Orphan Works): The ARROW project developed a system to manage rights information for the purposes of any DL program and, in principle, for any other use. It is conceived to facilitate diligent search to identify the rights status of any work that a library wishes to digitize and make available online. ARROW is an open, standard-based system that provides interoperability among existing resources and fosters the collection of additional data or enrichment of existing data within a network. This complex system has been named Rights Information Infrastructure (RII). ARROW Plus (2011–2013) was started with the goal to form a Best Practice Network by building on and furthering the implementation of the ARROW system after its piloting phase in Germany, France, Spain, and the UK. The objective was also to increase the number of countries in which ARROW is used, and broaden the types of works for which it is used to include visual material. The project contributed to the goal of the EU to make European CH legally accessible through an innovative way of establishing rights status in and facilitating rights clearance of copyright works.

> http://cordis.europa.eu/project/rcn/191892_en.html
> http://pro.europeana.eu/project/arrow
> https://www.arrow-net.eu/

ATHENA: ATHENA is a network of best practices within the eContentplus program that took its origins from the existing MINERVA network. Its goal was to bring together relevant stakeholders and content owners from museums and other cultural institutions all over Europe and to evaluate and integrate specific tools, based on a common agreed-on set of standards and guidelines to create harmonized access to their content. ATHENA is contributing in the content provision to Europeana.

> http://www.athenaeurope.org/

BRICKS (Building Resources for Integrated Cultural Knowledge Services): BRICKS was an Integrated Project of the FP6 program from 2004 until 2007. The BRICKS project established a network of cultural institutions to share digital cultural resources. These institutions included: the European Library, the MICHAEL Project, the British Museums, Libraries and Archives Council, and the Russian Culture Heritage Network. The target audience was very broad and heterogeneous and involved CH and educational institutions, the research community, industry, and citizens. This project has created a basis for a new generation of DLs by establishing the organizational and technological foundations of the European Digital Memory (EDM). The EDM has been reinforced through user support from the BRICK'S Community and conceived as an open, networked system to integrate distributed collections of multimedia resources in museums, libraries, and archives.

> http://cordis.europa.eu/project/rcn/71256_en.html
> http://cordis.europa.eu/result/rcn/46065_en.html
> https://www.ercim.eu/publication/Ercim_News/enw61/meghini.html

CALIMERA (Cultural Applications: Local Institutions Mediating Electronic Resource Access): Working with a network of support groups, practitioners, national authorities, and suppliers in European countries, the Coordination Action CALIMERA had produced a vast array of resources with key products that included reports on every country in the network, guidelines for local cultural institutions on social, management, and technical issues underlying digital service delivery, a research roadmap, and other documents and tools (2003–2005). CALIMERA built upon the achievements of the Pulman Network of Excellence that had already set the scene for promoting best practices among local institutions (LAMs) throughout Europe. One of the most important outcomes of the Pulman Network were the Pulman "Guidelines for Public Libraries in the Age of Digitization" and the "Oeiras Manifesto," a policy document paving the way for the implementation of eEurope in local cultural institutions

> http://cordis.europa.eu/ist/digicult/calimera.htm

CAMiLEON (Creative Archiving at Michigan and Leeds: Emulating the Old on the New): The CAMiLEON project developed and evaluated a range of technical strategies for the long-term preservation of digital materials. User evaluation studies and a preservation cost analysis provided answers as to when and where these strategies would be used. The project is a joint undertaking between the Universities of Michigan (U.S.) and Leeds (UK) and is funded by JISC and NSF. Emulation was proposed as a digital preservation strategy that would enable obsolete systems to run on future unknown systems, making it possible to retrieve, display, and use digital documents with their original software.

> http://www.dcc.ac.uk/resources/external/camileon-creative-archiving-michigan-and-leeds-emulating-old-new

CASLIN: The Union Catalog of the Czech Republic started the Caslin project in 1995. Today it contains information on books and serial publications held in the collections of libraries and other public institutions of the Czech Republic—about 6.2 millions records of foreign and domestic production.

http://www.caslin.cz/caslin-en/about-us

CASPAR (Cultural, Artistic and Scientific knowledge for Preservation, Access and Retrieval): CASPAR, a four-year, multi-partner, EU-funded initiative that aimed to research, implement, and disseminate innovative solutions for digital preservation based on the project, was also investigating digital preservation challenges and validating the potential of proposed solutions from the perspective of three distinct domains—scientific, CH, and creative arts. The CASPAR consortium was established to ensure adequate coverage from each of the three specialist areas and also includes commercial partners and information preservation experts.

http://cordis.europa.eu/project/rcn/92920_en.html; http://www.dcc.ac.uk/resources/briefing-papers/technology-watch-papers/caspar

CEDARS (CURL Exemplars in Digital ARchiveS): CEDARS is a UK digital preservation project funded by JISC through eLib. The project goal was to promote awareness of the importance of digital preservation, to produce strategic frameworks for digital collection management policies, and to promote methods appropriate for long-term preservation. An important strand of concerned metadata to be used as a means of recording migration and emulation strategies, ensuring the authenticity of digital objects, noting rights management and collection management issues, and for resource description and discovery.

http://www.ukoln.ac.uk/services/elib/projects/cedars/

COVAX: COVAX is the EU-funded project that aimed to test the use of XML with a goal to combine document descriptions with digitized surrogates of cultural documents. The goal was to build a global system for search and retrieval, increasing accessibility via the internet to the digital collections of memory institutions regardless of their location.

https://www.ercim.eu/publication/Ercim_News/enw49/bordoni.html

DC-NET (Digital Cultural heritage NETwork: DC-NET supported cooperation for research infrastructure in the digital CH field. The project's main goal was to develop and strengthen the coordination, among European countries, of public research programs in the sector of the DCH. The project intended to contribute to the integration of the research capacities of the participant member states in order to initiate the deployment of a wide and comprehensive European e-Infrastructure available to all ministries of cultures.

http://cordis.europa.eu/project/rcn/93066_en.html

DELOS: DELOS was first funded in 1997–1999 as a working group by the ESPRIT Long Term Research Program of the 4th Framework Program (4FP) in the frame of the Information Society Technologies Program (IST). The DELOS Network of Excellence investigated a number of topics, including methods and tools for semi-automatic indexing and semantic annotation of non-textual objects, such as music, speech and images, preservation issues, etc. It was also aimed at integrating DL research in Europe, as well as projects targeting archives and, in particular, audiovisual resources.

> http://delosw.isti.cnr.it/ (frozen in 2009)
> https://cordis.europa.eu/pub/ist/docs/digicult/delos.ppt

DESIRE: DESIRE addressed the needs of European researchers to locate and retrieve information relevant to their research activities. It is a project within the Telematics for Research area of the EU's FP4. DESIRE was a large project examining many issues to do with the use of the web (security, authoring, caching, training, and other areas) and was coordinated by Surfnet in the Netherlands.

> http://cordis.europa.eu/project/rcn/104212_en.html

DPE (DigitalPreservationEurope): This project's main activities were in field digital preservation with the following goals: to raise awareness among the general public, libraries, archives, museums, government bodies, and institutions across Europe; advocacy; building up certified repositories and mobilizing centers or networks of competency; spreading and exchanging knowledge of crucial technological issues; pooling of complementary existing expertise; contributing to audit and certification standards; and enabling training and collaboration services. The consortium was built on the work of the Electronic Resource Preservation and Access Network (ERPANET), which operated from 2001–2004, with funding from the EC. In 2009 EC funding of DPE ended and the Humanities Advanced Technology and Information Institute (HAITII) of the University of Glasgow assumed responsibility for managing DPE.

> http://cordis.europa.eu/project/rcn/101694_en.html
> http://www.digitalpreservation.gov/series/edge/dpe.html

eContentplus: eContentplus started in 2005 (until 2008) as the successor to the eContent program (2001–2004). One of its targets was the setting up of European information networks for accessing and using European digital scientific and cultural resources through the linking of virtual libraries or community memories. It aimed to support the development of interoperable collections and objects available in various cultural institutions and of solutions to facilitate the exhibition, discovery, or repatriation of such resources. Since 2009, such measures have continued under the ICT Policy Support Program (ICT PSP), one of three specific programs implemented to support establishing a Competitiveness and Innovation Framework Program (2007-2013) ("CIP").

> http://cordis.europa.eu/econtent

eLib Program: The eLib Program was a Hybrid Libraries project aimed at integrating electronic products and services with the traditional functions of a library. The goal was for a library user to be able to use a single interface to discover and retrieve all of a library's resources, both internal (physical materials) or external (internet resources). In 1994, eLib was set up by the JISC, paid for by the UK's funding councils, and was active until 2001. One of the many projects funded by eLib was an experimental magazine, *Ariadne*, an online journal originally produced in both print and web versions.

> http://www.ukoln.ac.uk/services/elib/

EPOCH (Excellence in Processing Open Cultural Heritage): This Network of Excellence, co-funded under the FP6 program, collected information on the use of ICTs in CH and performed research on toolkits for creating CH applications. EPOCH also helped spread excellence through dissemination and training activities, studying the socio-economic impact of CH, and exploring mechanisms for ICT deployment in heritage organizations. EPOCH's aim was to create a holistic view of the DL area by integrating and enhancing the previously fragmented efforts in research directed toward intelligent ICT for tangible CH.

> http://cordis.europa.eu/ist/digicult/epoch.htm

ERPANET (Electronic Resource Preservation and Access Network of Excellence): This project's goal was to make viable and visible information, best practices, and skills development in the area of digital preservation of CH and scientific objects. It was funded in 2004 under RP5-IST and by a Swiss Confederation. Coordinator, HATII; Glasgow University, UK, parters: Italy, theNetherlands and Switzerland, and PADI from Australia. The dominant feature of ERPANET was the provision of a virtual clearinghouse and knowledge base on state-of-the-art developments in digital preservation and the transfer of that expertise among individuals and institutions.

> http://www.erpanet.org/about.php
>
> http://cordis.europa.eu/project/rcn/61043_en.html

HUSLONET: The Hungarian-Slovak Network between five HEI libraries in two Hungarian and one Slovak town (close to the border and with Hungarian minorities) was an initiative, implemented in the summer of 1995, with an extensive planning phase to select hard- and software and secure finances (by the MellonFoundation) to network OPACs via the Hungarian research network and share CD-ROMs via a common gateway. This networked cooperation, together with the PHARE project for Hungarian-Romanian public library cooperation, had a special meaning in the context of the bilateral negotiations concerning Hungarian minorities in the neighboring countries.

> https://webcache.googleusercontent.com/search?q=cache:http://cordis.europa.eu/libraries/
> en/cee/hungary.html&gws_rd=cr&ei=Ha0AWd_BOcnEgAa826OICw

IMPACT project: This project focused on digitization of printed materials, with the aim of improving the technologies for optical character recognition, structuring documents, and working with different languages.

http://www.impact-project.eu/faqs/impact-strategic-faq-answers/

INDICATE: INDICATE started as a two-year project (2010–2012), funded in the FP7 (e-Infrastructure). The goals of the project were to coordinate policy and best practices regarding the use of e-Infrastructures for DCH in countries all around the Mediterranean and to develop consistent policies and best practices governing research.

http://www.indicate-project.org

InterPARES (The International Research on Permanent Authentic Records in Electronic Systems): The InterPARES Project was launched in 1999 as InterPARES 1 (1998–2001) and continued as InterPARES 2 (2002–2007), InterPARES 3 (2007–2012), and InterPARES Trust, which focuses on digital records entrusted to the Internet (2013–2018). In general, this project aims to develop the knowledge essential to the long-term preservation of authentic records created and/or maintained in digital form and to provide the basis for standards, policies, strategies, and plans of action capable of ensuring the longevity of such material and the ability of its users to trust its authenticity.

http://www.interpares.org

MALVINE (Manuscripts and Letters via Integrated Networks in Europe): This is a project under the Telematics for Libraries, which started in 1998. Its goal was to open new, and enhance access to, disparate modern manuscript holdings that are kept and cataloged in European libraries, archives, documentation centers, and museums. MALVINE provided a common multilingual user interface in a clear terminology with the help of metadata. The project incorporates databases in the field of biographical documentation, publishing projects, and related sectors.

http://cordis.europa.eu/libraries/en/projects/malvine.html

MEMORIES: A design of an audio semantic indexation system allowing information retrieval for the access to archive content. This project created a generic software library in order to facilitate the extraction of high-level information from audio signals. The main innovations of the MEMORIES project were a user-friendly system that matched archivist needs for information retrieval in audio databases, the definition of a format for database structuring of information content descriptors, and an efficient tool for audio restoration.

http://cordis.europa.eu/ist/digicult/memories.htm

MICHAEL and MICHAEL Culture: Founded in 2007 as the Michael European Portal, the Multilingual Inventory of Cultural Heritage in Europe, its purpose was to continue the work on the portal beyond the period of EU funding and to make the network of MICHAEL partners sustainable. The

Michael Culture Association became a key actor in the promotion and valorization of the digital cultural content, and gathered a strong network of more than 100 institutions all over Europe.

http://www.michael-culture.eu

MINERVA and MINERVAPLUS (Ministerial Network for Valorising Activities in Digitization): MINERVA and MINERVAPLUS were set up in 2002 as a network of EU member states' ministries and cultural agencies with the mission to facilitate the adoption of the Lund action plan on the coordination of digitization programs and policies. The network aimed at harmonizing activities carried out for the digitization of cultural and scientific content and coordinating national programs. Under FP6, the MINERVA network was extended to "MINERVAplus" and also included new EU member states, Russia, and Israel.

http://cordis.europa.eu/ist/digicult/minervaplus.htm

MOSAICA: Semantically Enhanced, Multifaceted, Collaborative Access to Cultural Heritage, MOSAICA designed a technology toolbox for intelligent presentation, knowledge-based discovery, and interactive and creative educational experience of CH resources.

http://cordis.europa.eu/ist/digicult/mosaica.htm

MultiMATCH (Multilingual/Multimedia Access to Cultural Heritage): The project focus was on multilingual information retrieval for cultural objects of different media formats, and designing systems to support diverse user groups. Its outcome was a multilingual search engine specifically designed for access, organization, and personalized presentation of CH information of different formats (text, images, audio, video). The system was designed to support diverse user classes and assist CH institutions to disseminate their content widely and raise their visibility.

http://cordis.europa.eu/ist/digicult/multimatch.htm

NEDLIB (Networked European Deposit Library): This was initiated by CoBRA+, a permanent Standing Committee of the Conference of European National Libraries (CENL) launched in 1998, with funding from the EC's Telematics Application Program. Eight national libraries in Europe, one national archive, two ICT organizations, and three major publishers participated in the project, led by the Koninklijke Bibliotheek, National Library of the Netherlands. The goal was to develop a common architectural framework and basic tools for building deposit systems for electronic publications (DSEP). The Open Archival Information System (OAIS) model was accepted as a reference model following the approach of similar projects such as CEDARS in the UK and PANDORA in Australia. The project also recognized the need to address the issue of long-term digital preservation focusing on the technical issues of preservation but taking into account other important issues, such as cost-effectiveness, legal restrictions, agreements with publishers, and user access requirements that all relate to long-term preservation.

http://cordis.europa.eu/project/rcn/43331_en.html

NEWSPLAN 2000: This project began in 1986. Since 1992, the Newspaper Library offered a concessionary rate for NEWSPLAN microfilming in recognition of the importance of NEWSPLAN and the contribution that the work makes to the preservation of BL's own collections. To assist in this, Guidelines for the Microfilming of Newspapers were prepared and published under the auspices of NEWSPLAN in 1994.

> http://www.bl.uk/reshelp/bldept/news/newsplan/newsplan.html

PATHTS (Personalized Access To Cultural Heritage Spaces): This project, funded under the EC's FP7 program, investigated alternative approaches to enhance information access as a means of discovery and exploration. The project consisted of partners from multiple disciplines, including CH, LIS, and CS, from both academic and non-academic institutions. A selection of artifacts from Europeana was used as a source of CH artifacts and additional semantic enrichment was carried out on the content, together with the development of user interfaces to support users in their exploration of digital CH. The latest prototype is used by Europeana.

> http://labs.europeana.eu/apps/paths

PLANETS (Preservation and Long-term Access to our Cultural and Scientific Heritage): PLANETS delivered a distributed service environment for the management of digital information preservation, with a special focus on the needs of organizations that have the preservation of social and cultural memory as a core task. This included planning services, methodologies, tools, and services for the characterization of digital objects, innovative solutions for preservation actions, and an interoperability framework to seamlessly integrate tools and services in a distributed service network.

> http://cordis.europa.eu/project/rcn/99184_en.html

PRESTOSPACE: This project investigated the digital preservation of film heritage, in particular, issues of storage and access. Its goal was to standardize practices for audio-visual contents in Europe that could be useful for institutions traditionally responsible for preserving audio-visual collections (broadcasters, research institutions, libraries, museums, etc.). The project developed technical tools and a semi-automated integrated system, the "Preservation factory," for digitization and preservation of all types of audio-visual collections. Two large-scale projects will test OAIS-based systems and tools to support longer-term availability and accessibility of multi-sourced and multi-formatted resources (CASPAR) and to integrate preservation functions and services into organizational workflows and processes (PLANETS).

> http://cordis.europa.eu/ist/digicult/digital-lib.htm

ROADS (Resource Organization and Discovery in Subject-based services): A major objective of ROADS is to provide a set of software tools for the eLib subject-based services. These tools aimed to allow the construction of distributed services and provide some data creation and other tools. ROADS was developed by the University of Loughborough (technical development), UKOLN at the University of Bath (metadata issues, requirements), SOSIG at the University of Bristol (coordination and project management, liaison with services and information providers, requirements), and Bunyip (technical consultancy). ROADS introduced the concept of "trusted information provider," arguing that the collection of descriptions from approved authors and website administrators was essential to a sustainable service.

http://www.ukoln.ac.uk/metadata/roads/what/

SCRAN (Scottish Cultural Resource Access Network): SCRAN was founded in 1995 and in its first five years was engaged in a wide-ranging scheme of grant awards that allowed cultural organizations to digitize parts of their collections to be made available for educational purposes. This was the Millennium Commission, funded through the UK Lottery. It developed an advanced licensing system, which was commended by many, in which the institution retained ownership of the digitized assets but made these available under license to SCRAN.

https://www.scran.ac.uk/

SHAMAN (Sustaining Heritage Access through Multivalent ArchiviNg): This project's goal was to develop and test a new generation digital preservation framework for long-term digital preservation (including tools for analyzing, ingesting, managing, accessing, and reusing information objects and data) and to explore the potential of recent developments in the areas of GRID computing, federated digital library architectures, multivalent emulation, and semantic representation and annotation.

http://cordis.europa.eu/project/rcn/85468_en.html

https://www.sub.uni-goettingen.de/en/projects-research/project-details/projekt/shaman/

SHERPA (Securing a Hybrid Environment for Research Preservation and Access): SHERPA was initiated by and in part funded by the Consortium of University Research Libraries (CURL). It was a three-year project (2002–2005) aimed at setting up a series of institutional OAI-compliant e-print repositories (using e-prints.org software) in the partner institutions. The project investigated key issues in populating and maintaining e-print collections. It concentrated on advocacy for the research community in order to get content.

http://www.sherpa.ac.uk/projects/

TEL (The European Library): This project's goal was to create a cooperative framework and specify a system for integrated access to the major collections of the European national libraries. It comprised portal and client functionality running completely in the browser, resulting in a low-implementation barrier and maximum scalability, as well as giving users control over the search interface and what collections to search. The metadata model used by TEL was a Dublin Core Application

Profile. TEL was a collaboration of a number of European national libraries under the auspices of CENL, coordinated by the British Library.

http://www.theeuropeanlibrary.org/tel4/

TEL-ME-MOR (The European Library: Modular Extensions for Mediating Online Resources): This project supported the national libraries of the ten new EU member states of 2004 in becoming part of The European Library (TEL), a networked service that provided unified access to the electronic resources of many national libraries across Europe. TEL-ME-MOR also included activities in the new member states to raise awareness of the opportunities for participation in EU-funded IST research.

http://cordis.europa.eu/ist/digicult/tel-me-mor.htm

TNT (The Neanderthal Tools): The TNT project built the largest collection of Neanderthal findings in Europe in an online database. Virtual representations created with state-of-the-art technology made fragile and dispersed fossils and artifacts continuously accessible for scientists and the interested public, independent of their location. The main results of the TNT project are: NESPOS—the Neanderthal Studies Professional Online Service; the VISICORE Suite (tools for 3D visualization and annotation); and the National Geographic ArchChannel, a dissemination web portal.

https://artcom.de/project/the-neanderthal-tools/

Bibliography

Aabø, S. (2005). The role and value of public libraries in the age of digital technologies. *Journal of Librarianship and Information Science*, 37(4), 2005–211. DOI: 10.1177/0961000605057855. 25, 43

Abdullahi, I. and Kajberg, L. (2004). A study of international issues in library and information science education: survey of LIS schools in Europe, the USA and Canada. *New Library World*, 105, 345–356. DOI: 10.1108/03074800410557303. 104

Abu-Zayed, A. (2009). Digitisation workflow and guidelines: digitisation processes. Exeter: University of Exeter https://projects.exeter.ac.uk/charter/documents/DigitisationWorkflow-Guidev5.pdf. 31

Agosti, M., Esposito, F., and Thanos, C. (eds) (2007). Post-proceedings of the Third Italian research Conference on Digital Library Systems (IRCDL 2007), Padova, 29-30 January 2007. (Information Society technologies).

Agosti et al. (2007a). The DELOS Digital library reference model: Foundations for digital libraries. In: *Post-proceedings of the Third Italian research Conference on Digital Library Systems (IRCDL 2007), Padova, January 29–30, 2007. (Information Society technologies).* 79

Agosti, et al. (2007b). DelosDLMS: The Integrated DELOS digital Library management system. In: Thanos, C., Borri, F. and Candella, L. (eds). *Digital Libraries: Research and development: Firts International DELOS Conference, Pisa, Italy, February 2007: Proceedings: revised selected papers.* Berlin, Heildeberg : Springer: 36–45. 81

Agosti, M. et al. (2007c). Agosti, M., Ferro, N., Fox, E. A., and Gonçalves, M.A. Modeling DL quality: a comparison between approaches: the DELOS reference model and the 5S Model. In: Thanos, T.; Borri, F. and Launaro, A. (eds). *Second DELOS Conference, December 5–7, 2007, Tirrenia – Pisa: Proceedings.* 81

Agosti, M., Braschler, M., Ferro, N., Petersm C., and Siebinga, S. (2007d). Roadmap to multilingual information access in the European Library. In: Kovacs, L., Fuhr, N. and C. Meghini (eds). *Research and advanced technology for digital libraries: 11th European Conference, ECDL 2007, Budapest, Hungary, September 2007 : Proceedings.* Berlin, Heildeberg:Springer:136–147. 78

Akimov, S. I., Elizarov A. M., Eršova T. B., Kogalovskiji M. P., Fedorov A. O, Hohlov, Ju. E. (2005). Naučno-metodičeskaja poderžka razrabotki naučnjih elektronjih bibliotek (Research and methodological support to the development of scientific digital libraries). *Russian Digital Library*, 8, 1. http://www.elbib.ru/index.phtml?page=elbib/rus/journal/2005/part1/AEEKFH. 44

Albrecht, Y. (2016). Preface. In: Segers, S. and Y. Albrecht (eds.) (2016). *Re-thinking Europe: Thoughts on Europe: Past, Present and Future.* Amsterdam:Amsterdam University Press. 15

Altenhöner, R., Brantl, M., and Ceynowa, K. (2011). Digitale Langzeitarchivierung in Deutschland – Projekte und Perspektiven. *Zeitschrift für Bibliothekswesen und Bibliographie*, 58, 184–196. DOI: 10.3196/18642950115834150. 34, 53

Anguelova, K. (2005). Libraries and digital academic knowledge in Bulgaria: Need for digital competence: Development in LIS education. In: *Proceedings of the International workshop on IT Profiles of Digital Librarian, Parma, October 13-14, 2005.* http://www.docfoc.com/libraries-and-digital-academic-knowledge-in-bulgaria-need-for-digital-competence. 44

Anghelescu, H. G. B. (2005). European integration: Are Romanian libraries ready? *Libraries & Culture*, 4(3), 435–454. DOI: 10.1353/lac.2005.0042. 43

Aparac, T. and Vrana, R. (2001). Advancement of academic communication by use of networked information: a Croatian perspective. *International Information and Library Review*, 33(2/3), 133–148. DOI: 10.1080/10572317.2001.10762545. 46

Aparac-Jelušić, T. (2007). Interdisciplinarni diplomski studij u polju informacijskih znanosti – digitalizacija pisane baštine: združeni studiji. (Interdisciplinary graduate program in the field of information sciences: Joint studies). In: Lučin, P. and Kovačević, M. (eds.). *Združeni studiji. Rijeka : Nacionalna zaklada za znanost*: 19–32. 116

Arnold, D. and G. Gezer (2008). *EPOCH Research Agenda for the Applications of ICT to Cultural Heritage: Full Report.* http://public-repository.epoch-net.org/publications/RES_AGENDA/research_agenda.pdf. 16, 39, 69

Artini, M., Atzori, C., Bardi, A., and Zoppi, F. (2014). The Heritage of the People's Europe project: An Aggregative data infrastructure for cultural heritage. *Communications in Computer and Information Science* 385, 77–80. DOI:10.1007/978-3-642-54347-0_9. 50

Athanasopoulos G., L. Candela, D., Castelli, P., Innocenti, Y.. Ioannidis, A., Katifori, A., Nika, A, Vullo, G., and Ross, S. (2010). *The Digital Library Reference Model version 1.0, DL.org: Coordination Action on Digital Library Interoperability, Best Practices and Modelling Foundations.* http://bscw.research-infrastructures.eu/pub/bscw.cgi/d222816/D3.2b%20Digital%20Library%20Reference%20Model.pdf. 79, 81

Attanasio, P. (2010). Rights information infrastructures and Voluntary Stakeholders Agreements in Digital Library programmes. *JLIS.it.* (*Italian Journal of Library, Archives, and Information Science*), 1(2), 237–261. 55

Audunson, R. (2005). Editorial: LIS and the creation of a European educational space. *Journal of Librarianship and Information Science*, 37, 171–174. DOI: 10.1177/0961000605058091. 25, 108, 110

Audunson R. A. and Shuva, N. Z. (2016). Digital library education in Europe: A Survey. *SAGE Open* January-March 2016, 1–17. Retrieved from: https://us.sagepub.com/en-us/nam/open-access-at-sage. DOI: 10.1177/2158244015622538. 107, 111, 117, 120

Authenticity (s.a.). *Authenticity Task Force Report. InterPARES 1 Project Book.* http://www.interpares.org/book/interpares_book_d_part1.pdf. 93

Baker, T. (1996). Library networks in Germany. *ERCIM News*, 27 https://www.ercim.eu/publication/Ercim_News/enw27/baker.html. 73

Baker, D. and Evans, W. (2009). *Digital Library Economics: An Academic Perspective.* London:Chandos. DOI: 10.1533/9781780630090. 31, 41

Bakó, R. K. (2007). Information Society discourse in Romania: Role modeling Western factors. In: *The Fifth Critical Management Studies Conference: "Reconnecting Critical Management"* Manchester, July 11–13, 2007 https://www.mngt.waikato.ac.nz/ejrot/cmsconference/2007/proceedings/criticalviewsacrosscultures/bako.pdf. 43

Ball, R. (2009). German perspective. In: Baker, D. and Ewans, W. (eds). *Digital Library Economics.* Cambrige:Chandos:130–144. 42, 55

Bangemann Report. (1994). *Recommendations to the European Council.* Brussels, May 24. http://www.cyber-rights.org/documents/bangemann.htm#section20. 9, 21, 40

Bardi, A., La Bruzzo, S., and Zoppi, F. (2011). *HOPE Heritage of the People's Europe.* http://www.peoplesheritage.eu/pdf/D4_1_Grant250549_HOPE_AggregatorDetailedDesign1_0.pdf. 50

Bates, J., Bawden, D., Cordeiro, I., Steinerova, J., Vakkari, P., and Vilar, P. (2005). Information seeking and information retrieval. In: Kajberg L. and Lörring, L. (eds.) (2005). *European Curriculum Reflections on Library and Information Science Education.* Copenhagen: The Royal School of Library and Information Science. http://euclid-lis.eu/wp-content/uploads/2014/02/european-curriculum-reflections.pdf. 113, 114

Bawden, D. and I. Rowlands. (1999). Digital libraries: assumptions and concepts. *Libri*, 49, 181–191. DOI: 10.1515/libr.1999.49.4.181. 77

Bawden, D., Vilar, P. and Zabukovec, V. (2005), Education and training for digital librarians:a Slovenia/UK comparison. *Aslib Proceedings: New Information Perspectives*, 571:185-98. 117

Bawden, D. and L. Robinson. (2013). *Introduction to Information Science*. Chicago:Neal Schuman. An imprint for the American Library Association. 10, 31

Beagrie N. and Jones M. (2001). *Preservation Management of Digital Materials: A Handbook*. London: The British Library. 31

Beagrie, N. (s.a.). *Going Digital: Issues in Digitisation for Public Libraries*. Earl: the Consortium of Public Libraries Networking, www.ukonl.ac.uk/public/earl/issuepapers/digitisation.htm. 33

Beagrie, N. (2003). *National digital preservation initiatives: An overview of developments in Australia, France, the Netherlands, and the United Kingdom and of related international activity*. Commissioned for and sponsored by the National Digital Information Infrastructure and Preservation Program, Library of Congress. Washington, D.C. : Council on Library and Information Resources and Library of Congress. 91

Beagrie, N. (2004). The Continuing access and digital preservation strategy for the UK Joint Information Systems Committee (JISC). *D–Lib Magazine*, 10(7/8). http://dlib.org/dlib/july04/beagrie/07beagrie.html. DOI: 10.1045/july2004-beagrie. 74

Bearman, D. (2006). Digital Libraries. *Annual Review of Information Science and Technology (ARIST)*: 223–271. 31, 85

Beaudoin, J. E. (2012). Context and its role in the digital preservation of cultural objects. *D–Lib Magazine* 18(11/12). http://dlib.org/dlib/november12/beaudoin/11beaudoin1.html. DOI: 10.1045/november2012-beaudoin1. 33, 93

Béquet, G. (2014). *Trois bibliothèques européennes face à Google: aux origines de la bibliothèque numérique (1990–2010)*. Paris: École des chartes. 30

Benhabib, S. (2002). *The Claims of Culture: Equality and Diversity in the Global Era*. Princeton:Princeton University Press. 17

Berman, F., Wilkinson, R., and Wood, J. (2014). Building Global Infrastructure for data sharing and exchange through the Research Data Alliance. *D–Lib Magazine*, 20(1/2). http://dlib.org/dlib/january14/01guest_editorial.html. DOI: 10.1045/january2014-berman. 48

Berting, J. (2007). *Europa: un'eredità, una sfida, una promessa*. Rome:Armando. 2, 8, 9

Bestandsaufnahme. (2007). *Bestandsaufnahme zur Digitalisierung von Kulturgut und Handlungsfelder*. Karlsruhe : Bundesregierung für Kultur und Medien (BKM); Karlsruhe Fraunhofer Institut intelligente Analye- und Informationssysteme. Available at: www.iais. fraunhofer.de/bkm-studie.html. 31

Blandford, A. and Bainbridge, D. (2009). The pushmepullyou of design and evaluation. In: G. Tsakonas and C. Papatheodorou (eds.) *Evaluation of Digital Libraries*. Chandos Publishing. DOI: 10.1016/B978-1-84334-484-1.50008-9. 31

Bochmann, K. (1990). L'idée d'Europe jusqu'au XXè siècle. In: Villain-Gandossi, C. et al. *Le concept del'Europe dans le processus de la CSCE*. Tübingen: Günther Narr Verlag: 62–63. 1

Bologna (1999). *Bologna Declaration*. AHEA. https://www.eurashe.eu/library/modernising-phe/Bologna_1999_Bologna-Declaration.pdf. 103

Boot, P. (2009). Towards a TEI-based encoding sheme for the annotation of parallel texts. *Literature and Lingvistic Computing* 24(3), 347–361. DOI: 10.1093/llc/fqp023. 30

Borbinha, J., J. Kunze, A. Spinazze, P. Mutschke, H.-J. Lieder, M. Mabe, L. Dixson, H. Besser, B. Dean, and C. Warwick. (2005). Reference models for digital libraries: actors and roles. *International Journal on Digital Libraries* 5(4), 325–330. DOI: 10.1007/s00799-004-0095-7.

Borbinha, J. (2010). SHAMAN: Sustaining Heritage Access Through Multivalent Archiving. *ERCIM News*, 80 (January) http://ercim-news.ercim.eu/en80/special/shaman. 92

Bordoni L. and F. Poggi. (2004). Un archivio virtuale in XML: il progetto COVAX. *Bollettino AIB* 44(1), 19–28. 92

Borgman, C. (2000). *From Gutenberg to the Global Information Infrastructure*. Cambridge, MA:MIT. 6, 40, 41, 43, 45, 112

Borrego, Á. (2015). Library and information education in Europe: An overview. *BiD: textos universitaris de biblioteconomia i documentació* 35. http://bid.ub.edu/pdf/35/en/borrego.pdf. 108, 111, 115, 120

Borup Larsen, J. (2005). A survey of library and information science schools in Europe. In L. Kajberg and L. Lorring (Eds.), *European Curriculum Reflections on Library and Information Science Education*. Copenhagen, Denmark: The Royal School of Library and Information Science: 232–241. Retrieved from http://www.library.utt.ro/LIS_Bologna.pdf. 119, 120

Božić-Vrbančić, S. (2008). Rasprava: diskurzivne teorije i pitanje europskog identiteta. (Discourse theory and European identity). *Etnološka tribina: Godišnjak Hrvatskog etnološkog društva* 31(38), 9–38. 5, 8

Brahms, E. (2001). Digital library initiatives of the Deutsche Forschungsgemeinschaft. *D-Lib Magazine*, 7(5). http://dlib.org/dlib/may01/brahms/05brahms.html. DOI: 10.1045/may2001-brahms. 42

Brancolini, K. R. and Mostafa, J. (2006). Developing a digital libraries education program: JCDL 2006 Workshop report. *D-Lib Magazine* 12(7/8). http://www.dlib.org/dlib/julyO6/brancolini/07brancolini.html. DOI: 10.1045/july2006-brancolini. 113

Brindley, L. (2008). The Intemational dimensions of digital science and scholarship: Aspirations ot the British Library in serving the international scientific and scholarlv communities. In: Earnshaw, R. and J. Vince (eds). *Digital Convergence: Libraries of the Future*. London: Springer: 65–73. 38, 41, 51, 53, 56

British Library. (2008). *Digitisation Strategy* 2008–2011. http://www.bl.uk/aboutus/stratpolprog/digi/digitisation/digistrategy.

British Library. (2013). *Digital Preservation Strategy*, 2013–2016. http://www.bl.uk/aboutus/stratpolprog/collectioncare/digitalpreservation/strategy/dpstrategy.html.

BRTF. (2010). *The Blue Ribbon Task Force (BRTF) Report*. http://blueribbontaskforce.sdsc.edu/biblio/BRTF_Final_Report.pdf. 88

Buckland, M. K. (2003). Five grand challenges for library research. *Library Trends* 51, 675–686. 85

Burchard, M. (2001). NUKat: Union National Universal Catalog in Poland. *Slavic and East European Information Resources* 2(1), 5–16. DOI: 10.1300/J167v02n01_02. 45

Caidi, N. (2001). Technology and values: Lessons from Central and Eastern Europe. *Joint Conference on Digital Libraries*, June 24–28, 2001, Roanoke, Virginia, USA. https://www.researchgate.net/profile/Nadia_Caidi/publications/3. DOI: 10.1145/379437.379477. 44, 45

Cameron, F. and S. Kenderdine. (eds) (2007). *Theorizing Digital Cultural Heritage: A Critical Discourse*. MIT Press. DOI: 10.7551/mitpress/9780262033534.001.0001. 9, 18, 19, 30

Candella, L., Castelli, D., and Pagano, P. (2007a). A Reference architecture for digital library systems: Principles and applications. In: Thanos, C., Borri, F. and L. Candella. (eds). *Digital Libraries: Research and Development: Firts International DELOS Conference, Pisa, Italy, February 2007.: Proceedings: Revised Selected Papers*. Berlin, Heildeberg:Springer: 22–35.

Candella, L., Castelli, D., Pagano, P., Thanos, C., Ioannidis,Y., Koutrika, G., Ross, S., Schek, H.-J., and Schuldt, H. (2007b). Setting the foundations of Digital Libraries: The DELOS Manifesto. *D-Lib Magazine* 13(3/4). 79, 81, 97

Carr, R. (2007). *The Academic Research Library in a Decade of Change*. Oxford:Chandos 2007. DOI: 10.1533/9781780630991. 31

Casarosa, V., Agosti M., and Tammaro, A. M. (2011a) Report on the Workshop "Linking Research and Education in Digital Libraries." *D-Lib Magazine* 17(11/12). http://dlib.org/dlib/november11/casarosa/11casarosa.html. DOI: 10.1045/november2011-casarosa.

Casarosa, V., Castelli, D., and Tammaro, A. M. (2011b). Report on the Workshop "Linking Research and Education in Digital Libraries." *D-Lib Magazine* 17(11/12). http://dlib.org/dlib/november11/casarosa/11casarosa.html. 113

Castells, M. (2000). *Uspon umreženog društva. Knj. 1: Informacijsko doba.* (The Rise of the network society; Vol. 1: Information age). Zagreb:Golden marketing. 6, 10

Chapman, A. (2005). Collection description: The state of play. *Library Information Update*, 4(4), 35–37. 53

Chobanova, R. (2003). *Information Society Development in Bulgaria*. Sofia: Publishing House of the Union of Scientists in Bulgaria https://www.iki.bas.bg/RePEc/BAS/ecbook/B_information_society_development.pdf. 43

Chowdhury, G. G. (2010). From Digital Libraries to Digital Preservation Research: the importance of users and context. *Journal of Documentation*, 66 (2), 207–23. DOI: 10.1108/00220411011023625. 86

Chowdbury, G.G. (2014). Sustainability of digital libraries: a conceptual model and a research framework. *International Journal on Digital Libraries*, 14(3/4), 181–195. DOI: 10.1007/s00799-014-0116-0.

Chowdbury, G. G. (2015a). iSchools: connecting information, technology and people around the globe. *Presentation at the Third International Seminar on LIS Education and Research (LIS-ER),* Barcelona, Spain, June 5, 2015. https://www.youtube.com/watch?v=x-wvKV-gI8Y. 111

Chowdhury, G. G. (2015b). Management of cultural heritage information: Policies and practices. In: Ruthven, I. and Chowdhury, G. G. (eds) (2015). *Cultural Heritage Information Access and Management*. Facet Publishing: 37–62. 32

Chowdhury, G. G. and Chowdhury, S. (1999). Digital library research: major issues and trends. *Journal of Documentation*, 55(4), 409–448. DOI: 10.1108/EUM0000000007154. 34

Chowdhury, G.G and Chowdhury, S. (2003). *Introduction to Digital Libraries*. London:Facet Publishing.

Chowdhury, G. G. and Chowdhury, S. (2011). *Information Users and Usability in the Digital Age*. London: Facet Publishing. 31

Chowdhury, G. G. and Foo, S. (eds). *Digital libraries and Information Access: Research Perspectives*. London Facet.

Chowdhury, S. (2015). Cultural heritage information: users and usability. In: Ruthven, I. and Chowdhury, G. G.. (eds). *Cultural Heritage Information Access and Management*. Facet Publishing:135–151.

Clouah, P., Goodale, P., Hali, M., and Stevenson, M. (2015). Supporting exploration and use of digital cultural heritage materials: the PATHS perspective. In: Ruthven, I. and Chowdhury, G. G. (eds). *Cultural Heritage Information Access and Management*. Facet Publishing: 197–220. 82

Cohen, D. and R. Rosenzweig. (2006). *Digital History: A Guide to Gathering, Preserving, and Presenting the Past on the Web*. Philadelpia, PA: University of Pennsylvania Press. 30

Coyle, K. (2004). Rights management and digital library requirements. *Ariadne*, 40 http://www.ariadne.ac.uk/issue40/coyle. 55

Cowen, T. (2002). *Creative Destruction: How Globalization is Changing the World's Cultures*. Princeton University Press.

Croisier, D., Purser, L., and Smidt, H. (2007). *Trends V: Universities Shaping the European HE Area*. http://www.eua.be/fileadmin/user_upload/files/Publications/Final_Trends_Report_May_10.pdf. 104

Cronin, B. (1998). Information professionals in the Digital Age. *International Information and Library Review*, 30, 37–50. DOI: 10.1080/10572317.1998.10762464. 101, 107

Dahlström, M. (2015). Critical transmission. In: Svensson, P. and Goldberg, D. T. (eds). *Between Humanities and the Digital*. Cambridge, MA:The MIT Press: 467–481. 39

Dahlström, M. and Doracic, A. (2009). Digitization education: Courses taken and lessons learned. *D-Lib Magazine* 15(3/4). Retrieved from http://dlib.org/dlib/march09/dahlstrom/03dahlstrom.html. DOI: 10.1045/march2009-dahlstrom. 30, 116, 118, 119

Dalbello, M. (2004). Institutional shaping of cultural memory: Digital Library as environment for textual transmission. *Library Quarterly* 74(3), 265–99. DOI: 10.1086/422774. 30, 79

Dalbello, M. (2009a). Cultural dimensions of Digital Library development. Part II: The Cultures of innovation in five European national libraries (Narratives of development). *Library Quarterly* 79(1), 1–72. 30, 32

Dalbello, M. (2009b). Digital cultural heritage: Concepts, projects, and emerging constructions of heritage. *Proceedings of the Libraries in the Digital Age (LIDA)*. Dubrovnik, Croatia, May 25–30, 2009. 18

Dalbello, M. (2011). A genealogy of digital humanities. *Journal of Documentation*, 67(3), 480–506. DOI: 10.1108/00220411111124550. 60

Dalbello, M. (2015). Digital convergence: The Past in the present. In: Spence Richards, P., Wiegand, W. A, and Dalbello, M. (eds). *A History of Modern Librarianship: Constructing the Heritage of Western Cultures*. Libraries Unlimited: 2005–224. 30

Darányi, S., Wittek, P., and Dobreva, M. (2010). Toward a 5M Model of Digital Libraries. In: *Digital Libraries for International Development. Surfers Paradise, Gold Coast: Joint JCDL/ ICADL Conference*. https://www.academia.edu/2826780/Toward_a_5M_model_of_digital_libraries?auto=download. 79, 82

Davison, J. (2016). Fostering Open Science practice through recognising and rewarding research data management and curation skills In: Bisto, C. and Raju, R. (eds.) *LIS Education and Research in a Dynamic Information Landscape: Proceedings of the Library and Information Studies Centre 75 Years Commemorative Conference*. University of Cape Town Libraries: Cape Town: 63–75. www.//eprints.gla.ac.uk/116867. 74

Deegan, M. and Tanner, S. (2001). *Digital Futures: Strategies for the Information Age*. London: Library Association Publishing. 31

Deegan, M. and Tanner S. (2006a). *Digital Futures: Strategies for the Information Age*. 2nd ed. London:Library Association.

Deegan, M. and Tanner, S. (2006b). *Digital Preservation*. London, Library Association Publishing. 31, 34, 96

Deegan, M. and Tanner, S. (2008). Some key issues in digital preservation. In: Earnshaw, R. and J. Vince (eds). *Digital Convergence: Libraries of the Future*. London: Springer: 219–237. 19, 20

Dempsey, L. (1996). Meta Detectors. *Ariadne*, 3. http://www.ariadne.ac.uk/issue3/metadata. 73

Derr, M. and Arnold, D. (2011). ICT and education for future cultural heritage professionals: Introduction to the special theme. *ERCIM News*, 10–12. 74

Díez Carrera, C. (2013). *La biblioteca digital*. Madrid: Trea. 31

Digitisation. (2004). *Digitization of Cultural and Scientific Heritage in Russia: State-of-the-art, Problems, Perspectives*. http://www.minervaeurope.org/structure/nrg/statusreports/russia0604.pdf. 44, 56

Dillon, A. (2012). What it means to be an iSchool. *Journal of Library and Information Science Education*, 53(4), 267–273. 111

Dixon, P. and Tammaro A. M. (2003). Strengths and issues in implementing a collaborative inter-university course: the International Masters in Information studies by distance. *Education for Information*, (2/3), 12–27. 109

DPimpact. (2009). *Socio-economic Drivers and Impact of Longer Term Digital Preservation: D.5 Final Report*. http://cordis.europa.eu/fp7/ict/telearn-digicult/dpimpact-final-report.pdf. 35, 94

Dragulanescu, N.-G. (2002a). Social impact of the 'Digital Divide' in a Central-Eastern European country. *International Information and Library Review* (34), 139–51. DOI: 10.1080/10572317.2002.10762570. 43

Dragulanescu, N.-G. (2002b). Emerging Information Society and history of Information Science in Romania. *Journal of the American Society for Information Science and Technology* 53, 41–46. DOI: 10.1002/asi.10007. 43

Drake, K.-M, Justrell-Riksarkivet, B., and Tammaro, A. M. (eds) (2003). *Good Practice Handbook: Minerva: Digitizing Together*. Minerva eEurope. 31

Duranti, L. (1995). Reliability and authenticity: The Concepts and their implications. *Archivaria*, 39, 5–10. 92

Duranti, L. (2001). Concepts and principles for the management of electronic records. *The Information Society. An International Journal*, 17, 1–9.

Eagleton, T. (2000). *The Idea of Culture*. Blackwell. 14

Earnshaw, R. (2008). Introduction. In: Earnshaw, R. and J. Vince (eds). *Digital Convergence: Libraries of the Future*. London: Springer: XXIII-XXXII. 41

EHEA. (2007). *EHEA London Comunique*. http://www.ehea.info/Uploads/Declarations/London_Communique18May2007.pdf. 103

EHEA. (2015). *The European Higher Education Area in 2015: Implementation Report*. European Commission: EACEA: Eurydice. http://eacea.ec.europa.eu/education/eurydice/documents/thematic_reports/182EN.pdf. 103

EPOCH. (2008). *Excellence in processing open cultural heritage: D.4.13: Final State of the Union: A Proposed Curriculum for Digital Heritage Studies Policies, Practices and Developments in Europe*. Vol. 3. (ed. by Sorin Hermon). 115

Ershova, T. V. and Hohlov, Y. E. (1999). Russian digital libraries programme: Approaches and perspectives. *Russian Digital Library*, 2. http://www.elbib.ru/index.phtml?page=elbib/eng/journal/1999/part2/ershova. 44

EuroMACHS. (s.a). Curriculum for the Joint-Degree-Master-Programme Europe, Digital Media, Arts and Cultural Heritage Studies (EuroMACHS)at Karl-Franzens-University Graz. http://hfi.uni-graz.at/euromachs/EuroMACHS-curriculum_EN.pdf. 115

European Commission. (2000). *E-Europe: An Information Society for All.* https://www.w3.org/WAI/References/eEurope. 21

European Commission. (2001). *eEurope Digitizing Content Togheter: Lund Action Plan.* https://cordis.europa.eu/pub/ist/docs/digicult/lund_action_plan-en.pdf. 22, 56

European Commission. (2002). *The DigiCULT Report: Technological Landscape for Tomorrow's Cutural Economy: Unlocking the Value of Cultural Heritage: Full Report.* Luxembourg:Office for Official Publications of the European Communities. 4, 19, 21, 23, 24, 31, 34, 35, 44, 53, 54, 57, 59, 61

European Commission. (2003). *Promoting Language Learning and Linguistic Diversity An Action Plan 2004—06.* http://www.saaic.sk/eu-label/doc/2004-06_en.pdf. 4

European Commission. (2004). *MINERVA Project: Coordinating Digitization in Europe: Progress Report of the National Representative Group Coordination Mechanism for Digitisation Policies and Programmes 2003.* Lunghi, M. (ed). Roma:Ministero per i Beni e le Attività Culturali. 23, 35, 43, 61

European Commission. (2005a). *i2010 – A European Information Society for Growth and Employment.* http://eur-lex.europa.eu/LexUriServ/LexUriServ.do?uri=COM:2005:0229:FIN:EN:PDF (30-11-2016). 24, 62

European Commission. (2005c). *A New Framework Strategy for Multilingualism* http://eur-lex.europa.eu/LexUriServ/LexUriServ.do?uri=COM:2005:0596:FIN:en:PDF. 4

European Commission. (2006a). *Commission Recommendation on the Digitisation and Online Accessibility of Cultural Material and Digital Preservation.* https://ec.europa.eu/digital-single-market/en/news/commission-recommendation-digitisation-and-online-accessibility-cultural-material-and-digital. 25, 28

European Commission. (2006b). *European Commission Communication. Fostering Entrepreneurial Mindsets through Education and Learning.* http://www.eesc.europa.eu/?i=portal.en.soc-opinions.18027. 105

European Commission. (2007a). *DigiCult: Digital Culture and Digital Libraries Research.* (brochure). 24, 86

European Commission. (2007b). *European Agenda for Culture in a Globalizing World.* http://eur-lex.europa.eu/legal-content/EN/TXT/?uri=celex:52010DC0390. 24, 101

European Commission. (2007c). *European i2010 Initiative on e-Inclusion: To Be Part of the Information Society.* http://ec.europa.eu/smart-regulation/impact/ia_carried_out/docs/ia_2007/sec_2007_1470_en.pdf. 62

European Commission. (2008a). *Best Procedure Project. Entrepreneurship in Higher Education, Especially within Non-business Studies. Final Report of the Expert Group.* Brussels: European Commission. 75, 105

European Commission. (2008b). *Europe's Cultural Heritage at the Click of a Mouse Progress on the Digitisation and Online Accessibility of Cultural Material and Digital Preservation across the EU.* http://register.consilium.europa.eu/doc/srv?l=EN&f=ST%2012580%202008%20ADD%201. 35

European Commission. (2008c). *i2010: Digital Libraries.* http://eur-lex.europa.eu/legal-content/EN/TXT/?uri=URISERV%3Al24226i. 24, 25

European Commission. (2008d). *Access to and Preservation of Cultural Heritage: 25 European Research Projects.* http://cordis.europa.eu/pub/ist/docs/digicult/digicult-fp6-projects_en.pdf. 75

European Commission. (2009a). *Europeana - Next Steps.* SEC. Bruxelles. http://ec.europa.eu/information_society/newsroom/cf/document.cfm?ac. 25, 65, 68, 69

European Commission. (2009b). NUMERIC: Developing a statistical framework for measuring the progress made in the digitisation of cultural materials and content: Study Report: Study findings and proposals for sustaining the framework. http://cordis.europa.eu/fp7/ict/telearn-digicult/numeric-study_en.pdf. 35, 57, 61

European Commission. (2009c). *Regulatory Framework for Electronic Communications in the European Union.* https://ec.europa.eu/digital-single-market/sites/digital-agenda/files/Copy%20of%20Regulatory%20Framework%20for%20Electonic%20Communications%202013%20NO%20CROPS.pdf. 47

European Commission. (2009d). *Technology Enhanced Learning in FP7: 13 European Research Projects.* http://cordis.europa.eu/fp7/ict/telearn-digicult/telearn-projects-fp7_en.html. 75, 76

European Commission. (2010a). *EUROPE 2020 – A Strategy for Smart, Sustainable and Inclusive Growth.* Bruxelles. http://ec.europa.eu/eu2020/pdf/COMPLET%20EN%20BARROSO%20%20%20007%20-%20Europe%202020%20-%20EN%20version.pdf. 25, 59

European Commission. (2010b). *Digital Libraries, Digital Preservation: Cultural Heritage Research in FP7 11 ICT Projects.* http://cordis.europa.eu/fp7/ict/telearn-digicult/digicult-fp7-projects_en.pdf. 48, 76, 78, 87

European Commission. (2010c). *Second Progress Report on the Digitisation and Online Accessibility of Cultural Material and on Digital Preservation in the European Union: Working Document.* https://ec.europa.eu/digital-single-market/sites/digital-agenda/files/2010%20Digitisation%20report%20overall.pdf. 35, 56, 58, 59, 61, 63, 67

European Commission. (2011a). *An Agenda for the Modernisation of Europe's Higher Education Systems.* Brussels. http://ec.europa.eu/education/library/policy/modernisation_en.pdf. 105

European Commission. (2011b). Commission Recommendation of 27 October 2011 on the Digitisation and Online Accessibility of Cultural Material and Digital Preservation. *Official Journal of the European Union* (29-10-2011). http://eur-lex.europa.eu/LexUriServ/LexUriServ.do?uri=OJ:L:2011:283:0039:0045:EN:PDR. 28, 62

European Commission. (2012). *Europeans and their Languages: Report.* http://ec.europa.eu/public_opinion/archives/ebs/ebs_386_en.pdf. 35

European Commission. (2013). *Opening up Education: Innovative Teaching and Learning for All through New Technologies and Open Educational Resources.* Bruxelles. http://ec.europa.eu/transparency/regdoc/rep/1/2013/EN/1-2013-654-EN-F1-1.Pdf. 105

European Commission. (2014a). *Mapping of Cultural Heritage actions in European Union Policies, Programmes and Activities.* Bruxelles. https://europa.eu/european-union/topics/digital-economy-society_en. 76, 79

European Commission. (2014b). *Digital Agenda for Europe: a Europe 2020 Initiative: Digitiziation and Digital Preservation.* http://ec.europa.eu/digital-agenda/en/digitisation-digital-preservation. 26, 89

European Commission. (2014c). *Cultural Heritage Digitisation, Online Accessibility and Digital Preservation: REPORT on the Implementation of Commission Recommendation 2011/711/EU 2011-2013.* file:///C:/Users/Toshiba/Downloads/Recommendation-2011-2013-progress-report-final%20(2).pdf. 35, 58, 59, 61

European Commission. (2015a). *Getting Cultural Heritage to Work for Europe: Report of the Horizon 2020 Expert Group on Cultural Heritage.* file:///C:/Users/Toshiba/Downloads/KI-0115128ENN_002.pdf. 29

European Commission. (2015b). *Broadband Coverage in Europe 2014. Mapping Progress toward the Coverage Objectives of the Digital Agenda: Final Report.* https://ec.europa.eu/digital-single-market/en/news/study-broadband-coverage-europe-2014. 47

European Commission. (2016a). *Cultural Heritage Digitisation, Online Accessibility and Digital Preservation: REPORT on the Implementation of Commission Recommendation 2011/711/*

EU 2013-2015. http://ec.europa.eu/information_society/newsroom/image/document/2016-27/2013-2015_progress_report_9-06-2016_16531.pdf. 35, 58, 59, 61, 78

European Commission. (2016b). *The European Cloud Initiative.* https://ec.europa.eu/digital-single-market/en/%20european-cloud-initiative. 28

European Council. (2001). *European Content in Global Networks Coordination Mechanisms for Digitisation Programmes: The Lund Principles.* https://cordis.europa.eu/pub/ist/docs/digicult/lund_principles-en.pdf. 22

European Council. (2008). *Resolution of 21 November 2008 on a European Strategy for Multilingualism.* http://eur-lex.europa.eu/legal-content/EN/TXT/PDF/?uri=CELEX:32008G1216(01)&from=EN. 4

European Council. (2012). *Draft Council Conclusions on the Digitisation and Online Accessibility of Cultural Material and Digital Preservation: Adoption of Council Conclusions.* Bruxelles. https://eceuropa.eu/digital-agenda/sites/digital-agenda/files/Council%27s%20conclusions_0.pdf. 27

European Union. (2008). *Council Conclusions on the Promotion of Cultural Diversity and Intercultural Dialogue in the External Relations of the Union and its Member States.* http://www.consilium.europa.eu/ueDocs/cms_Data/docs/pressData/en/educ/104189.pdf. 24

Europeana. (2010). *Europeana Public Domain Charter.* http://pro.europeana.eu/publication/the-europeana-public-domain-charter. 66

Europeana Strategy. (2014). *Europeana Strategy Impact, 2015–2020.* http://pro.europeana.eu/files/Europeana_Professional/Publications/Europeana%20strategy%20impact.pdf. 66

Fabian, C. and Schreiber, C. (2013). Piloting a national programme for the digitization of medieval manuscripts in Germany. *LIBER*, 23(2), 2–16. (Selected papers from LIBER's 42nd Annual Conference 2013, Munich, Germany). 53

Faletar Tanacković, S.(2005). Mogućnosti suradnje baštinskih ustanova - odabrane europske inicijative i projekti. (Possibilities of the collaboration between heritage institutions: selected European initiatives and projects. In: Aparac-Jelušić, T. (ed.). *Izazovi pisane baštine : zbornik radova u povodu 75. obljetnice života A. Stipčevića.* Osijek:Filozofski fakultet: 193–205. 53

Feather, J. (2006). Managing the documentary heritage: issues fro the present and future. In: Gorman, G. E. and Sydney J. Shep (eds.). *Preservation Management for Libraries, Archives and Museums.* London: Facet: 1–18. 30

Follett, B. (1993). *Joint Funding Council's Libraries Review Group: Report*. Bristol: Higher Education Funding Council for England. http://www.ukoln.ac.uk/services/papers/follett/report/. 41

Follett B. K, Sir. (2008). World class universities need World-class libraries and information resources: But how can they be provided? In: *Earnshaw, R. and Vince, J. (eds). Digital Convergence: Libraries of the Future*. London: Springer. 39

Fox, E. A. and Urs, S. R. (2002). Digital libraries. *ARIST*, 36, 503–589. DOI: 10.1002/aris.1440360113. 31

Fox E. A., Gonçalves, M. A. and Shen, R. (2012). *Theoretical Foundations for Digital Libraries: The 5S (Societies, Scenarios, Spaces, Structures, Streams) Approach*. San Rafael, CA : Morgan and Claypool. (Synthesis Lectures on Information Concepts, Retrieval, and Services). DOI: 10.2200/s00434ed1v01y201207icr022. 79, 82

Fresa, A. (2013). A Data infrastructure for digital cultural heritage: Characteristics, requirements and priority services. *Journal of Humanities & Arts Computing: A Journal of Digital Humanities*, (7), 29–46. DOI: 10.3366/ijhac.2013.0058. 42

García-Marco, F.-J. (2009). Teaching digital libraries in Spain: Context and experiences. *Education for Information*, 27, 127–155. DOI: 10.3233/EFI-2009-0878. 116

Gardašević, S. (2010). International master in digital library learning: Size the opportunity. *INFOtheca*, 11(2), 73–77. 114

Geser G. and Mulrenin A. (2002). *The DigiCULT Report: Technological Landscapes for Tomorrow's Cultural Economy: Unlocking the Value of Cultural Heritage*. European Commission, Directorate-General for the Information Society. http://www.digicult.info/pages/report.php. 34

Giaretta, D. (2006). CASPAR and a European Infrastructure for Digital Preservation. *ERCIM News*, 47–49. https://www.ercim.eu/publication/Ercim_News/enw66/EN66.pdf. 75

Gielen P. (ed). (2016). *No Culture, No Europe: On the Foundation of Politics*. Metahaven:Grafisch ontwerp. 8

Gill, T. and Miller, P. (2002). Re–inventing the wheel? Standards, interoperability and digital cultural content. *D–Lib Magazine*, 8(1). http://www.dlib.org/dlib/january02/gill/01gill.html. DOI: 10.1045/january2002-gill.

Gillman, D. (2010). *The Idea of Cultural Heritage*. Cambridge:Cambridge University Press. 31

Giordano, T. (2001). Library cooperation on ICT in Italy: An Overview. *Program*, 36(3), 144–151. DOI: 10.1108/00330330210440430. 54

Gleick, J. (1999). *Faster: Acceleration of Just About Everything*. Abacus. 10

Gleick, J. (2000). *Faster: Acceleration of just about Everything*. Abacus.

Gonçalves, M.A., Fox, E. A., Watson, L. T., and Kipp N. A. (2004) Streams, structures, spaces, scenarios, societies (5s): A formal model for digital libraries. *ACM Transactions on Information Systems (TOIS)*, 22 (2), 270–312. http://eprints.cs.vt.edu/archive/00000653/01/5s11.pdf. 80

Gore, A. (1994). *The National Information Infrastructure* (Transcript). http://www.speeches-usa.com/Transcripts/al_gore-internet.html.

Görtz, M.; Mandl, T., Werner, K. and Womser-Hacker, C. (2012). Challenges for globalized information systems in a multilingul and multicultural context. In: Spink, A. and Heinstrom, J. (eds.). *Library and Information Science Trends and Research: Europe* 6, 169–191. 85

Grabowska, M. and Ogonowska, A. (1993). *The Information Society policy in the European Union and Poland*. http://www.ce.uw.edu.pl/pliki/pw/16-2013_grabowska.pdf.43

Graham, B., Ashworth, G. J., and Tunbridge, J. E. (2000). *A Geography of Heritage*. London:Arnold. 15, 16

Gradmann, S. (2010). Knowledge = Information in Context. On the Importance of Semantic Contextualisation in Europeana. *Europeana White Paper 1*. http://pro.europeana.eu/files/Europeana_Professional/Publications/Europeana%20White%20Paper%201.pdf. 63

Greengrass, M. and Hughes, L. (2008). *The Virtual Representation of the Past*. Ashgate. 31

Griffin, S., Peter, C. and Thanos, C. (2005). Toward the new-generation digital libraries: recommendations of the NSF/EU DELOS working groups. *International Journal on Digital Libraries*, 5(4), 253–254. DOI: 10.1007/s00799-004-0093-9. 78

Guercio, M. (2012). Digital Preservation in Europe Strategic Plans, Research Outputs and Future Implementation. The Weak Role of the Archival Institutions. In: Duranti, L. and Shaffer, E. (eds). *The Memory of the World in the Digital Age: Digitization and Preservation: An International Conference on Permanent Access to Digital Documentary Heritage:Conference Proceedings*. / Vancouver : UNESCO. Memory of the World Programme, Knowledge Societies Division: 467–481. http://ciscra.org/docs/UNESCO_MOW2012_Proceedings_FINAL_ENG_Compressed.pdf. 60

Gundersen, R. (1997). BIBSYS: An information system for the Norwegian academic community. *Proceedings of the IATUL Conferences*. Paper 6. http://docs.lib.purdue.edu/cgi/viewcontent.cgi?article=1390&context=iatul. 52

Hakkala, J. (2003). *Archiving the Web: European Experiences*. Paper presented at CONSAL XII, October 20-23, 2003. https://www.kansalliskirjasto.fi/extra/tietolinja/0203/webarchive. html. 54

Häkli, E. (2002). Towards a national digital library: the case of Finland. *Alexandria*, 14(3), 141–149. DOI: 10.1177/095574900201400303. 52

Hamilton, M. (2016). Back to the moon: eLib and the future of the library. *Ariadne*, 75. http://www. ariadne.ac.uk/issue75/hamilton. 73

Hansen K. P. (2003). *Kultur und Kulturwissenschaft*. 3. Auflage. A. Francke. UTB. 15

Hargreeves, I. (2011). *Digital Opportunity: A Review of of Intellectual Property and Growth: An Independent Report*. https://www.gov.uk/government/publications/digital-opportunity-review-of-intellectual-property-and-growth. 34, 35

Harvey, R. (2005). *Preserving Digital Materials*. München:Saur. DOI: 10.1515/9783598441080. 31, 91

Hazan, S. (2010). When is a library not a library. In: Verheul, I., Tammaro, A. M. and Witt, S. (eds.). D*igital Library Futures: User Perspectives and Institutional Strategies*. München: De Gruyter Saur: 87–95. DOI: 10.1515/9783110232196.61. 68, 69

Hecken, T. (2007). *Theorie der Populärkultur: dreissig Positionen von Schiller bis zu den cultural studies*. Bielefeld. DOI: 10.14361/9783839405444. 14

Hill, T., Haskiya, D., Isaac, A., Manuinhas, H. and Charles, V. (2016). *Europeana Search Strategy*. (Europeana Foundation R&D). http://pro.europeana.eu/files/Europeana_Professional/ Publications/EuropeanaSearchStrategy_whitepaper.pdf. 64, 66, 68, 69, 87

House of Lords. (2015). Select Committee on Digital Skills Report of Session 2014–15. *Make or Break: The UK's Digital Future*. Available at: http://www.publications.parliament.uk/pa/ ld201415/ldselect/lddigital/111/111.pdf. 106

Howarth, D. (2005). Applying discourse theory: The Method of articulation. In: Howarth, D. and Torfing, J. (eds). D*iscourse Theory in European Politics: Identity, Policy and Governance*. New York: Palgrave: 316–345. DOI: 10.1057/9780230523364. 8

Hughes, L. (2004). *Digitizing Collections: Strategic Issues for the Information Manager*. London: Facet. 31

Hughes, L. (ed.) (2011a). *Evaluating and Measuring the Value, Use and Impact of Digital Collections*. London: Facet Publishing. 31

Hughes, L. (2011b). Introduction: the value, use and impact of digital collections. In Hughes, L. (ed.). *Evaluating and Measuring the Value, Use and Impact of Digital Collections.* London: Facet Publishing: 1–10. DOI: 10.1080/00020184.2011.594623. 80, 96

Hunter D., and Brown, K. (2010). Thriving or Surviving? National Library of Scotland in 2030. http://www.nls.uk/about/policy/docs/future-national-libraries.pdf. 55, 112

Huntington, S. P. (1993). The Clash of civilizations? *Foreign Affairs*, 72(3), 22–49. DOI: 10.2307/20045621. 7

IFLA/UNESCO. (2011). *IFLA/UNESCO Manifesto for Digital Libraries: Bridging the Digital Divide: Making the World's Cultural and Scientific Heritage Accessible to All.* http://www.ifla.org/files/assets/digital-libraries/documents/ifla-unesco-digital-libraries-manifesto.pdf. 57

Ingwersen, P. and Järvelin, K. (2005). *The Turn: Integration of Information Seeking and Retrieval in Context.* Dordrecht, The Netherlands:Springer. 86

Invest to Save (2003). *Report and Recommendation of the NSF-DELOS Working Group on Digital Archiving and Preservation.* Pisa and Washington DC. Prepared by: Hedstrom M., Ross S., Ashley K., Christensen-Dalsgaard B., Duff W., Gladney H., Huc C., Kenney, A.R., Moore R., and Neuhold, E. https://www.researchgate.net/publication/31869588_Invest_to_Save_Report_and_Recommendations_of_the_NSF-DELOS_Working_Group_on_Digital_Archiving_and_Preservation. 91

Ioannidis, Y. (2005). Digital libraries at a crossroads. *International Journal on Digital Libraries* 5(4), 255–265. DOI: 10.1007/s00799-004-0098-4. 96

Jacobs, N. (2006). *Open Access: Key Strategies, Technical and Economic Aspects.* Oxford:Chandos. DOI: 10.1533/9781780632117. 31

Jeffery, K. G. (2006). Introducing Beyond-The-Horizon. In: Beyond the horizon: Anticipating future and emerging information society technologies. *Ercim News*, 1–3. 47

JISC. (2005). *Digitisation in the UK – the Case for a UK Framework.* London: JISC: CURL. 56

JISC. (2010). *Sustainable Economics for a Digital Planet: Ensuring Long Term Access to Digital Information.* www.jisc.ac.uk/publications/reports/2010/blueribbontaskforcefinalreport.aspx. 79

Johnson, I. (2013). The impact on education for librarianship andinformation studies of the Bologna process and related European Commission programmes – and some outstanding issues in Europe and beyond. *Education for Information*, 30, 63–92. DOI: 10.3233/EFI-130933. 3, 103

Johnson, L.; Adams, S., Becker, V., Estrada, A., and Freeman. (2015) *NMC Horizon Report: 2015 Higher Education Edition. Austin, Texas): The New Media Consortium.* https://net.educause.edu/ir/library/pdf/HR2015.pdf. 106, 110

Jochum, U. and Schlechter, A. (eds) (2011). *Vom Wert des Analogen.* Frankfurt am Main: V. Klostermann. 31

Jones, C. (2007). *Institutional Repositories: Content and Culture in an Open Access Environment.* Oxford:Chandos. 31

Justrell, B. (2002). Sweden. In: *Coordinating Digitalisation in Europe: Progress Report of the National Representative Group Coordination Mechanisms for Digitisation Policies and Programmes 2002.* European Commission: The Information Society Directorate-General. http://www.minervaeurope.org/publications/globalreport/globalreppdf02/svezia.pdf. 112

Justrell, B. (2003). Sweden. In: *Coordinating Digitalisation in Europe: Progress Report of the National Representative Group Coordination Mechanisms for Digitisation Policies and Programmes 2003,* European Commission: The Information Society Directorate-General. http://www.minervaeurope.org/publications/globalreport/globalrepdf03/sweden.pdf. 23, 112

Južnič, P. and Badovinac, B. (2005). Toward library and information science education in the European Union: A comparative analysis of library and information science programmes of study for new members and other applicant countries to the European Union. *New Library World,* 106, 173–186. DOI: 10.1108/03074800510587372. 117

Kajberg, L. (2003a). Cross country partnerships in international library and information science education. *New Library World,* 104(1189), 218–226. DOI: 10.1108/03074800310481894. 108

Kajberg L. and L. Lörring (eds.) (2005). *European Curriculum Reflections on Library and Information Science Education* (Copenhagen: The Royal School of Library and Information Science.) http://euclid-lis.eu/wp-content/uploads/2014/02/european-curriculum-reflections.pdf. 30, 119

Kajberg, L. (2007). The European LIS curriculum project: An overview. *Journal of Education for Library and Information Science* 48(2), 68–81. 108, 119

Kajberg, L. (2008). The European LIS Curriculum Project:Findings and Further Perspectives. *Zeitschrift für Bibliothekswesen und Bibliographie* 55(3/4), 184–185. DOI: 10.3196/18642950085534135. 108, 118, 119

Kalvet, T. (2007). *The Estonian Information Society Developments Since the1990s. Praxis Working Paper 29.* http://praxis.ee/wp-content/uploads/2014/03/2007-Estonian-information-society-developments.pdf. 43

Kampylis, P. G., Bocconi, S., and Punie, Y. (2012). Towards a mapping framework of ICT enabled innovation for learning. Luxemburg: European Commission. *JRC Scientific and Policy Reports*. Publications Office of the European Union. http://ftp.jrc.es/EURdoc/JRC72277.pdf. 105, 107

Khoo, M., Buchanan, G., and Cunningham, S. J. (2009). Lightweight user-friendly evaluation knowledge for digital libraries. *D-Lib Magazine* (July/August). http://www.dlib.org/dlib/july09/khoo/07khoo.html.

Klas, C.-P., Tsakonas, G., Albrechtsen, H., and Hansen, P. (2007). A Qualitative evaluation of The European Library. In: *Second DELOS Conference*, December 5–7, 2007, Tirrenia – Pisa: Proceedings. https://www.academia.edu/14891253/A_Qualitative_Evaluation_of_The_European_Library. (26-05-2016). 88

Knoll, A. (2006). TEL-ME-MOR or from what do we build a European Digital Library. In: *Proceedings ELPUB2006 Conference on Electronic Publishing* – Bansko, Bulgaria – June 2006: 383–384. 50

Koch, T., Neuroth, H. and Day, M. (2001). Renardus: Cross-browsing European subject gateways via a common classification system (DDC). In: McIlwaine, I. C. (ed.). *Subject Retrieval in a Networked World: Proceedings of the IFLA Satellite Meeting* held in Dublin, OH, 14-16 August 2001. München: K. G. Saur: 25-33.

Kolb, I. (2008). *Auf dem Weg zur Deutschen Digitalen Bibliothek (DDB)*. Bundesbeauftrager für Kultur und Medien, Deutschland; Fraunhofer-Institut Intelligente Analyse- und Informationssysteme -IAIS- Sankt Augustin. http://www.iais.fraunhofer.de/uploads/media/DDB-Studie_01.pdf. 31

Kolbmüller, B. (2006). HERMES: Culture, communication and sustainable development in Central and Eastern Europe. In: Hassenpflug, D., Kolbmüller, B., and Schröder-Esch, S. (eds). *Heritage and Media in Europe*. Hermes project, 3: 15–25. 112

Koltay, T. and Boda, I. (2008). Digital library issues in Hungarian LIS curricula: Examples from three library schools. *Library Review* 57, 430–441. DOI: 10.1108/00242530810886706. 114

Konrád, G. (2016). The special quality of Europe is culture. IN: Segers, M. and Albrecht, Y. *Re-thinking Europe: Thoughts on Europe: Past, Present and Future*. Amsterdam:Amsterdam University Press, 243–50. 8

Krzysztofek, K. (1997). Central Europe: Changing patterns of cultural identities. In: Švob-Đokić, N. (ed.). *The Cultural Identity of Central Europe: Proceedings of the Conference "Europe of*

Cultures: Cultural identity of Central Europe," Zagreb, November 22-24, 1996. Zagreb : Institute for International Relations:Europe House Zagreb: 65–71. 7

Kyriaki-Manessi, D. (2003). Library education in Greece: New challenges, new dimensions: European convergence and European diversity. *Education for Information,* 21, 21–29. 111

Lee, S. D. (2001). *Digital Imaging: A Practical Handbook.* London:Facet. DOI: 10.1007/BF03190342. 31

Le Glatin, M. (2007). *Internet, le séisme dans la culture.* Toulouse, Editions de l'attribut. 17

Le Goff, J. (1995). Series Editor's Preface. In: Eco, U. T*he Search for the Perfect Language.* Translated by J. Fentress. Oxford; Cambridge, MA:Blackwell.

Lehmann, K.-D. (ed.) (2004). *Digital Resources from Cultural Institutions for use in Teaching and Learning: A Report of the American/German Workshop The Andrew W. Mellon Foundation / Stiftung Preussischer Kulturbesitz Berlin.* München:K.G. Saur. DOI: 10.1515/9783110936179.11. 31

LIBER (2009). *LIBER Response to the Public Consultation "Europeana - Next Steps.* http://libereurope.eu/wp-content/uploads/LIBER-Response_COM_future-Europeana_final.pdf. 68

Liu, J. (2005). Digital Library activities in Europe: A brief overview. *Journal of Educational Media and Library Sciences* 42(4), 455–69. 30, 34, 50, 51, 53, 55, 59, 61, 111

Liew, C. L. (2009). Digital library research 1997–2007: Organizational and people issues. *Journal of Documentation,* 66(2), 245–266. DOI: 10.1108/00220410910937606. 76, 77

Liew, C. L. (2012). Towards accessible and inclusive digital libraries. In: Chowdhury, G. and Foo, S. (eds.). *Digital Libraries and Information Access: Research Perspectives.* London: Facet Publishing: 97–111. 33

London Communiqué. (2007). *Towards the European HE Area: Responding to Challenges in a Globalised World.* http://www.dfes.gov.uk/bologna/uploads/documents/LondonCommuniquefinalwithLondonlogo.pdf.

Lossau, N. (2008). Digital services in academic libraries: the Internet is setting benchmarks. In: In: Earnshaw, R. and J. Vince (eds). *Digital Convergence: Libraries of the Future.* London: Springer: 11–30. 55

Lowenthal, D. (1998). T*he Heritage Crusade and the Spoils of History.* Cambridge University Press. DOI: 10.1017/cbo9780511523809. 15

MacColl, J. (1996). JISC projects ahead. *Ariadne,* 5. http://www.ariadne.ac.uk/issue5/jisc. 73

Manghi, P., Bolikowski, L., Manola, N., Schirrwagen, J. and Smith, T. (2012) OpenAIREplus: the European scholarly communication data infrastructure. *D-Lib Magazine,*

18(9/10). http://dlib.org/dlib/september12/manghi/09manghi.html. DOI: 10.1045/ september2012-manghi. 49, 62

Mansell, R. and Tremblay, G. (2013). *Renewing the Knowledge Societies Vision for Peace and Sustainable Development.* Paris:UNESCO. 10

Manson, P. (2010). Digital preservation research: An evolving landscape. *ERCIM News,* 80: 3. 90, 93

Manžuch, Z., Huvila, and Aparac-Jelušić, T. (2005). Digitization of cultural heritage. In L. Kajberg and L. Lörring (Eds.), *European Curriculum Reflections on Library and Information Science Education.* Copenhagen:Royal School of Library and Information Science: 37-59. 18, 30, 113, 114, 115, 118

Manžuch, Z. (2007). Towards the European digital library: management of cultural heritage in the national libraries. *INFORUM: 13th Conference on Professional Information Resources* Prague, May 22-24, 2007. https://www.researchgate.net/publication/267919971. 85

Manžuch, Z. and Knoll, A. (2007). Building digital access to cultural heritage in Europe: national libraries context. In: Achleitner, H. K. and Dimchev, A. (eds). *Globalization, Digitization, Access and Preservation of Cultural Heritage*: 65–76. 17, 77

Manžuch, Z. (2009). Archives, libraries and museums as communicators of memory in the European Union projects. *Information Research,* 14(2), 1–25. 17

Manžuch, Z. (2009). Monitoring digitisation: lessons from previous experiences. *Journal of Documentation,* 65(5), 768–796. DOI: 10.1108/00220410910983100.

Marchionini, G. and Moran, B. (eds.) (2012). *Information Professionals 2050: Educational Possibilities and Pathways.* North Carolina: School of Information and Library Science of University of North Carolina at Chapel Hill. http://sils.unc.edu/sites/default/files/news/ Information-Professionals-2050.pdf. 107

Marchionini, G., Plaisant C., and Komlodi A. (2003). The people in digital libraries: multifaceted approaches to assessing needs and impact. In: Peterson Bishop, A., Van House, N. A., and Buttenfield, B. P. *Digital Library Use: Social Practice in Design and Evaluation.* Cambridge, MA; London:The MIT Press: 119–160. 95

Macevičiūtė, E. and Wilson, T.D. (2010). Information behaviour research and information systems development: the SHAMAN project: an example of collaboration. *Information Research,* 15(4) http://InformationR.net/ir/15-4/paper445.html. 92, 93, 96

McKinsey and Co. (2013). Re-Establishing the European Union's competitiveness with the next wave of investment in telecommunications. In: Bilbao-Osorio, B.; Soumitra, D., and

Lanvin, B. (eds.). *The Global Information Technology Report 2013: Growth and Jobs in a Hyperconnected World: Inside Report*. World Economic Forum: 93–100.

Miller, M. and Yudice, G. (2002). *Cultural Policy*. Sage. 20

Miller, P., Dawson, D. and Perkins, J. (2003). Understanding the international audiences for digital cultural content. *D-Lib Magazine*, 9(6) http://dlib.org/dlib/june03/miller/06miller.html. DOI: 10.1045/june2003-miller. 86

Milne, R. (2008). From "boutique" to mass digitization: The Google Library project at Oxford. In: In: Earnshaw, R. and J. Vince (eds). *Digital Convergence: Libraries of the Future*. London: Springer: 3–9. 52, 53

Mongili, A. and Pellegrino, G. (2014). *Information Infrastructure(s): Boundaries, Ecologies, Multiplicity*. Newcastle u/T.:Cambridge Scholars Publishing. 40

Moniarou-Papaconstantinou, V., Chatzimari, S., and Tsafou, S. (2008). Revamping the LIS curriculum in the Department of Library Science and Information Systems at the TEI of Athens. *Education for Information* 26, 121–132. DOI: 10.3233/EFI-2008-26208. 118

Monteiro, E., Pollock, N., and Williams, R. (2014). Innovation in Information Infrastructures: Introduction to the Special Issue. *Journal of the Association for Information Systems* 15(4), I-X. http://www.research.ed.ac.uk/portal/files/19373652/Innovation_in_Information_Infrastructures.introduction.pdf. 40

Mulrenin, A. and Greser, G. (2002). *The DigiCult Report: Technological Landscapes for Tomorrow's Cultural Economy: Unlocking the Value of Cultural Heritage*. Salzburg Research, on behalf of the European Commission. 44

Müller, U., Severiens, T., Malitz, R., and Schirmbacher, P. (2009). OA Network: An integrative Open Access infrastructure for Germany. *D-Lib Magazine*, 15(9/10) http://dlib.org/dlib/september09/mueller/09mueller.html. 49

Müller-Funk, W. (2006). *Kulturtheorie.: Eiführung in Schlüsseltexte der Kulturwissenscahften*. Tübingen ; Base : A. Francke Verlag. 14

Murzyn-Kupisz, M. and Dziazek, J. (2013). Cultural heritage in building and enhancing social capital. *Journal of Cultural Heritage, Management and Sustainable Development* 3(1), 35–54. DOI: 10.1108/20441261311317392.

Myburgh, S. and Tammaro, A. M. (2013). *Exploring Education for Digital Librarians: Meaning, Modes and Models*. Oxford, UK:Chandos. DOI: 10.1533/9781780633008. 30

Nauta G. J. and van den Heuvel, W. (2015). *Survey Report on Digitisation in European Cultural Heritage Institutions 2015. DEN Foundation (NL) on Behalf of Europeana/ENUMER-*

ATE. Public version. http://www.den.nl/art/uploads/files/Publicaties/ENUMERATE_ Report_Core_Survey_3_2015.pdf. 59, 90, 94, 97Németh, M. (2014). Hungarian libraries and librarianship, 1990–2013: An overview. *Library Trends*, 63(2), 212–232. DOI: 10.1353/lib.2014.0034. 44, 45

NMC. (2014). *The New Media Consortium: The NMC Horizon Report: 2014 Higher Education Edition*. http://cdn.nmc.org/media/2014-nmc-horizon-report-he-EN-SC.pdf. 106

Nicholas, D. and Rowlands, I. (eds) (2008). *Digital Consumers: Reshaping the Information Professions*. London:Facet Publishing. 31

Nicholas, D. and D. Clark. (2013). The second digital transition: to the mobile space — an analysis of Europeana. *Learned Publishing*, 26(4). DOI: 10.1087/20130402. 87

Nicholas D., Clark D., Rowlands I., and Jamali H.R. (2013). Information on the go: A case study of Europeana mobile users. *Journal of the American Society for Information Science and Technology* 64: 1311–1322. DOI: 10.1002/asi.22838. 87

Nicholson, S. (2004). A conceptual framework for the holistic measurement and cumulative evaluation of library services. *Journal of Documentation*, 60(2), 164–182. DOI: 10.1108/00220410410522043.

Niccolucci, F. (ed) (2006). *Training Offerings and Needs in Europe on ICT Applications to Cultural Heritage Report on an EPOCH Survey on the State of Higher Education in European Countries in the Field of Applications of Information and Communication Technologies to Cultural Heritage*. Budapest. 115, 116

Niegaard, H. (1999). *National Information Policy: National IT Strategies*: A survey. http://www.ifla. org/publications/national-information-policy-national-it-strategies-a-survey. 45

NPLD. (s.a). *European Network to Promote Linguistic Diversity's: The European Roadmap for Linguistic Diversity towards a New Approach on Languages as Part of the European Agenda 2020*. http://www.npld.eu/uploads/publications/313.pdf. 4, 5

NUA. (2003). *NUA Internet Surveys*. http://www.mefacts.com/cache/html/statistics/10187.htm. 43

Oppenheim, C and Smithson, D. (1999). What is the hybrid library? *Journal of Information Science* 25(2). DOI: 10.1177/016555159902500202.

Orgel, T., Höffernig, M., Bailer, W., and Russegger, S. (2015). A metadata model and mapping approach for facilitating access to heterogeneous cultural heritage assets. *International Journal of Digital Libraries* 15, 189–207. DOI: 10.1007/s00799-015-0138-2. 37, 79

Ortiz-Repiso, V. (2015). Rethinking Library and Information Studies in Spain: Crossing the Boundaries. *BiD: Textos Universitaris de Biblioteconomia i Focumentació*, 35(Desembre), 1–13. http://bid.ub.edu/en/35/ortiz.htm. 117

Østby, J. B. (2003). The new cross-sectorial agency in Norway for archives, libraries and museums: plans and perspectives. *LIBER Quarterly*, 13(3-4), 190–200 https://www.liberquarterly.eu/articles/10.18352/lq.7733/. DOI: 10.18352/lq.7733. 47

Peacock, D., Ellis D., and Doolan, J. (2004). Searching for meaning: Not just records. In: Bearman, D. and Trant, J. (eds). M*useums and the Webe 2004: Conference Proceedings, Toronto, Archives and Museum Informatics.* http://www.museumsandtheweb.com/mw2004/papers/peacock/peacock.html. 55

Pennock, M. (2008). *Supporting Digital Preservation & Asset Management in Institutions: JISC Programme Synthesis Study.* http://www.ukoln.ac.uk/ukoln/staff/m.pennock/publications/docs/404publicreport-2008.pdf. 74

Pieters, J. (1996). The SURF Foundation. *Ariadne*, 5. http://www.ariadne.ac.uk/issue5/surf. 42

Pinfield, S. (2004). eLib in retrospect: A National strategy for digital library development in the 1990s. IN: Andrews, J. and D. Law (eds). *Digital Libraries: Policy, Planning and Practice.* London : Ashgate: 19–34. 41

Pinninger, D. (2008). *Controlo de pragas em museums, arquivos e casas históricas.* Lisboa:Biblioteca Nacional de Portugal. 31

Poole N. (2010). *The Cost of Digitising Europe's Cultural Heritage: A Report for the Comité des Sages of the European Commission. The Collections Trust.* https://www.academia.edu/1520040/The_Cost_of_Digitizing_Europes_Cultural_Heritage. 27, 32, 65

Pomerantz, J., Wildemuth, B. M., Yang, S., and Fox, E. (2006). Curriculum development for digital libraries In *Proceedings of the 6th ACM/IEEE-CS Joint Conference on Digital Libraries New York: Association for Computing Machinery*: 175–184. http://doi.acm.org/10.1145/1141753.1141787. 113, 118

Prott, L. V. and O'Keefe, P. J. (1992). 'Cultural Heritage' or 'Cultural Property'? *International Journal of Cultural Property*, 1, 307. DOI: 10.1017/S094073919200033X.

Purday, J. (2009). Think culture: Europeana.eu from concept to construction. *The Electronic Library*, 27(6), 919–37. DOI: 10.1108/02640470911004039. 65

Purday, J. (2010). Intellectual property issues and Europeana, Europe's digital library, museum and archive. *Legal Information Management*, 10, 174–180. DOI: 10.1017/S1472669610000678. 66

Quirk, R., Martin O., Hammond, M., and Davies, C. (2008). *The Guide to Researching Audiences, JISC Strategic Content Alliance.* http://sca.jiscinvolve.org/wp/2009/02/05/download-audience-analysis-toolkit/. 89

Raitt, D. (2000). Digital library initiatives across Europe. *Computers in Libraries* 20, 10: 26-34. 30, 34, 42, 50, 53, 61, 73

Rajabi, H. and S. Virkus (2013). The Potential and readiness of Tallinn University to establish Massive Open Online Courses (MOOCs). *Qualitative and Quantitative Methods in Libraries (QQML)*, 4, 431–439. http://www.qqml.net/papers/December_2013_Issue/249QQML_Journal_2013_Rajabi_Virkus_4_431_439.pdf. 106, 110

Renhart, E. (2013). Manuscript fragments the hidden library. In: Willer, M. and Tomić, M. (eds). *Proceedings/Summer School in the Study of Historical Manuscripts.* Zadar:Sveučilište: 133–143. 54

Riding, A. (2005). France detects a cultural threat in Google. *New York Times* (April 11). http://www.nytimes.com/2005/04/11/technology/france-detects-a-cultural-threat-in-google.html. 38

Rodriguez, R., Warmerdam, J., and Triomphe, C. E. (2010). *The Lisbon Strategy, 2000–2010: An Analysis and Evaluation of the Methods Used and Results Achieved.* Bruxelles: EMPL. 22

Ross S. and Economou, M. (1998). Information and communications technology in the cultural sector: The need for national strategies. *D-Lib* 6(1998) http://www.dlib.org/dlib/june98/06ross.html.

Ross, S. (2004). Reflections on the impact of the Lund Principles on European approaches to digitization. In: *Strategies for a European Area of Digital Cultural Resources: Towards a Continuum of Digital Heritage.* Den Haag:Dutch Ministry of Culture: 88–98. 95

Ross, S. (2012). Digital preservation, Archival Science and methodological foundations for digital libraries. *New Review of Information Networking*, 17(1), 43–68. DOI: 10.1080/13614576.2012.679446. 34, 79, 92, 94, 95

Ross, S. and Hedstrom, M. (2005). Preservation research and sustainable digital libraries. *International Journal of Digital Libraries*, (5), 317–324. DOI: 10.1007/s00799-004-0099-3. 61, 91, 93

Rouhana, K. (2011). ICT and cultural heritage: Research, innovation and policy. *ERCIM News*, (86), 3. 26, 89

Rowlands, I. and Bawden, D. (1999). Digital libraries: a conceptual framework. *Libri*, 49, 192–202. DOI: 10.1515/libr.1999.49.4.192. 79, 117

Rupnik, J. (1989). *The Other Europe*. Pantheon Books. 2

Rusbridge, C. (1998). Towards the hybrid library. *D-Lib Magazine*, 7, (7/8) http://www.dlib.org/dlib/july98/rusbridge/07rusbridge.html. DOI: 10.1045/july98-rusbridge. 41

Ruthven, I. and Chowdhury, G. G. (eds) (2015). *Cultural Heritage Information: Access and Management*. Croydon:Facet. 30, 32, 33, 77

Rydberg-Cox and Jeffrey, A. (2006). *Digital Libraries and the Challenges of Digital Humanities*. Oxford:Chandos. DOI: 10.1533/9781780630816. 31

Sable, K. A. and Kling, R.W. (2001). The Double public good: A conceptual framework for "shared experience" values associated with heritage conservation. *Journal of Cultural Economics* 25, 77–89. DOI: 10.1023/A:1007675701979. 15

Salarelli, A. and Tammaro, A. M. (2006). *La Biblioteca Digitale*. Editrice Bibliografica. 30

Saracevic, T. (2001). Digital library evaluation: toward an evolution of concepts. *Library Trends* 49(2), 350–368. 95, 96

Saracevic, T. (2004). *Evaluation of Digital Libraries: An Overview*. Presentation at the DELOS WP7 Workshop on the Evaluation of Digital Libraries, 4-5 October 2004, Department of Information Engineering, University of Padua, Italy. 95

Saracevic, T. and Dalbello, M. (2001). A survey of digital library education. In: *Proceedings of the American Society for Information Science and Technology* 38, 209-223. 54

Sassoon, D. (2012). *The Culture of the Europeans: From 1800 to the Present*. Harper Press (kindle ed.). 8

Savenije, B. (2009). The Dutch perspective. In: Baker, D. and Ewans, W. (eds). *Digital Library Economics*. Cambrige:Chandos: 145–159. 52, 53

Schmiede, R. (1999). *Digital Library Activities in Germany: The German Digital Library Program GLOBAL INFO*. http://www.ssoar.info/ssoar/bitstream/handle/document/25555/ssoar-1999-schmiede-digital_library_activities_in_germany.pdf?sequence=1. DOI: 10.1109/adl.1999.777694.

Schöpfel, J. (2004). The workshops of the UKSC Annual Conferences 1990-2004. *Serials*, 17(3), 243–251. DOI: 10.1629/17243. 112

Schreibman, S., Siemens, R., and Unsworth, J. (eds.) (2004). *A Companion to Digital Humanities*. Oxford: Blackwell. Available at http://www.digitalhumanities.org/companion. DOI: 10.1002/9780470999875. 30

Schreibman, S., Siemens, R., and Unsworth, J. (eds.). (2016). *A New Companion to Digital Humanities*. Willey. 30

Segers, S. and Albrecht, Y. (eds.) (2016). *Re-thinking Europe: Thoughts on Europe: Past, Present and Future*. Amsterdam:Amsterdam University Press. 9

Seljak, M. and Seljak, T. (2002). The development of the COBISS system and services in Slovenia. *Program* 36(2), 89–98. DOI: 10.1108/00330330210429316. 46

Shore, C. (2004). Whither European citizenship? Eros and civilisation revisited. *European Journal of Social Theory* 7(1), 27–44. DOI: 10.1177/1368431004040018. 5

Siemens, R. and Schreibman, S. (eds.) (2008). *A Companion to Digital Literary Studies*. Oxford: Blackwell. http://www.digitalhumanities.org/companion_DLS. 30

Sigurdsson, E. (1998). The National Electronc Library: Iceland. *LIBER Quarterly*, 8(1), 38–46. 53

Silberman, N. (2007). *Cultural Heritage and the Information Technologies: Facing the Grand Challenges and Structural Transformations of the 21st Century*. http://works.bepress.com/neil_silberman/35. 14

Skarstein, V. M. (2012). Editorial: The digital library. *Scandinavian Library Quarterly*, 45(2), 1–2. 59

Snow, K., Ballaux, B., Christensen-Dalsgaard, B., Hofman, H., Hofman Hansen, J., Innocenti, P., Poltorak Nielsen, M., Ross, S., and Thøgersen, J. (2008). Considering the user perspective: Research into usage and communication of digital information. *D-Lib Magazine*, 14(5/6). http://dlib.org/dlib/may08/ross/05ross.html. 92

Spink, A. and Cool, C. (1999a). Developing digital library education: International perspective on theory and practice. In: Aparac, T. et al (ed.) Digital Libraries: Interdisciplinary concepts, challenges and opportunities. *Proceeding of the Third International Conference on Conceptions of Library and Information Science (CoLIS3)*. Dubrovnik, Croatia: 55–62. 111

Spink, A. and Cool, C. (1999b). Education for Digital Libraries. *D-Lib Magazine*, 5(5), 1–7. http://www.dlib.org/dlib/may99/05spink.html. DOI: 10.1045/may99-spink. 111

Spink, A. and Heinstrom, J. (eds.) (2012). *Library and Information Science Trends and Research: Europe*. Bingley, UK:Emerald Group. DOI: 10.1108/S1876-0562(2012)6. 31

Stavrakakis, Y. (2005). Strasti identifikacije: diskurs, užitak i europski identitet (Passions of identification: Discourse, pleasure and European identity). *Politička Misao*, 42(3), 89–115. 8

Steenbakkers, J. (2000). The NEDLIB guidelines – Setting up a deposit system for electronic publications. *NEDLIB Report Series*, 5. Amsterdam:Koninklijke Bibliotheek. 54

Steinerová, J. (2003). In search for patterns of user interaction for digital libraries. In: *Proceedings of the 7th European Conference on Research and Advanced Technology for Digital Libraries* 13–23. DOI: 10.1007/978-3-540-45175-4_2. 86

Stiller, J. and Petras, V. (2015). A framework for classifying and comparing interactions in cultural heritage information svstems. In: Ruthven, I. and Chowdhury, G. G. (eds) (2015). *Cultural Heritage Information Access and Management.* Facet Publishing: 153–176. 88

Stivenson, N. (2003). *Cultural Citizenship: Cosmopolitan Questions.* Maidenhead, Bershire:Open University Press. DOI: 10.1080/13621020302214. 9

Stoklasová, B. and Krbec, P. (2002). *CASLIN Uniform Information Gateway.* http://jib-info.cuni.cz/dokumenty/tallin/html/Tallin.html. 45

Strathmann, S. and Osswald, A. (2012). Digital curation training: The Nestor activities. *IASSIST Quarterly* (Fall/Winter), 13–16. 112

Stroeker, N. and Vogels, R. (2012). Survey report on digitisation in European cultural heritage institutions 2012. *Panteia (NL):ICT Policy Support Programme part of the Competitiveness and Innovation Framework Programme.* 89

Stroeker, N. and Vogels, R. (2014). Survey Report on Digitisation in European Cultural Heritage Institutions 2014. *Panteia (NL):ICT Policy Support Programme part of the Competitiveness and Innovation Framework Programme.* 89

Sula, C. A. (2013). Digital humanities and libraries: A Conceptual model. *Journal of Library Administration* 53, 10–26. DOI: 10.1080/01930826.2013.756680. 11

Sursock, A. (2015). *Trends 2015: Learning and Teaching in European Universities.* Brusselles: European University Association. http://www.eua.be/Libraries/Publications_homepage_list/EUA_Trends_2015_web.sflb.ashx. 104, 106

Sursock, A. and Smidt, H. (2010). *Trends 2010: A Decade of Change in European Higher Education.* EUA http://www.eua.be/Libraries/publications-homepage-list/Trends2010. 104

Syuntyurenko, O. V and Hohlov, Y. E. (2000). Distributed library networks and digital libraries. *Russian Digital Libraries Journal* 3(5). http://www.elbib.ru/index.phtml?page=elbib/eng/journal/2000/part5/HS. 44, 52

Šimić, D. (2007). e-Croatia 2007: Fostering the development of Information Society in Croatia. In: Seljan, S. and Stančić, H. (eds). *The Future of Information Sciences (INFuture 2007): Digital Information and Heritage.* Zagreb:Odsjek za informacijske znanosti, Filozofski fakultet: 7–15. 44

Škiljan, D. (2001). Languages with(out) frontiers. In: Švob-Đokic, N. (ed) (2001). *Redefining Cultural Identities: Southeastern Europe: Collection of Papers from the Course.* Dubrovnik, May 14–19, 2001. Zagreb:Institute for International Relations: 87–100. 4

Šola, T. S. (2015). *Mnemosophy: An Essay on the Science on Public Memmory.* Zagreb: European Heritage Association. 15

Švob-Đokić, N. (ed.) (1997). The Cultural identity of Central Europe. *Proceedings of the Conference "Europe of Cultures: Cultural identity of Central Europe,"* Zagreb, November 22–24, 1996. Zagreb:Institute for International Relations : Europe House Zagreb. 7

Švob-Đokić, N. (ed.) (2004). *Cultural Transitions in Southeastern Europe.: Collection of Papers from the Course on "Managing Cultural Transitions: Southeastern Europe, Inter-University Centre Dubrovnik,"* May 9–16, 2004. Zagreb:Institute for International Relations. 7

Tammaro, A. M. (2007a). A curriculum for digital librarians: A reflection on the European debate. *New Library World* 108, 229–246. DOI: 10.1108/03074800710748795. 113, 115, 119

Tammaro, A. M. (2011). Library and information science (LIS) education: A Conceptual framework towards "Europeisation." *Journal of the Bangladesh Association of Young Researchers,* 1(1), 1–13. DOI: 10.3329/jbayr.v1i1.6950. 104

Tanner, S. (2001). Librarians in the digital age: Planning digitization projects. *Program* 35(4), 327–337. DOI: 10.1108/EUM0000000006951.

Tanner, S. (2005). *Digital Libraries and Culture: A Report for UNESCO.* London:KDCS Digital Consultatcy. 16, 33, 34

Tanner, S. (2006). The Economic opportunities and cost of developing digital libraries and resources. In: Deegan, M. and Tanner S. (2006). *Digital Futures: Strategies for Information Age.* London:Library Association. 16

Tanner, S. (2010). Technological trends and developments and their future influence on digital national libraries: Appendix A. In Hunter D. and Brown, K. (eds). *Thriving or Surviving? National Library of Scotland in 2030.* NLS. http://www.nls.uk/about/policy/docs/future-national-libraries.pdf. 40

Tanner, S. (2012). *Measuring the Impact of Digital Resources: The Balanced Value Impact Model.* King's College London. 79, 83, 84

Tanner, S. (2016). Using impact as a strategic tool for developing the digital library via the Balanced Value Impact Model. *Library Leadership and Management,* 30(3). 79, 84, 96, 97

Tariffi, F., Morganti, B. and Segbert, M. (2004). Digital cultural herirateg projects in Europe: an overview of TRIS and takeup trial projects. *Program* 38(1), 15–28. DOI: 10.1108/00330330410523120. 34

Tedd, L. A. and Large A. (2005). *Digital Libraries: Principles and Practice in a Global Environment.* Muenchen:K.G. Saur. 31

Terras, M. (2012). Digitization and digital resources in the Humanities. In: Warwick, C., Terras, M. and Nyhan, J. (eds). *Digital Humanities in Practice*, Facet Publishing: 47–70. 37, 38

Terras, M. (2015). Cultural heritage information: Artefacts and digitization technologies. In: Ruthven, I. and Chowdhury, G. G. (eds). *Cultural Heritage Information Access and Management*. Facet Publishing: 63–88. 37

Thorhauge, J. (2000). Danish research libraries: Danish models. *LIBER Quarterly*, 10, 417–426. DOI: 10.18352/lq.7612. 52

Thorhauge, J. and Petersen, J. H. (2001). Organisational development in Denmark's Electronic Research Library In: Gorman, G. E. (ed). *International Yearbook of Library and Information Management* 2001-2002. London: Scarecrow Press. 43

Thanos, C., Borri, F., and Candella, L. (2007). Preface. I: Thanos, C., Borri, F. and Candella, L. (eds). *Digital Libraries: Research and Development: First International DELOS Conference*, Pisa, Italy, February 2007. Proceedings: revised selected papers. Berlin; Heildeberg:Springer. 79

Throsby, D. (2003). Determining the value of cultural goods: How much (or how little) does contingent evaluation tell us? *Journal of Cultural Economics* 27(3/4), 275–85. 15

Trunel, L. (2009). A snapshot of some current digitisation projects in French art libraries. *Art Libraries Journal* 34(1), 17–21. DOI: 10.1017/S0307472200015716. 53

Tsakonas, G. and Papatheodorou, C. (2011). An ontological representation of the digital library evaluation domain. *Journal of the American Society for Information Science & Technology* 62(8), 1577–1593. DOI: 10.1002/asi.21559. 79, 80, 81, 96

Tuck, J. (2008). From intergration to web archiving. In: Earnshaw, R. and J. Vince (eds). *Digital Convergence: Libraries of the Future*. London:Springer. 92

Tuominen, K., Talja, S. and Savolainen, R. (2003). Multiperspective digital libraries: The implications of constructionism for the development of digital libraries. *Journal of the American Society for Information Science and Technology* 54, 561–569. DOI: 10.1002/asi.10243. 86

UNESCO (1972). *Convention Concerning the Protection of the World Cultural and Natural Heritage*. Adopted by the General Conference at its seventeenth session Paris, November16, 1972. http://whc.unesco.org/archive/convention-en.pdf. 13

UNESCO. (2003a). *UNESCO's Convention on the Preservation of Digital Heritage*. UNESCO:Paris. http://portal.unesco.org/en/ev.php-URL_ID=17716&URL_DO=DO_TOPIC&URL_SECTION=201.html. (02-12-2016).13

UNESCO. (2003b). *UNESCO's Convention on the Safeguarding of the Intangible Cultural Heritage.* UNESCO : Paris. http://www.unesco.org/new/en/santiago/culture/intangible-heritage/convention-intangible-cultural-heritage.13

UNESCO. (2003c). *UNESCO Charter on the Preservation of Digital Heritage.* UNESCO : Paris. http://portal.unesco.org/en/ev.php-URL_ID=17721&URL_DO=DO_TOPIC&URL_SECTION=201.html. 13, 18

UNESCO. (2003d). *Guidelines for the Preservation of Digital Heritage.* Paris: UNESCO.

UNESCO (2005). *Towards Knowledge Societies.* Paris:UNESCO. 10

van der Zwand, R. (1996). Ticer Summer School on the digital library at Tilburg University, The Netherlands. *Ariadne,* (6) http://www.ariadne.ac.uk/issue6/tilburg. 53, 112

Van Rij, V. (2015). *21st Century Higher Education: Quick Scan of Foresight and Forward Looks on Higher Education in the ICT Age: Discussion Paper.* http://iite.unesco.org/files/news/639201/Foresight_on_HE_and_ICT_Discussion_paper.pdf. 9, 106

van Veen, T. (2005). Renewing the Information Infrastructure of the Koninklijke Bibliotheek. *D-Lib Magazine,* 11(3). http://dlib.org/dlib/march05/vanveen/03vanveen.html. DOI: 10.1045/march2005-vanveen. 41

Verheul, I., Tammaro, A. M., and Witt, S. (eds.) (2010). *Digital Library Futures: User Perspective and Institutional Strategies.* Berlin: De Gruyter Saur. DOI: 10.1515/9783110232196. 31

Virkus, S. and Harbo, O. (2002), The internationalization of Baltic Library and Information Science education with emphasis on the cooperation with Nordic partners. *Education for Information,* 20(3/4), 217–35. DOI: 10.3233/EFI-2002-203-404. 109

Virkus, S. (2008). LIS education in Europe: Challenges and opportunities. In Neugebauer, V. (ed.). *Informationskonzepte für die Zukunft: ODOK '07*: 191–204. http://eprints.rclis.org/14978/1/odok07_virkus.pdf. 116

Virkus, S. (2015). Change and Innovation in European Library and Information Science Education. *BiD: Textos Universitaris de Biblioteconomia i Documentació,* 35. http://bid.ub.edu/en/35/virkus.htm. 106, 110, 121

Warwick, C., Terras, M., and Nyhan, J. (eds.) (2012). *Digital Humanities in Practice.* Facet Publishing: 47–70. 30, 87

Weech, T. (2007). Multidisciplinarity in education for digital librarianship. *Proceedings of the 2007 Informing Science and IT Education Conference.* https://www.researchgate.net/publication/33436440_Education_for_Digital_Librarianship. 115

Wilson, T.D. (2001). Mapping the curriculum in information studies. *New Library World*, 102(11), 436–42. DOI: 10.1108/03074800110411875. 110

Wilson, T. D. and Macevičiūtė, E. (2012). Users' interaction with digital libraries. In: Chowdhury, G. G. and Foo, S. (eds.). *Digital Libraries and Information Access: Research Perspectives.* London Facet: 113–128. 92

Zemskov A. I. (2003). Elektronije biblioteki i razvitie Informacionovo obščestva v Rosiji. Digtal Libraries and development of Information Society in Russia. *Russian Digital Library*, 6(4).

Zhang, Y. (2010). Developing a holistic model for digital library evaluation. *Journal of the American Society for Information Science and Technology*, 61(1), 88–110. DOI: 10.1002/asi.21220.

Author Biography

Tatjana Aparac-Jelušić received her Ph.D. in Information Sciences (IS) at the University of Zagreb (1991). She graduated in Comparative Literature and Italian Language and Literature, Faculty of Philosophy in Zagreb (1972). She was the Head of the Department of IS at the University of Zadar from 2007 until 2012, and Head of the Department of IS at the University of Osijek from 2003 until 2007. In 2008 she designed the new Ph.D. program Knowledge Society and the Information Transfer at the University of Zadar and acted as the dean of the program from 2008 until 2015.

She is the author of one book, nine chapters in other books, over 120 research and professional papers (in Croatian and English), and over 30 reviews and opinion papers. She edited 25 books and started several series such as *Croatian Librarians*, *Handbooks in LIS*, and *Advances in IS*. She is the supervisor of over 200 diploma papers and 13 MS and 9 Ph.D. theses of Croatian and Slovenian (L)IS students.

She was a member of the editorial board of *Information Processing and Management* (2003–2008). She is currently a member of the editorial boards of the *Journal of Documentation*, *JELISE*, and *Bibliotekarstvo, Serbia*.

She was the Chair, ASIST/European Chapter, 2003–2009; Chair, Euclid—European HEI for LIS education and research, 2008–2014; and Chair, Croatian Council on Libraries, from 2013. To the international IS community she has been known as the co-director of LIDA Conferences from 2000–2014 together with Professor Tefko Saracevic. She was/is a member of PC for a number of international conferences in IS. She was PI for two Croatian research projects: Organization, Preservation and Usage of Croatian Written Heritage, 2002–2006 and 2007–2010, and Croatian Written Heritage, 2007–2012; and started several projects aimed at reorganizing and digitizing rich but neglected collections of monastery libraries in Croatia, Bosnia, and Hercegovina, as well as a project for several library buildings in Croatia.

In 1998 she received Kukuljević's Award (Croatian highest award in LIS field); in 2006 she was given by ASIST Thompson/ISI an Outstanding Teacher of Information Science Award.

She retired in 2015 from the University of Zadar as Distinguished Professor in Information Sciences.

Printed in the United States
by Baker & Taylor Publisher Services